Writing
Across the Curriculum

Writing
Across the Curriculum

An Annotated Bibliography

Compiled by
Chris M. Anson, John E. Schwiebert,
and Michael M. Williamson

Bibliographies and Indexes in Education, Number 13

Greenwood Press
Westport, Connecticut • London

Library of Congress Cataloging-in-Publication Data

Writing across the curriculum : an annotated bibliography / compiled
by Chris M. Anson, John E. Schwiebert, and Michael M. Williamson.
    p. cm. — (Bibliographies and indexes in education, ISSN
0742-6917 ; no. 13)
  Includes bibliographical references (p.) and index.
  ISBN 0-313-25960-7
  1. English language — Composition and exercises — Bibliography.
  2. Interdisciplinary approach in education — Bibliography.
I. Anson, Christopher M. II. Schwiebert, John E.
III. Williamson, Michael M. IV. Series.
Z5818.E5W75 1993 LB1576
016.808′042′07 — dc20   93-29897

British Library Cataloguing in Publication Data is available.

Library of Congress Catalog Card Number: 93-29897
ISBN: 0-313-25960-7
ISSN: 0742-6917

First published in 1993

Greenwood Press, 88 Post Road West, Westport, CT 06881
An imprint of Greenwood Publishing Group, Inc.

Printed in the United States of America

The paper used in this book complies with the
Permanent Paper Standard issued by the National
Information Standards Organization (Z39.48-1984).

10 9 8 7 6 5 4 3 2 1

Contents

Acknowledgments

The compiling of a substantive annotated bibliography is a lengthy and sometimes wearisome task. At times when we felt buried beneath mounds of unread material, each of us wondered how we had ever become involved in so time-consuming and difficult a project. As we saw our way toward publication, however, we began to recognize the benefits of several years of labor—the benefits to our own learning from gathering together, reading, and distilling the work of many scholars and teachers; the benefits to our students, who now had many more resources for their own research; and the benefits, ultimately, to the many practitioners, administrators, scholars, and researchers in the field of writing studies, and their counterparts in other disciplines, who will make use of this resource in their work.

We could not have harvested the crop without the significant help of our colleagues and students. We thank especially the many scholars and friends who brought to our attention works that we might otherwise have passed over, especially Judy Self, who sent us a long list of works on language across the curriculum, and Rick Henry, for his excellent compilation of references on writing to learn in mathematics. We also extend our sincere gratitude to the following people for locating and abstracting some of the references included in the bibliography: Dennis Hock of Consumnes River College; William Yanner and Doris Cooper of Indiana University of Pennsylvania; Duane Molnar of Westmoreland County Community College; David Wallace of Carnegie Mellon University; and Jianping Wang and James Maertens of the University of Minnesota. Without their contributions to this volume, we might still be neck deep in a swamp of references.

From the start, the editorial staff at Greenwood Press supported this project and gave us invaluable advice along the way. In particular, we would like to thank Mary Sive, our original developmental editor at Greenwood Press; Loomis Mayer, who assumed her duties when she moved to another division, and who untiringly advised us about the preparation of the final manuscript; and Mildred Vasan, who saw the project to completion.

We also express our thanks to our wives and children for their patience and support during the several years it took us to compile the bibliography: to

Geanie, Ian, and Graham Anson; to Ann Jefferds; and to Suzie, Sarah, and Cay Williamson.

Finally, a note about our authorship of this work and our relative contributions to it. The order of authorship is purely alphabetical. Chris Anson and Mike Williamson originated the project when, during a discussion at a conference, they decided to merge their fairly substantive bibliographies on writing across the curriculum. Chris sought and obtained a contract at Greenwood Press and soon after solicited the help of John Schwiebert. Chris oversaw the project until the summer of 1992, when his other responsibilities had caused it to stall. It was John Schwiebert, however, who tirelessly worked throughout 1992 and into 1993 to finish the bibliography, adding several hundred new entries and seeing to the enormously complicated process of preparing the final manuscript for submission. Without John's dedication and perseverance, the bibliography might never have reached production. Special thanks go to the Research and Professional Growth Committee, the College of Arts and Humanities, the English Department, and the Writing Across the Curriculum program at Weber State University for providing John with partial release time from teaching to complete the project.

CMA
JES
MMW

Organization of the Bibliography

Format

This bibliography is divided into two parts, "Scholarship" and "Pedagogy," to accommodate readers who are interested in either of these main areas of writing across the curriculum (WAC). Within each part, we have organized references around more specific categories to help readers locate materials appropriate to their own interests or needs.

Part One: Scholarship

Bibliographies and Literature Reviews. In our search for references for the present bibliography, we located as many other bibliographies as we could and then read and annotated or reannotated any works we did not already have in our own bibliography. Since some readers may want to obtain copies of shorter bibliographies, perhaps to circulate among colleagues or distribute at WAC workshops, we decided to include these and describe them briefly.

We also included in this section works clearly designed to review or synthesize existing literature on WAC. On occasion, we ran across articles with substantive reviews of literature as prefaces to research studies. Since such reviews are secondary to the goals of reporting *new* research, these were placed in "Research Studies" below.

Collections and Special Issues. This section includes the major collections of articles and essays, as well as a few special issues of scholarly journals, focusing on WAC. The annotations provide a general description of each collection and are followed by the names of individual authors therein, so that the reader may locate more detailed annotations in other sections by checking the author index.

History and Implementation. In this section, we included essays on the history and development of WAC as a movement, descriptions of specific WAC programs, discussions of faculty workshops, and any other special projects not included in "Research Studies" below.

Research Studies. Here we have included all those works that report the results of original research. While there is much current debate about what constitutes "formal research" in composition studies, we have made no attempt to differentiate studies that, for example, have "statistical validity" from those that do not. We have included ethnographic studies, surveys and questionnaires, observations and text analyses, interviews and case studies. Whenever a study focuses on writing in a particular content area (e.g., science, mathematics, history, etc.), we included it here if it seemed markedly oriented toward research or the analysis of data. Those works that seem clearly oriented toward teaching are included in Part II, under "Pedagogy."

Theory and Rationale. Works not fitting any of the categories above, but not clearly pedagogical in focus, we placed into this general category. Under this rubric, a work that does not report the results of research, synthesize existing research studies, describe specific programs, or trace the history of WAC is considered theoretical, focusing on the goals of the movement and its various manifestations. Readers seeking general background on WAC will most likely find the best preliminary reading in this section.

Part Two: Pedagogy

The second part of the bibliography contains references to works focusing primarily on teaching. Included are explanations of particular techniques, descriptions of entire courses in various curricular areas in which writing plays a central role, practical guides for interested teachers, and textbooks. Researchers of WAC will find this part of the bibliography useful as a reflection of how underlying theory is translated into practice. Teachers can turn to sections relevant to their own disciplines and find ideas and techniques useful in their own teaching or in staff development workshops.

We have grouped references into six sections. The first section, "General Pedagogy," includes works clearly focused on the particulars of instruction but not geared toward a specific discipline. These works are of general interest to teachers of all subject areas. The next four sections include works focused on writing in the arts and humanities; math, science, and engineering; the social and behavioral sciences; and business, law, finance, and economics.

In dividing up the curriculum in this way, we relied on the most common classifications used in colleges and universities for defining disciplinary areas (and ultimately for structuring the departments or colleges of the university as an institution). Such divisions may wrongly encourage further curricular fragmentation, but we offer them as an aid to teachers who want to find information about their own fields without having to wade through lots of less relevant material.

The final section of Part Two lists textbooks claiming to be cross-disciplinary or identified as such. We made no attempt to choose works on the basis of any formal criteria; we leave it to the reader to decide if a particular textbook merits the title "cross-disciplinary."

Substance of Entries

We have tried whenever possible to avoid making evaluative judgments on the works annotated. The field of WAC is so varied, with audiences at so many curricular levels and with such wide practical, theoretical, or empirical interests, that it would have been inappropriate and perhaps misleading for us to make subjective judgments on the coverage or arguments of particular works. From the perspective of a researcher of college writing, a lively, anecdotal work describing an informal project in the fourth grade of a small, rural elementary school might not merit as much attention as a carefully designed longitudinal study of writing-to-learn at a major university. On the other hand, a work deserving accolades among the research community—one that includes statistical formulas and complicated rationales for complex research designs—might be met with indifference or frustration by a teacher seeking workable ideas described in plain English. Consequently, the annotations are almost entirely unbiased. We have avoided qualifications ("readable," "difficult," "excellent," "confusing," "dry," "useful," etc.) and have tried instead to provide a thorough, accurate precis for each work.

We have undoubtedly left out some important and perhaps many not so important works on WAC. That we began the bibliography thinking we might reach 100 references and ended up with over 1000 suggests something of the field's tremendous vitality. We do, however, take full responsibility for any glaring omissions; for those, we blame only the maze-like complexity of our task and our limited resources to explore every path therein.

Reference Style

The bibliographic style of the American Psychological Association (as described in the Third Edition of its style manual) offers several advantages over other styles in the context of WAC. First, the majority of researchers in WAC publish their findings in journals which adhere to APA style; of those journals that do not, most follow the style of the Modern Language Association, which includes the same information as the APA but provides authors' first names. Second, the initial elements in the APA style are author's name and year of publication. We find this a useful style for a bibliography: scholars can easily keep track of works they are citing or intend to consult. If they too are using the APA style, then their own within-text references will correspond to the entries listed here.

Introduction

The Future of Writing Across the Curriculum: Consensus and Research

Chris M. Anson

WAC and the Limits of Apparent Consensus

Language educators have long argued that writing is a key to intellectual development, fostering improved thinking abilities and enhancing both the quality and quantity of learning. Only recently, however, has the educational community considered ways to act on this assumption, particularly through the increased use of writing in the many academic disciplines that make up our school and university curricula.

In the past several years, the movement now widely known as "writing across the curriculum" (WAC) has burgeoned, and with it attention to writing in diverse subject areas has increased dramatically. Scores of testimonials from enlightened teachers—both within and beyond traditional contexts for teaching and learning writing—have appeared in the pages of academic journals. Dozens of new textbooks have been published under the rubric of "cross-disciplinary writing." National networks on writing across the curriculum have formed, creating special sessions at educational conferences and publishing newsletters to disseminate information. And, by some estimates, over 400 colleges and universities now have well-integrated programs in writing across the curriculum (Griffin, 1985; Haring-Smith & Stern, 1985; McLeod & Shirley, 1988).

Unlike many educational trends, however, WAC has not been accompanied by much empirical research that might lend support to the movement and provide it with coherence (Anson, 1988). In the past, claims about the effectiveness of specific instructional methods—invention heuristics, sentence-combining, peer-revision conferences, and composing on computers, to name a few—have been generally supported or refuted by carefully designed research studies (see Hillocks, 1986). Even larger-scale and often controversial instructional trends such as the recent "back-to-basics" movement typically follow the lead of government-sponsored studies whose findings suggest a decline in basic skills, a loss of "cultural literacy," or a "crisis" in levels of educational attainment. In contrast, WAC seems to have grown from a grass-roots consensus that writing is central to learning and should be a part of all academic contexts. Instead of revealing and trying to understand the complexities of writing as both an interdisciplinary and a discipline-specific activity, most efforts in WAC have focused on the need to persuade faculty in a variety of content areas to include more extended writing in their instruction.

Of course, WAC has not emerged from a theoretical vacuum. Years of scholarship on writing have led to some degree of functional consensus about the acquisition of written literacy and what sorts of educational processes best encourage its growth.   The rationale for WAC has been traced at least as far back as Dewey, whose philosophy led to an interdisciplinary, project-oriented curriculum in the twenties, thirties, and forties (Yates, 1983, p. 4) and was responsible, in part, for the "progressive education" and "cooperative" movements which, as Russell has well documented, represented an organized attempt to share the responsibility for writing instruction among various academic disciplines (see Russell, 1990; 1989; 1987; 1986). More recently, WAC has gained much of its impetus from the work of British scholars who, throughout the 1970's, argued for the increased role of language in all learning contexts (Barnes, 1976; Britton et al., 1975; Martin et al., 1976; for overviews, see Applebee, 1977; Fillion, 1979; Bailey, 1983; Knudson, 1978). But in spite of these theoretical foundations, the bulk of the literature on WAC has been discursive and testimonial, sometimes citing general scholarship on the writing process but very rarely reporting original research on writing within or across specific academic disciplines.

Coming from educators who are not often involved in research, the growing pleas for WAC may be a predictable response to larger social and educational concerns about students' writing abilities.   Teachers who are dismayed by the poor quality of student writing in their subject-area courses often turn angrily to their English department or composition program for not adequately preparing students to write. In defense of their own positions, composition faculty argue that writing cannot be relegated to a single-term course assumed to give students all they need to succeed. Instead, writing must be central to learning within every discipline and must continue throughout each person's intellectual development (for a typical example, see Zinsser, 1986).

A second explanation for the growth of WAC may be found in the recent criticism of curricular fragmentation and what Marland (1977) has called the "extraordinary separation of subject teachers" that characterizes today's schools. Beginning in the late nineteenth century with the division of the academic community into discrete, seemingly self-contained bodies of knowledge (Berlin, 1984, p. 9), many global intellectual processes were reduced to individual skills to be studied and practiced in isolation.   Subsequently, imaginative discourse was housed in departments of English or language arts, where it took on a literary or essayist orientation. All other writing instruction fell within the province of composition, where over the years it found itself increasingly mechanized, skills-oriented, and stripped of context. Driven to the periphery of the curriculum, writing became reductive and behavioristic, and faculty soon began equating writing ability with simple, generic skills (see Rose, 1985).

Whatever its historical origins, WAC has enjoyed a surge of consensus from the growing conviction that a limited quantity of composition instruction, by itself, is not dramatically improving students' written literacy. But such tacit endorsements are rarely self-sustaining. In tracing the characteristic patterns of change in composition practice, Phelps (1989) suggests that beneath new instructional movements often lie different theoretical assumptions that lead to disparate or even competing practices. As it becomes clear that competing methodologies will not yield definitive solutions, research must begin to explore the constituent processes and activities that underlie surface behavior or its products. Until it does, the foundation of consensus for WAC will begin to weaken as what was once a set of shared beliefs turns into a multitude of controversies and debates about pedagogy, implementation, and assessment. If we do not begin more formal and carefully charted explorations of WAC , and if we continue to rely exclusively on testimony and impassioned pleas, no unified theory can be constructed, making it difficult to effect large-scale methodological change.

The Second Stage: Consensus Through Research

At present, the movement toward writing in all academic disciplines seems to be entering a second stage, revealing its methodological complexity as competing beliefs surface about the nature and function of writing in different disciplines and about the most appropriate implementation of WAC programs. Still heartily endorsed in principle, the philosophy that writing should be integrated into all academic disciplines is nonetheless approached now with less emotional zeal and more intellectual caution. What does it mean to "write" in an academic discipline? What are the ultimate goals of increasing the use of writing across all curricular contexts? Do the criteria for successful writing differ among diverse disciplines? How should "learning" be measured as a function of writing across the curriculum? What sorts of beliefs about writing are held by faculty in different disciplines, and to what extent are they influenced by the conventions, styles, and formats of the writing produced in their fields beyond academia?

In our review of some 1070 works represented in this bibliography, we have seen several signs that the almost religious zeal of WAC is giving way to a more careful and intellectual stance. Quick-fix solutions have yielded to a more hesitant but theoretically rich questioning. Grandiose, romantic visions of an entire nation of schoolchildren writing in art classes, the music room, and the gymnasium are fading as educators squarely face the realities of the school curriculum and the habits and attitudes of its teachers. And, most importantly, a plea for carefully designed research is revealing cracks in the very foundation of WAC, in those areas where it has been built from the mortar of blind conviction.

To illustrate these shifts in the demeanor of WAC, I want to consider briefly one area that has yielded a variety of conflicting interpretations and data: how is writing being used across the curriculum in schools and colleges today? Has it disappeared, largely, from all but English and composition? Are teachers using it productively, or only as a means of assessment? How much writing does the typical high school or college student do?

As I have pointed out in my review of research on WAC (Anson, 1988), there are many discrepancies in the large body of survey research exploring the kinds and quantities of writing in secondary and college curricula. Some studies, for example, show that the amount of writing tends to decrease as students advance in age or grade level, and that it is dominated by mechanical functions often used for the sake of classroom management and control (Donlan, 1974; Applebee, 1981; 1982; 1984; Bader & Pearce, 1983). Teachers seem to use writing more often for reporting information and rehearsing facts than for exploring ideas (Donlan, 1980). Other scholars, however, are much more sanguine in their reports of the great diversity of writing they find in college curricula and the relative frequency of writing tasks (Eblen, 1983; Bernhardt, 1985; Scharton, 1983; Bridgeman & Carlson, 1984). Set against the experiences of many researchers who have watched writing dry up in their own universities, these findings give us pause: is the picture, in fact, as bleak as many WAC scholars would have us believe?

This is a prime example of the movement's development into a second, more questioning stage. Initially, those involved in WAC relied almost entirely on subjective impressions, anecdotal evidence, and reports from colleagues in reaching the conclusion—which has fueled WAC for some time now—that our schools and universities no longer use much writing at all as a way to build literacy or help students learn various subjects. As educators began to test this notion through the use of surveys and questionnaires, the consensus weakened: the issue was not as simple as we had thought. Some studies showed a healthy attention to writing even in the absence of WAC crusaders or well-established cross-curricular programs, which implied that good practices would probably exist at schools with even limited efforts at WAC. At the same time, scholars such as Knoblauch and Brannon (1983) claimed that, on closer scrutiny, many efforts to integrate writing into various academic disciplines appear to be nothing more than programs in "grammar across the curriculum."

Typically, the shift away from tacit endorsement carries with it some very rough (and quite preliminary) sorts of investigations, without much methodological or theoretical rigor. Now we must somehow explain discrepancies in the survey data: are they simply showing idiosyncratic tendencies at individual schools? Why then are so many writing teachers skeptical about positive conclusions from these studies?

A partial answer begins to form if we look beneath the surveys themselves to the theories of writing informing their design. Apart from the obvious limitations of survey research in general—e.g., biased samples based on the dispositions of those willing to fill out and return questionnaires (see Zemelman, 1977; Rose, 1979) or unreliable reports (see Anderson, 1985), any survey designed to measure the types or amounts of writing used in a particular classroom or department reflects the researcher's rubric for classifying "functions" or "uses" of writing. Although we no longer adhere to the outmoded "modes" of discourse (see Connors, 1981), we have not yet created an adequate functional taxonomy of writing in different disciplines; nor have we studied differences in the characteristics of written discourse which are given functional labels in these disciplines.

Consider, for example, Britton's study, *The Development of Writing Abilities (11-18)*, (Britton et al., 1975), one of the most influential and frequently cited pieces of research in the entire WAC movement. Britton and his team classified discourse into various functions and audiences in order to study the uses of writing in British secondary schools and to map any changes in these uses over the course of the public school curriculum. But where Britton looked for "poetic," "expressive," and "transactional" functions, Applebee's team (1981, 1982) assigned terms based on an earlier scheme developed and later rejected by Britton (1971): mechanical uses, informational uses, personal uses, and imaginative uses, each of which contains several sub-categories. Where Donlan's (1974) survey employed a traditional mode-driven scheme (narration, exposition, argumentation, and reporting), Eblen's surveys (1983) included responses for essay tests, abstracts of readings, lab reports, and personal journals. Bridgeman and Carlson (1984) relied on "topic types" combining kinds or genres of discourse (personal essay) with processes common to many different kinds of discourse (compare and contrast, summarize a passage, etc.).

Faced with such a range of classification systems, how can we generalize from survey research about the status of writing instruction either within particular institutions or across the country as a whole? A teacher may interpret an "informational" use of writing in several ways—a test of knowledge in which the reader (teacher) already possesses the information; a report of original findings; or a discursive and more exploratory essay about some social condition. What counts as a "lab report" to one teacher may be another's "journal," and an "abstract of a reading" in one class may be highly subjective and "imaginative" while in another it may be assessed using formal criteria for its adherence to proper disciplinary conventions. At this stage, discourse taxonomies have failed to correlate the textual characteristics of writing (mode, genre, conventions) with the pragmatic characteristics of its use (purpose, surrounding context, etc.). Before we can say with any certainty that a given school or classroom uses writing for intellectually impoverished and mechanical purposes, we must rethink not only our research methods but also the theoretical constructs beneath them—and that questioning may well lead us to pursue alternative kinds of research models, such as ethnographies or a combination of methods.

Other conflicts in existing scholarship on WAC abound. In fact, many teachers and researchers appear to disagree on the very goals of WAC. Herrington (1985), for example, has shown that faculty tend to fall into one of two groups with respect to the integration of writing in their courses. One group explains writing from the perspective of a school community, and their purpose is to use writing to foster the acquisition of knowledge and the development of intellect. The second group views writing from a disciplinary perspective, and their goal is to indoctrinate students into the kinds of discourse expected of them in particular professions. The first group thus favors "writing to learn," while the second favors "learning to write."

This distinction has more recently suggested a large split in the entire WAC movement, one that partly explains why apparent consensus has shifted into some preliminary conflict and debate. Teachers' ideological differences concerning the processes of literacy may explain why some programs fail while others flourish. In my study of 15 pedagogical journals across the curriculum, for example, I found that not only has the number of published articles about writing in these content-area journals increased over the past twenty years, but that their focus has shifted quite dramatically away from "learning to write" and toward "writing to learn" (Anson, 1987). Encouraged by these findings, I erroneously judged interest in WAC among faculty to be much higher than I now suspect it is. In the absence of further research, I had not seen how strongly these journals appeal to educators who take an active interest in the *teaching* of their subject; by contrast, no such evidence of an increased interest in writing (even as a professional activity) is apparent in the corresponding "professional" journals in those same fields. As a movement, WAC may well be influencing those who see themselves primarily as teachers; but many faculty, particularly in large universities with research agendas, hardly know that the movement exists.

The Third Stage: Assessment Across the Curriculum

More diverse research paradigms in WAC, and a richer theoretical questioning, may well push us through conflict and restore to the movement a deeper and more sophisticated kind of consensus. At the same time, a continued focus on the writing process may only deter our research and do little to provide us with a fuller understanding of the relationships between writing and surrounding disciplinary cultures.

In the late 1970's and early 1980's, composition was preoccupied with studying the writing processes of students. As we have been made painfully aware recently, most of this research ignored context and purpose, choosing instead to hold a magnifying glass to the moment-by-moment activities of young inexperienced writers as they struggled to create meaning through text (Anson, 1988; Brandt, 1986; Faigley, 1985). Following the lead of "cognitivists," we became almost obsessed with trying to understand what was happening in writers' heads as they composed, through such research methods as protocol analysis (a procedure for tapping into the composing mind at work; see Flower & Hayes, 1984), and analyses of pauses during the writing process (Matsuhashi, 1982). Other researchers proposed conducting electroencephalograms during the writing process, and soon even discussions of right- and left-brain functions could be heard at professional conferences. Meanwhile the trickle-down effect was starting what would soon become a new attention to "process" in many secondary and elementary schools.

Recognizing the limitations of studying one kind of writer in one limited context, the more rigorous second phase of WAC might well turn toward the composing process as the object of its study, this time looking at writers in different disciplines. We have already seen many process studies of writers in non-academic settings (e.g., Odell & Goswami, 1985), and several important studies of students' writing behaviors across the curriculum have already appeared in the professional journals and academic presses (e.g., Applebee et al., 1984; Faigley & Hansen, 1985; Newell, 1984; McCarthy, 1987). Attention has also turned toward the development of reliable, rich methods for analysis (see Jolliffe, 1988).

An intense focus on composing processes alone, however, may not move us toward a much richer understanding of writing across the disciplines. Findings from studies of writers' composing processes in different settings tell us that the composing process varies considerably across contexts. Writers do different things in different places, and these differences are probably attributable to the relationship between the conventions of discourse in a discipline and the assumptions and processes of the people in it. Expanding this research, we might also discover significant differences in the kinds and quantities of revisions writers make in different academic and non-academic settings. And we might learn a good deal more about idiosyncrasies in writing processes by conducting case studies of writers in specific courses or disciplines.

Without significant attention to how communities of people define or assess the writing they produce, however, such process studies may tell us very little. Evaluation has, of course, been a topic of central importance to composition, and new studies of assessment have raised important questions about methods, criteria, and the goals of education (e.g., Greenberg, Wiener & Donovan, 1986). Yet much of this new work is preoccupied with large-scale assessment programs or the diagnostic and placement issues confronting English or composition departments, and does not explore what it means to assess the writing abilities of students in departments of psychology, philosophy, studio arts, or architecture. Integrated into research on WAC, the subject of assessment suggests a powerful new area for study.

Some existing literature already murmurs with implications for assessment across the curriculum. Most of it is informal and anecdotal, sharing the insights and experiences emerging from faculty workshops on WAC. As teachers from different disciplines come together to discuss and practice writing, it is clear that their own instructional and professional ideologies influence their often profoundly different perspectives (see Connelly & Irving, 1976; Freisinger, 1980; Fulwiler, 1981, 1984; Herrington, 1981; Maimon, 1979; Nochimson, 1980; Raimes, 1980). Clearly, the tacit understandings of the communities where these teachers work and write are expressed in judgments as well as processes, and the two must be seen as complimentary. As students acquire certain ways of thinking about texts, in other words, they are simultaneously building a sense of what it means to adhere to the norms and conventions of particular discursive communities. Attempts to understand faculty members' judgments of writing quality must therefore consider several simultaneous influences, including personal, professional, and pedagogical beliefs informing such judgments. Comparisons of the various educational contexts in which WAC is being implemented also suggest that we must consider the effects of institutional missions or goals on the way that faculty within and across disciplines at those institutions assess the writing of their students (see McCarthy, 1987).

The chief benefit of a research agenda focusing on assessment across the curriculum will be the driving force to *reach* consensus, even in the midst of disciplinary and ideological differences. As it becomes clear that our second stage of research, especially our focus on the writing process across the curriculum, will not yield this consensus, we will be compelled to move toward a study of assessment practices in different disciplinary contexts and the epistemologies that underlie those practices.

It is our hope that the present bibliography will sufficiently reflect the current state of scholarship and pedagogy in WAC to help us establish new and exciting research agendas like these. Armed with such agendas, we have the opportunity to push WAC in a direction that will ensure that it is not tossed onto the heaps of educational fads that lived out their brief lives without the benefit of sustained, meaningful research.

References

Anderson, P. V. (1985). Survey methodology. In L. Odell & D. Goswami (Eds.), *Writing in nonacademic settings* (pp. 453-502). New York: Guilford.

Anson, C. M. (1987, March). *Outside looking in: Charting the influence of composition theory on writing in other disciplines, 1966–1986.* Paper delivered at the Conference on College Composition and Communication, Atlanta, GA.

Anson, C. M. (1988). Toward a multidimensional model of writing in the academic disciplines. In D. A. Jolliffe (Ed.), *Writing in academic disciplines: Vol. 2 of advances in writing research* (pp. 1–33). New York: Ablex.

Applebee, A. N. (1977). Writing across the curriculum: The London projects. *English Journal, 66*(9), 81–85.

Applebee, A. N. (1981). *Writing in the secondary school: English and the content areas.* NCTE Research Report No. 21. Urbana, IL: NCTE.

Applebee, A. N. (1982). Writing and learning in school settings. In M. Nystrand (Ed.), *What writers know: The language, process, and structure of written discourse* (pp. 365–381). New York: Academic Press.

Applebee, A. N., Langer, J. A., Durst, R. K., Butler-Nalin, K., Marshall, J. D., & Newell, G. E. (1984). *Contexts for learning to write: Studies of secondary school instruction.* Norwood, NJ: Ablex.

Bader, L. A., & Pearce, D. L. (1983). Writing across the curriculum, 7–12. *English Education, 15*, 97–106.

Bailey, R. W. (1983). Writing across the curriculum: The British approach. In P. L. Stock (Ed.), *Fforum: Essays on theory and practice in the teaching of composition* (pp. 24–32). Upper Montclair, NJ: Boynton/Cook.

Barnes, D. (1976). *From communication to curriculum.* Harmondsworth, U.K.: Penguin.

Brandt, D. (1986). Toward an understanding of context in composition. *Written Communication, 3,* 139–157.

Berlin, J. A. (1984). *Writing instruction in nineteenth-century American colleges.* Carbondale, IL: Southern Illinois University Press.

Bernhardt, S. A. (1985). Writing across the curriculum at one university: A survey of faculty members and students. *ADE Bulletin, 82,* 55–59.

Brandt, D. (1986). Toward an understanding of context in composition. *Written Communication, 3,* 139–157.

Bridgeman, B., & Carlson, S. B. (1984). Survey of academic writing tasks. *Written Communication, 1,* 247–280.

Britton, J. (1971). What's the use? A schematic account of language functions. *Educational Review, 23,* 205–219.

Britton, J., Burgess, T., Martin, N., McLeod, A., & Rosen, H. (1975). *The development of writing abilities (11–18).* London: Macmillan Education.

Connelly, P. J., & Irving, D. C. (1976). Composition and the liberal arts: A shared responsibility. *College English, 37,* 668–670.

Connors, R. J. (1981). The rise and fall of the modes of discourse. *College Composition and Communication, 32,* 444–455.

Donlan, D. (1974). Teaching writing in the content areas: Eleven hypotheses from a teacher survey. *Research in the Teaching of English, 8,* 250–262.

Donlan, D. (1980). Teaching models, experience, and locus of control: Analysis of a summer inservice program for composition teachers. *Research in the Teaching of English, 14,* 319–330.

Eblen, C. (1983). Writing across-the-curriculum: A survey of a university faculty's views and classroom practices. *Research in the Teaching of English, 17,* 343–348.

Faigley, L. (1985). Nonacademic writing: The social perspective. In L. Odell & D. Goswami (Eds.), *Writing in nonacademic settings* (pp. 231–280). New York: Guilford.

Faigley, L. & Hansen, K. (1985). Learning to write in the social sciences. *College*

Composition and Communication, 36, 140–149.

Fillion, B. (1979). Language across the curriculum. *McGill Journal of Education, 14,* 47–60.

Flower, L. S., & Hayes, J. R. (1981). A cognitive process theory of writing. *College Composition and Communication, 32,* 365–387.

Fulwiler, T. (1981). Showing, not telling, at a writing workshop. *College English, 43,* 55–63.

Fulwiler, T. (1984). How well does writing across the curriculum work? *College English, 46,* 113–125.

Freisinger, R. R. (1980). Cross-disciplinary writing workshops: Theory and practice. *College English, 42,* 154–166.

Greenberg, K. L., Wiener, H. S., & Donovan, R. A. (1986). *Writing assessment: Issues and strategies.* New York: Longman.

Griffin, C. W. (1985). Programs for writing across the curriculum: A report. *College Composition and Communication, 36,* 398–403.

Haring-Smith, T., & Stern, L. (1985). Beyond the English department: Writing across the curriculum. In T. Haring-Smith, N. Hawkins, E. Morrison, L. Stern, & R. Tatu, *A guide to writing programs: Writing centers, peer tutoring programs, and writing-across-the-curriculum* (pp. 19–27). Glenview, IL: Scott Foresman.

Herrington, A. J. (1981). Writing to learn: Writing across the disciplines. *College English, 43,* 379–387.

Herrington, A. J. (1985). Classrooms as forums for reasoning and writing. *College Composition and Communication, 36,* 404–413.

Hillocks, G., Jr. (1986). *Research on written composition: New directions for teaching.* Urbana, IL: NCTE/NCRA.

Jolliffe, D. A. (1988). *Writing in academic disciplines: Vol. 2 of advances in writing research.* New York: Academic Press.

Knoblauch, C. H., & Brannon, L. (1983). Writing as learning through the curriculum. *College English, 45,* 465–474.

Knudson, R. (1978). How the English teach writing. *English Journal, 67*(8), 49–50.

Maimon, E. P. (1979). Writing in the total curriculum at Beaver College. *CEA Forum, 9,* 7–16.

Marland, M. (1977). *Language across the curriculum.* London: Heinemann.

Martin, N., D'Arcy, P., Newton, B., & Parker, R. (1976). *Writing and learning across the curriculum, 11–16.* London: Ward Lock.

Matsuhashi, A. (1982). Explorations in the real-time production of written discourse. In M. Nystrand (Ed.), *What writers know: The language process and structures of written discourse* (pp. 269–290). New York: Academic Press.

McCarthy, L. P. (1987). A stranger in strange lands: A college student writing across the curriculum. *Research in the Teaching of English, 21,* 233–265.

McLeod, S. H., & Shirley, S. (1988). National survey of writing across the curriculum programs. In S. H. McLeod (Ed.), *Strengthening programs for writing across the curriculum* (pp. 103–130). San Francisco: Jossey-Bass.

Newell, G. E. (1984). Learning from writing in two content areas: A case-study/protocol analysis. *Research in the Teaching of English, 18,* 265–287.

Nochimson, M. (1980). Writing instruction across the curriculum: Two programs. *Journal of Basic Writing, 2*(4), 22–35.

Odell, L., & Goswami, D. (Eds.). (1985). *Writing in nonacademic settings.* New York: Guilford.

Phelps, L. W. (1989). Images of student writing: The deep structure of teacher response. In C. M. Anson (Ed.), *Writing and response: Theory, practice, and research* (pp. 37–67). Urbana, IL: National Council of Teachers of English.

Raimes, A. (1980). Writing and learning across the curriculum: The experience of a faculty seminar. *College English, 41,* 797–801.

Rose, M. (1979). When faculty talk about writing. *College English, 41,* 272–279.

Rose, M. (1985). The language of exclusion: Writing instruction at the university. *College English, 47,* 341–359.

Russell, D. R. (1986). Writing across the curriculum in 1913: James Fleming Hosic on "cooperation." *English Journal, 75*(5), 34–37.

Russell, D. R. (1987). Writing across the curriculum and the communications movement: Some lessons from the past. *College Composition and Communication, 38,* 184–194.

Russell, D. R. (1989). The cooperation movement: Language across the curriculum and mass education, 1900–1930. *Research in the Teaching of English, 23,* 399–423.

Russell, D. R. (1990). Writing across the curriculum in historical perspective: Toward a social interpretation. *College English, 52,* 52–73.

Scharton, M. (1983). Composition at Illinois State University: A preliminary assessment. *Illinois English Bulletin, 71,* 11–22.

Yates, J. M. (1983). *Research implications for writing in the content areas.* Washington, DC: National Education Association.

Zinsser, W. (1986, April 13). A bolder way to teach writing. *New York Times* (Education Life), pp. 58–63.

Zemelman, S. (1977). How college teachers encourage students' writing. *Research in the Teaching of English, 11,* 227–234.

Writing
Across the Curriculum

PART ONE: SCHOLARSHIP

Bibliographies
and Literature Reviews

1. Anson, C. M. (1985, November). *Writing across the curriculum: The current state of research.* Paper presented at the meeting of the Assembly on Research, National Council of Teachers of English, Philadelphia, PA.
Based on a review of over 200 published works specifically focused on WAC, the paper documents the paucity of formal research in this area. The movement has grown from a grass-roots consensus that writing should be used as a tool for learning in all content areas. Unlike other movements in the teaching of writing, however, it is not accompanied by research that looks at writing as a process which may vary in important ways across diverse instructional and institutional contexts. Anson offers some new directions for further research based on unsolved problems and unanswered questions.

2. Anson, C. M. (1988). Toward a multidimensional model of writing in the academic disciplines. In D. A. Jolliffe (Ed.), *Advances in writing research, vol. 2: Writing in academic disciplines* (pp. 1–33). Norwood, NJ: Ablex.
Based on an extensive review of existing scholarship on WAC, this article points out important gaps and discrepancies in our knowledge of writing in the academic disciplines. Three research perspectives are explored: the professional, the curricular, and the developmental. By looking closely at specific lines of research in each perspective, Anson creates a multidimensional model of writing in the disciplines as a heuristic for further research.

3. Applebee, A. N. (1984). Writing and reasoning. *Review of Educational Research, 54,* 577–596.
Addresses the question of what contributions written language might make to intellectual development, particularly to "higher order" thinking skills and the ability to reason. Reviews studies of the cultural consequences of literacy, "the effects of particular writing experiences on individual learning, and the role of writing in the development of reasoning skills in school contexts." The article claims that while there is a general assumption that writing improves reasoning and increases knowledge of a given topic, "we know almost nothing about the nature of the understanding that develops." Applebee concludes by offering an agenda for further research.

4. **Bergman, C. A. (1983). Writing across the curriculum: An annotated bibliography. In B. L. Smith (Ed.), *Writing across the Curriculum* (pp. 33–38). Washington: American Association for Higher Education. (ERIC Document Reproduction Service No. ED 243 391)**
Includes over 40 annotated entries. Most citations may be found in the present bibliography.

5. **Bizzell, P., & Herzberg, B. (1985). Writing-across-the-curriculum textbooks: A bibliographic essay. *Rhetoric Review, 3* (2), 202–216.**
A review and critique of the most popular composition textbooks claiming to treat writing as a multidisciplinary activity. The authors begin with a brief history of WAC, and then examine whether its assumptions are reflected in textbooks "touted as cross-disciplinary." Eight books are reviewed; most are "organized along traditional rhetorical lines," emphasizing readings instead of composing processes. The authors raise questions about the future of textbooks on WAC.

6. **Burkett, E. M. (1977). *Writing in subject-matter fields: A bibliographic guide, with annotations and writing assignments.* Metuchen, NJ: Scarecrow Press.**
The bibliography includes seven sections: "About Writing," "Writing and Literature," "Writing in History, Autobiography and Biography, Law," "Writing in Science," "Technical and Business Writing," "Interdisciplinary Writing," and "Writing Articles for Newspapers and Magazines." Most works annotated are by and about professional writers rather than teachers and researchers. Chapters are followed by writing exercises based on annotated items.

7. **Clifton, L. J. (1985). Bibliography. In A. R. Gere (Ed.), *Roots in the sawdust: Writing to learn across the disciplines* (pp. 229–235). Urbana, IL: National Council of Teachers of English.**
A short annotated bibliography on WAC. Provides 37 entries, including general theories of and strategies for teaching writing. Emphasis is on books (27 entries) as opposed to articles (10 entries).

8. **Fillion, B. (1983). Let me see you learn. *Language Arts, 60* (6), 702–710.**
Reviews research on language and cognition and summarizes three basic tenets of the language-across-the-curriculum movement: that language develops through its purposeful use; that learning involves and occurs through talking and writing; and that language use contributes to overall cognitive development. In discussing these principles and supporting his generalizations with reference to specific studies, Fillion offers practical implications for effective teaching. Focuses mainly on the elementary grades.

9. **Freisinger, R., & Petersen, B. T. (1981). Writing across the curriculum: A theoretical background. *Fforum, 2,* 65–67, 92.**
Intended as an introduction for faculty, this article provides an overview of the theoretical underpinnings of WAC and describes the basic assumptions necessary to establish a program. Also includes an annotated bibliography.

10. **Gere, A. R. (1985). Glossary [of WAC terms]. In A. R. Gere (Ed.),** *Roots in the sawdust: Writing to learn across the disciplines* **(pp. 222–228). Urbana, IL: National Council of Teachers of English.**
A useful compendium of terms and concepts associated with WAC and contemporary composition theory, particularly those used by authors of articles in the collection. Terms are keyed to individual entries.

11. **Healy, M. K. (1987). A bibliography for writing and learning. In J. Self (Ed.),** *Plain talk: About learning and writing across the curriculum* **(pp. 101–103). Commonwealth of Virginia: Virginia Department of Education.**
Lists 42 sources under the following headings: "Writing Across the Curriculum," "Writing and Learning [General]," "Writing and Learning: K–6," and "Writing and Learning: Secondary and College."

12. **Johns, A. M. (1988). The discourse communities dilemma: Identifying transferable skills for the academic milieu.** *English for Specific Purposes,* 7 (1), 55–59.
As several researchers have pointed out, many skills and cognitive activities are area-specific and are difficult to "transfer" to other disciplines. In exploring the contradictions of teaching writing for many "discourse communities," Johns provides an overview of recent research and pedagogical literature aimed at increasing our understanding of those abilities that can be generalized across disciplines.

13. **Lehr, F. (1982). ERIC/RCS report: Promoting schoolwide writing.** *English Education,* 14, 47–52.
Surveys ERIC documents dealing with the practical implementation of cross-disciplinary writing programs at the high school and college levels. Documents are introduced under the following headings: "Getting Started," "Getting Other Departments Involved," and "Existing Programs." Lehr closes with suggestions for locating additional ERIC documents on WAC.

14. **McLeod, S. H. (1989). A brief WAC bibliography.** *ATAC Newsletter,* 1(1), 15.
Includes 19 unannotated references to books and articles on WAC programs and faculty seminars, specifically for directors of composition.

15. **Parker, R. (1985). The "language across the curriculum" movement: A brief overview and bibliography.** *College Composition and Communication,* 36, 173–177.
Briefly traces the origins of "language across the curriculum" (LAC) through three stages: root principles of LAC evolving from psychology, anthropology, philosophy, sociology, and linguistics, which collectively see knowledge as "a product of complex interactions between each person and what he or she observes or reads"; the beginnings of the LAC movement in London in 1966; and what has happened since in England, Australia, Canada, and the United States. Parker distinguishes between LAC as conceptualized in England and in the United States. The British movement concentrates on all forms of language and portrays language as a "dynamic instrument" and a "means of thinking and learning," while in the U.S. writing is separated from talking and

reading, and the movement concentrates on pedagogy and methods for evaluation. The article includes a comprehensive bibliography, which is offered for the purpose of "shifting discussion from WAC to LAC and from methods to ideas."

16. Petersen, B. T. (1982a). Additional resources in the practice of writing across the disciplines. In C. W. Griffin (Ed.), *Teaching writing in all disciplines* **(pp. 75–82). San Francisco: Jossey-Bass.**
Includes 47 annotated entries in the following categories: WAC programs; general pedagogy; business and economics; engineering; history; humanities, arts, and literature; pre-law; mathematics; and physics, chemistry and biology. Most of the references also appear in the present bibliography.

17. Petersen, B. T. (1982b). A select bibliography. In T. Fulwiler & A. Young (Eds.), *Language connections: Writing and reading across the curriculum* **(pp. 179–188). Urbana, IL: National Council of Teachers of English.**
Includes 77 annotated entries which collectively examine language from a heuristic perspective. Selections support the way that language promotes learning and the thesis that "talking, writing, listening, and speaking [are] essential elements in the development of knowledge in all fields." The bibliography includes both theoretical and practical works, as well as those intended for schools planning to develop a WAC program. Most of the references are also included in the present bibliography.

18. Thaiss, C. (1983). Supplementary sources for writing across the curriculum. In C. Thaiss (Ed.), *Writing to learn: Essays and reflections on writing across the curriculum* **(pp. 145–150). Dubuque, IA: Kendall Hunt.**
An unannotated bibliography which includes many of the books and articles cited in the collection to which it is appended, as well as "other resources useful to teachers and writers across the disciplines." Sections include "Language and Learning: Research and Theory," "Descriptions of 'Writing to Learn' Practices," "Designing a Writing-Across-the-Curriculum Program," "Histories of the Writing-Across-the-Curriculum Movement," and "The Teaching of Writing in any Setting."

19. Walvoord, B. F., & Smith, H. L. (1982). Coaching the process of writing. In C. W. Griffin (Ed.), *Teaching writing in all disciplines* **(pp. 3–14). San Francisco: Jossey-Bass.**
Discusses the recent emphasis on process in composition research and teaching, and its implications for WAC. The essay provides a concise review of the literature on writing as process and suggests four ways to increase "the potential of the new process research and the writing-across-the-curriculum movement."

20. Williams, D. N. (1991). Sources and information. In L. C. Stanley & J. Ambron (Eds.), *Writing across the curriculum in community colleges* **(pp. 97–105). San Francisco: Jossey-Bass.**
An annotated bibliography of recent ERIC literature on WAC programs at community and junior colleges.

Collections and Special Issues

21. Brown, P. A. (Ed.) (1984). Writing programs [Special issue]. *Forum for Liberal Education, 7.*
Theme issue devoted to examining ways colleges and universities provide opportunities for students to improve their writing. Reports from 15 institutions.

22. Copeland, J. S. (Ed.) (1987). *Essays grown from a writing across the curriculum institute at Indian Hills Community College: Fostering cooperation and cohesion in writing instruction.* **(ERIC Document Reproduction Service No. ED 294 182)**
Assembles 14 brief essays emerging from the WAC institute at Indian Hills. Articles address writing in diverse content areas, including history, physics, mathematics, speech, computer science, studio art, computer aided drafting, communication technology, high technology, and biology. [Not individually annotated.]

23. Dillon, D. (Ed.) (1983). Language across the curriculum [Symposium]. *Language Arts, 60,* 695–748.
Articles focus on the dynamics of individuals and processes and not on static objects. Many articles go beyond writing to include other sorts of "language events," such as speech and drama. Emphasis is on the elementary grades. See 1983 entries for: Fillion; Rouse; Mayher & Lester; Boutwell; Verriour; Ganz; and Dyson & Genishi.

24. Fulwiler, T., & Young, A. (Eds.) (1982). *Language connections: Writing and reading across the curriculum.* **Urbana, IL: National Council of Teachers of English.**
Designed primarily for teachers and administrators at the college level, this landmark collection introduces both the theory and practice of WAC. Contributions emerged from work in the WAC program at Michigan Technological University. The twelve articles cover a range of topics, including the conceptual frameworks of the WAC program at Michigan Tech.; journal writing across the curriculum; writing and problem solving; audience and purpose in writing; peer-critiquing; conducting research; responding to stu-

dent writing; and the role of the writing laboratory. Also includes a select bibliography. See 1982 entries for: Freisinger; Fulwiler; Berkenkotter; Fulwiler & Jones; Jobst; Young; Kalmbach & Powers; Petersen (2); Falke; Flynn; Schiff; and Freisinger & Burkland.

25. Gere, A. R. (Ed.) (1985). *Roots in the sawdust: Writing to learn across the disciplines.* **Urbana, IL: National Council of Teachers of English.**
This collection of 15 articles focuses specifically on "writing to learn," not, in the editor's words, on writing across the curriculum, which aims to improve the quality of written products. Each article discusses uses for writing in a different subject area across the curriculum, particularly as a way to foster better thinking and learning. Subject areas include literature, art, German, social studies, special education, science, math, philosophy, and history. The collection also includes an annotated bibliography, a glossary of terms used in the book and in WAC generally, and several more generic articles which discuss various strategies, such as journals, for weaving writing more fully into courses. See 1985 entries for: Pearse; Zimmerman; Peterson; Beaman; Marik; Johnston; Schmidt; Yoshida; Watson; Arkle; Forsman; West; Juell; Bronson; Stevens; Gere; and Clifton.

26. Griffin, C. W. (Ed.) (1982). *Teaching writing in all disciplines.* **San Francisco: Jossey-Bass.**
A collection of articles on the theory and practice of teaching writing in various disciplines. Includes pieces on writing in different content areas; descriptions of WAC programs; a historical sketch of WAC; and a bibliographic essay. See 1982 entries for: Walvoord & Smith; Fulwiler; Bean, Drenk, & Lee; King; Thaiss; Drenk; MacAllister; Maimon; Petersen; and Griffin.

27. Hayes, M. F., Morenberg, M., & Ziegler, J. (Eds.) (1981). *Teachers and writers: Articles from the Ohio Writing Project.* **Oxford, OH: Summer Institute, Miami University.**
A collection of 23 essays, including several pieces on writing-to-learn in the content areas. See 1981 entries for: Connors; Lidrbauch; and Brosmer.

28. Jolliffe, D. A. (Ed.) (1988). *Advances in writing research, vol. 2: Writing in academic disciplines.* **New York: Ablex.**
A collection of articles focusing specifically on research. Articles range from theoretical models for research on WAC to studies of writing in various disciplines or analyses of the rhetorical structures of texts. See 1988 entries for: Anson; Jolliffe & Brier; Williamson; Herrington; Hansen; and Rymer.

29. Killingsworth, J. (Ed.) (1988). *Designing writing assignments for vocational-technical courses.* **Lubbock, TX: Texas Tech University. (ERIC Document Reproduction Service No. ED 298 331)**
Includes 27 essays on implementing and developing WAC in two-year and vocational courses. Not individually annotated.

30. Martin, N. (Ed.) (1984). *Writing across the curriculum pamphlets.* **Upper Montclair, NJ: Boynton/Cook.**
First published individually in 1973–1975 by the project Writing Across the

Curriculum: Schools Council/London University Institute of Education English Department, these six pamphlets represent the innovations that grew out of the research program documented in Britton et al., *The Development of Writing Abilities (11–18)*. Each pamphlet focuses on a different aspect of WAC. See 1983 entries for: Martin, Medway, & Smith; Martin, Medway, Smith, & D'Arcy; Medway; D'Arcy; Watts; Shapland; Newton; and Medway & Goodson.

31. McLeod, S. H. (1988). *Strengthening programs for writing across the curriculum.* **San Francisco: Jossey-Bass.**
A collection of essays on the practical and theoretical dimensions of implementing WAC programs in public schools and universities. Articles focus on program development and evaluation, faculty workshops, funding, the relationship of colleges to local public schools, and problems specific to research universities and community colleges. See 1988 entries for: McLeod; Soven; Stout & Magnotto; Strenski; Barr & Healy; Tandy; Fulwiler; McCarthy & Walvoord; Thaiss; and McLeod & Shirley.

32. McLeod, S. H., & Soven, M. (Eds.). (1992). *Writing across the curriculum: A guide to developing programs.* **Newbury Park, CA: SAGE Publications.**
A collection of essays intended to help faculty and administrators with implementation of WAC programs at all types of post-secondary institutions. Contributors address a spectrum of issues, such as: how to start a WAC program; how to plan faculty workshops and sustain interest in WAC; the role of English departments in WAC; the role of writing-intensive courses; WAC and related support services, such as writing centers and writing fellow programs; and other topics. See 1992 entries for: McLeod; Walvoord; Magnotto & Stout; Sandler; Peterson; Farris & Smith; Thaiss; Graham; Kuriloff; Harris; Haring-Smith; and Soven.

33. Morris, B. S. (Ed.). (1989). *Disciplinary perspectives on thinking and writing.* **Ann Arbor: English Composition Board.**
A collection of essays on WAC by faculty at the University of Michigan, Ann Arbor. Not individually annotated.

34. Morris, B. S. (Ed.). (1991). *Writing to learn in disciplines: Detroit teachers combine research and practice in their classrooms.* **Detroit Public Schools/University of Michigan. (ERIC Document Reproduction Service No. ED 333 420)**
A WAC manual compiled by middle and high school science and humanities teachers in the Detroit public schools. The manual's seven sections include: "Writing in Science Classes"; "Writing in English Classes"; "Writing in Math Classes"; Writing about Social Studies Content"; "Using Writing to Learn to Improve Administration and Support Teaching"; "Student Voices"; and "Detroit Teachers' Plans and Concerns: Toward Dissemination of Writing to Learn throughout the Curriculum." Not individually annotated.

35. Nodine, B. F. (Ed.). (1990). Psychologists teach writing [Special issue]. *Teaching of Psychology, 17,* **4–61.**
Includes 16 articles divided into the following categories: "Managing Writing," "Writing Affects Thinking: Empirical Evidence," "Writing As a Mode of

Learning," and "Writing for Other Audiences." See 1990 entries for: McGovern & Hogshead; Willingham; Boice; Anderson; Friedrich; Madigan & Brosamer; Hinkle & Hinkle; Hettich; Jolley & Mitchell; Ventis; Nadelman; Price; Poe; Chrisler; Levine; and Lehmann.

36. Odell, L., & Goswami, D. (Eds.) (1985). *Writing in nonacademic settings.* **New York: Guilford.**
A collection of articles focusing mainly on professional writing beyond the schools, but including several important pieces on writing in academic disciplines. Relevant to WAC in its exploration of the varied social and institutional contexts of writing on the job. [Not individually annotated.]

37. O'Dowd, K. & Nolan, E. (Eds.) (1986). *Learning to write, writing to learn.* **Livonia, MI: Madonna College Humanities Writing Program.**
This "dissemination booklet," published with support from the National Endowment for the Humanities, contains 13 articles by faculty members across the curriculum at Madonna College in Livonia, Michigan. The booklet is an "unanticipated outcome of a writing program initiated at Madonna College in 1984." Its purpose is to describe the methods and experiments in WAC and writing-to-learn afforded by the program. Articles range from a "dean's eye view" of WAC to methods for integrating writing into music theory, history, the social sciences, and psychology. See 1986 entries for O'Dowd; Kujawa; Nolan; Popoff; Reilly; Bozyk; Sax; Maher; Charbonneau; Caulfield; Redmon; Herman; and Anderson.

38. Self, J. (Ed.). (1987). *Plain talk: About learning and writing across the curriculum.* **Commonwealth of Virginia: Virginia Department of Education.**
A book of "stories and conversations""about classroom instruction that integrates learning and writing. The collection consists of five sections: "Visualizing," which contains short articles by Virginia teachers on the way that writing has functioned in their math, science, social studies, and other classes; "Checking the Foundation," an article by a social studies teacher who traces research on WAC, followed by a short bibliography; "Framing," five articles discussing WAC programs and support groups in Virginia; "Building In," specific methods for using writing to learn; and "Viewing the Results," a single article which focuses on program evaluation and classroom implementation. See 1987 entries for Self (2); Owen; Grumbacher; Page; Walpole; Morgan (2); Glaze (3); McConachie; Healy; Shreve & Page; Hesson; Taylor et al.; Alvine; Bent; Strickland; and Nocerino.

39. Simmons, J. M. (Ed.) (1983). *The shortest distance to learning: A guidebook to writing across the curriculum.* **Los Angeles: Los Angeles Community College District. (ERIC Document Reproduction Service No. ED 241 073)**
Articles offering practical suggestions on the use of learning logs, assignment sequences, essay exams, and other write-to-learn activities. Not individually annotated.

40. Smith, B. L. (Ed.) (1983). *Writing across the curriculum.* **Washington: American Association for Higher Education. (ERIC Document Reproduction Service No. ED 243 391)**

Six articles on the WAC movement, including a review of the rationale for WAC by the editor; a discussion of recent changes in the teaching of writing consonant with WAC; an interview with Elaine Maimon, a leader in WAC and director of an important college-level program; and two practical essays on what works in WAC. Also includes an annotated bibliography. See 1983 entries for: B. Smith; Graham; Rideout; and Myers.

41. Stanley, L. C., & Ambron, J. (Eds.). (1991). *Writing across the curriculum in community colleges.* **San Francisco: Jossey-Bass.**
Addresses the concerns of faculty and administrators involved in initiating or sustaining WAC programs at community colleges. See 1991 entries for: Ambron; Stout & Magnotto; Odell; Spear, McGrath, & Seymour; Cummins; Stuchin-Paprin & Lambert; Bertch & Fleming; Stanley; Laipson; Durfee, Sova, Bay, Leech, Fearrien, & Lucas; Hughes-Wiener & Jensen-Cekalla; Hirsch, Nadal, & Shohet; Anderson, Eisenberg, & Wiener; Godwin; Witt; and Williams.

42. Thaiss, C. (Ed.) (1983). *Writing to learn: Essays and reflections on writing across the curriculum.* **Dubuque, IA: Kendall Hunt.**
A collection of 16 short essays written as part of the George Mason University Faculty Writing Program, sponsored by the State Council of Higher Education for Virginia. Mainly instructionally oriented, including pieces from faculty members in psychology, business law, computer science, nursing, history, and physical education. See 1983 entries for: Thaiss; Peters; Metcalf; Hollennbeck; Karlson; Holsinger; Jacobs; Pierce; Fauth, Gilstrap & Isenberg; Seligman; Coffinberger, Paik & Norris; Sanford; Lewis; and Shine.

43. Young, A., & Fulwiler, T. (1986). *Writing across the disciplines: Research into practice.* **Upper Montclair, NJ: Boynton/Cook.**
A collection of articles which evolved from the WAC workshops held at Michigan Technological University between 1977 and 1984. Written by leaders and participants in MTU's WAC program, the essays describe the impact of a particular program on the professional life of a single university department (Humanities) and on the pedagogical life of an entire campus community. Essays are grouped into four sections: 1) "Writing Across the Disciplines: Community and Purpose," which describes the rationale and context for collective research on WAC at MTU; 2) "Evaluation: Assumptions and Discoveries," which assesses the "global" impact of WAC on the entire campus; 3) "Research on Writing and Learning," which evaluates specific techniques (journals, peer groups, poetry writing, etc.) in individual classes such as psychology, biology, engineering, math, and English; and 4) "Writing in the Disciplines: Problems and Perspectives," which considers opportunities and problems—academic, political, theoretical, and practical—that accompany an interdisciplinary writing program. See 1986 entries for: Young; Fulwiler (2); Gorman; McCulley; Fulwiler, Gorman, & Gorman; Kalmbach & Gorman; Selfe & McCulley; Selfe, Gorman, & Gorman; McCulley & Soper; Gorman, Gorman & Young; Flynn, McCulley, & Gratz; Kalmbach (2); Selfe & Arbabi; Selfe, Petersen, & Nahrgang; Flynn; and Gorman.

History and Implementation

44. Alvine, L. (1987a). Buena Vista writing to learn: Teachers as agents for educational change. In D. Goswami & P. Stillman (Eds.), *Reclaiming the classroom: Teacher research as an agency for change* (pp. 107–125). Upper Montclair, NJ: Boynton/Cook.
Describes a project conducted in Buena Vista, Virginia, with several teachers of various grades. The project investigated the functions of writing as a tool for learning.

45. Alvine, L. (1987b). Fostering the teaching/learning community: Buena Vista writing to learn. In J. Self (Ed.), *Plain talk: About learning and writing across the curriculum* (pp. 131–138). Commonwealth of Virginia: Virginia Department of Education.
Describes a WAC teacher network which the author established in the Buena Vista (Virginia) city public schools.

46. Ambron, J. (1991). History of WAC and its role in community colleges. In L. C. Stanley & J. Ambron (Eds.), *Writing across the curriculum in community colleges* (pp. 3–8). San Francisco: Jossey-Bass.
Summarizes the rationale for WAC generally and traces the evolution of WAC as a movement at the community college level.

47. Anderson, J. R., Eisenberg, N., & Wiener, H. S. (1991). Literacy and learning: Integrated skills reinforcement. In L. C. Stanley & J. Ambron (Eds.), *Writing across the curriculum in community colleges* (pp. 79–84). San Francisco: Jossey-Bass.
Describes the ISR (Integrated Skills Reinforcement) project of LaGuardia Community College (NY), a program designed to integrate students' reading, writing, oral, and aural skills.

48. Anson, C. M. (1988, March). *Resistance to writing: Case studies of departmental ideology.* Paper presented at the Conference on College Composition and Communication, St. Louis, MO.
An examination of the political and ideological sources of resistance among faculty at large universities to the idea of increasing their attention to writing. Anson concludes that to bring about the effective and lasting implementation

of WAC, we must abandon our naive optimism, begin conducting fuller research on educational attitudes and processes, and work from the inside out to bring about change by creating ideological shifts before imposing WAC on the curriculum.

49. Applebee, A. N. (1977). Writing across the curriculum: The London projects. *English Journal, 66*(9), 81–85.
Discusses the University of London Institute of Education Writing Across the Curriculum Project and Writing Research Unit and the implications of its findings, particularly for writing instruction in secondary schools.

50. Bailey, R. W. (1983). Writing across the curriculum: The British approach. In P. L. Stock (Ed.), *Fforum: Essays on theory and practice in the teaching of writing* (pp. 24–32). Upper Montclair, NJ: Boynton/Cook.
"Educational programs in Great Britain differ in significant ways from those in the United States"; and so, says Bailey, has the impetus for integrating writing into all subject-area courses. The article documents WAC as a movement in Great Britain which gained much of its strength from the 1975 Bullock Report.

51. Barber, E. A. (1988). Creating a mirror for language and learning in the Southern Mountain Region. *Virginia English Bulletin, 38*, 92–103.
Describes a program which creates a mirror of regional culture and values to enhance children's self-esteem and learning. Story-telling and folklore are central to the program, which integrates a variety of language activities.

52. Barr, M. A., & Healy, M. K. (1988). School and university articulation: Different contexts for writing across the curriculum. In S. H. McLeod (Ed.), *Strengthening programs for writing across the curriculum* (pp. 43–53). San Francisco: Jossey-Bass.
Argues that WAC programs in secondary schools may have been fostered by the same body of knowledge as those in the universities, but their evolution has been shaped by a different set of circumstances. WAC directors at the college level who wish to set up articulation programs with secondary schools must understand the nature of early WAC staff development programs and of testing at the secondary level before they begin to discuss articulation.

53. Barton, T. L., & Zelm, S. J. (1983). Beyond the Bay Area: A description of the Washington State University Writing Project. *English Education, 15*, 36–44.

54. *Bay Area Writing Project/California Writing Project/National Writing Project: An overview* (1979). Berkeley, CA: University of California. (ERIC Document Reproduction Service No. ED 184 123)
Discusses the initiation and development of the Bay Area Writing Project, the proliferation of programs based on the Bay Area model, and the establishment of the National Writing Project (NWP).

55. Bean, J. C. (1981). Involving non-English faculty in the teaching of writing and thinking skills. *International Journal of Instructional Media, 9*, 51–59.
Suggests ways for non-English faculty to incorporate writing into their courses

and discusses a model for curricular change among business faculty at Montana State University.

56. Bergman, C. A. (1984). Writing across the curriculum: Students as scholars, scholars as students. *Journal of Advanced Composition*, **5, 79–86.**
Discussing the faculty workshops on WAC at Pacific Lutheran University in Tacoma, Washington (led by Kenneth Bruffee), Bergman suggests the importance of engaging faculty in the writing process as an inductive method for helping them to see new possibilities for their teaching.

57. Bertch, J., & Fleming, D. R. (1991). The WAC workshop. In L. C. Stanley & J. Ambron (Eds.), *Writing across the curriculum in community colleges* **(pp. 37–43). San Francisco: Jossey-Bass.**
Offers advice on planning WAC workshops and on recruiting participants, handling logistical problems, and developing follow-up activities.

58. Blair, C. P. (1988). Only one of the voices: Dialogic writing across the curriculum. *College English, 50,* **383–389.**
Argues that WAC should be the responsibility of all departments and should not be housed within departments of English. A theoretically consistent WAC program will become dialogic, through "fruitful, growth-producing, creative interaction" among colleagues with different perspectives toward discourse and knowledge. Includes specific strategies for building and maintaining a dialogic program.

59. Blake, R. W. (1978). *Rationale; Composing as the curriculum: A guide for instruction in written composition, grades K–12.* **Albion, NY: Albion Central School District 1. (ERIC Document Reproduction Service No. ED 162 319)**
Gives the rationale for the Albion Central School District's writing program.

60. Booher, S. C. (1982). *A report on the tutorial outreach model for reading and writing across the curriculum at Los Medanos College.* **Pittsburgh, CA: Los Medanos College. (ERIC Document Reproduction Service No. ED 221 252)**
Describes the peer tutoring approach to WAC used at Los Medanos College.

61. Bronson, B. (1985). An impartial observer's view of write-to-learn classes. In A. R. Gere (Ed.), *Roots in the sawdust: Writing to learn across the disciplines* **(pp. 202–210). Urbana, IL: National Council of Teachers of English.**
A non-participant in the Writing-in-the-Humanities Program that evolved from work in the Puget Sound Writing Project, Bronson interviewed teachers and students in the program and observed classroom techniques during a three-month period in the spring of 1982. She describes four representative classes: special education in a suburban school, literature in a large city, humanities in a moderately rural school, and literature in a very rural school.

62. Brunetti, G. J. (1978). The Bullock Report: Some implications for American teachers and parents. *English Journal, 67(8),* **58–64.**
In an article directed at language arts teachers in America, Brunetti discusses the major features and implications of the Bullock report (*A Language for Life*, London, 1975).

63. Carson, J. (1992, March). *Recognizing and using context as a survival tool for WAC.* Paper presented at the annual meeting of the Conference on College Composition and Communication, Cincinnati, OH.   (ERIC Document Reproduction Service No. ED 346 497)
Based on his experience with WAC at Robert Morris College, Carson argues that WAC proponents can best sustain their programs by tailoring them to the particular contexts of their institutions.

64. Caywood, C. L., & Overing, G. R. (1987). Writing across the curriculum: A model for a workshop and a call for change. In C. L. Caywood & G. R. Overing (Eds.), *Teaching writing: Pedagogy, gender, and equity* (pp. 185-200). Albany, NY: State University of New York Press.
Analyzes a WAC workshop held for 25 faculty and administrators at a small liberal arts university.

65. Connelly, P. J., & Irving, D. C. (1976). Composition in the liberal arts: A shared responsibility. *College English, 37,* 668–670.
Describes WAC seminars offered by the English Department at Grinnell College.   The authors suggest that the quality of student writing correlates closely with the quality of writing assignments.

66. Covington, D., Brown, A. E., & Blank, G. (1985). An alternative approach to writing across the curriculum: The writing assistance program at North Carolina State's School of Engineering. *WPA: Writing Program Administration, 8*(3), 15–23.
Arguing that writing centers located in English departments often have no idea of the writing needs of students in departments at some intellectual distance from them, the authors offer an alternative to the centralized campus writing center.   The decentralized center responds to the needs of students and faculty in specialized programs.   The authors discuss their own writing assistance program, including its cost, efficiency, and effectiveness.

67. Cullen, R. J. (1985). Writing across the curriculum: Adjunct courses. *ADE Bulletin, 80,* 15–17.
Proposes the use of "adjunct" writing courses to avoid several of the problems outlined by Kinneavy (1983) that emerge from the "centralized" and the "single-subject" approaches to college programs. Adjunct courses are intensive writing courses linked to specific disciplines and taught by faculty in the writing program.

68. Cummins, M. Z., Stuchin-Paprin, J., & Lambert, J. R. (1991). A solution to student-faculty mismatch. In L. C. Stanley & J. Ambron (Eds.), *Writing across the curriculum in community colleges* (pp. 31–36). San Francisco: Jossey-Bass.
Describes two programs, at community colleges in the Bronx and in Dallas, that successfully address the problem of disparities between faculty expectations for students and students' ability to perform.

69. Daigle, S. L. (1985). *Writing and critical reading for learning across the disciplines: Academic challenges.* Long Beach: Office of the Chancellor, California State University. (ERIC Document Reproduction Service No. ED 262

684)
Describes grant projects sponsored by California State University during 1980–
1982 to improve writing and critical reading across the disciplines.

**70. Deaux, G. (1981). The writing project for faculty from disciplines other than
English.** In A. Humes (Ed.), *Moving between practice and research in writing:
Proceedings of the NIE-FIPSE grantee workshop* (pp. 75–79). Los Alamitos, CA:
SWRL Educational Research and Development.
Describes a faculty development project at Temple College funded by a grant
from the Fund for the Improvement of Post-Secondary Education. Trainees in
the program were teachers in various disciplines at Temple preparing to teach
the freshman composition course.

**71. Delmar, P. J. (1978). Composition and the high school: Steps toward fac-
ulty-wide involvement.** *English Journal, 67,* 36–38.
Argues that the English department must take the initiative to motivate
faculty members in all disciplines to use writing more fully in their classes.
Delmar offers suggestions for such initiatives and gives an example of a
suitable writing assignment in each of six subject areas—biology, home economics, art, health, mathematics, and music.

**72. Dick, J. A. R., & Esch, R. M. (1985). Dialogues among disciplines: A plan for
faculty discussions of writing across the curriculum.** *College Composition and
Communication, 36,* 178–182.
Outlines a consulting method used at the University of Texas at El Paso for
helping faculty in other disciplines to use writing in their classes in a
principled way.

**73. Dixon, M. S., & Fry, M. S. (1991). Raising consciousness across the
curriculum: How faculty can own responsibility for student writing.** *The
Writing Lab Newsletter, 16*(2), 12–15.
Recounts the development of the writing center, WAC program, and related
writing programs at Wittenberg University in Ohio.

**74. Dowling, H. F., Jr. (1985). Towson State University's approach to im-
proving writing across the curriculum.** *College Composition and Communication, 36,* 240–242.
Describes the origins, structure, and history of the cross-curricular writing
program at Towson State University, Maryland, which began in 1976. The core
of the program involves the establishment of "second" writing courses which
students elect in any discipline.

75. Draper, V. (1991, March). *Can writing programs change the university?
Change from the margins.* **Paper presented at the annual meeting of the
Conference on College Composition and Communication, Boston, MA. (ERIC
Document Reproduction Service No. ED 336 739)**
Discusses challenges a WAC director faces in working with WAC faculty,
particularly in encouraging instructors and teaching assistants to involve and
assist students with writing. As a solution, Draper teaches students strategies
for actively eliciting constructive feedback from their teachers.

76. **Durfee, P., Sova, A., Bay, L., Leech, N., Fearrien, R., & Lucas, R. (1991). Formalizing WAC in the curriculum: Writing-emphasis courses. In L. C. Stanley & J. Ambron (Eds.),** *Writing across the curriculum in community colleges* **(pp. 57–63). San Francisco: Jossey-Bass.**
Describes diverse programs for writing-intensive courses at three community colleges: Broome Community College, Rockland Community College, and Kapiolani Community College.

77. **Eastman, A. M. (1981, December).** *The foreign mission of the university English department.* **Paper presented at the annual meeting of the Modern Language Association, New York, NY. (ERIC Document Reproduction Service No. ED 215 349)**
According to Eastman, the university English department's home mission is the teaching of reading and writing; its foreign mission is to "convert" to a higher literacy those outside the English department, particularly future teachers of high school English and teachers of other university subjects.

78. **Faery, R. B. (1987). Women and writing across the curriculum: Learning and liberation. In C. L. Caywood & G. R. Overing (Eds.),** *Teaching writing: Pedagogy, gender, and equity* **(pp. 201–212). Albany, NY: State University of New York Press.**
An examination of the role that WAC can play in the education of women, particularly in light of the attempt to "explore the possibilities offered by the new writing pedagogy for revising the educational circumstances of women students."

79. **Farris, C., & Smith, R. (1992). Writing-intensive courses: Tools for curricular change. In S. H. McLeod & M. Soven (Eds.),** *Writing across the curriculum: A guide to developing programs* **(pp. 71–86). Newbury Park, CA: SAGE Publications.**
Discusses a range of problems and issues involved in developing the Writing Intensive (WI) courses that undergird WAC at many institutions. Topics addressed include implementation, maintaining "faculty-centered control" of the WI requirement, encouraging and rewarding faculty involvement, and evaluation.

80. **Ferlazzo, P. J. (1982, April).** *Writing across the curriculum from the point of view of a department chair.* **Paper presented at the annual meeting of the College English Association, Houston, TX. (ERIC Document Reproduction Service No. ED 215 368)**
The Chair of the Montana State University English Department describes the origins and success of that school's WAC program. Some components of the program have included start-up workshops for non-English faculty, a discussion series on "solving the writing crisis," the establishment of a writing center, and summer workshops on collaborative learning and the training of peer tutors.

81. **Fincke, G. (1982). Writing across the curriculum in high school.** *Clearing House, 56,* **71–73.**
Explores ways of modifying WAC programs for use in high schools.

82. Fitzgerald, S. H. (1988). Successes and failures: Facilitating cooperation across the curriculum. *Writing Lab Newsletter*, 13(1), 13–15.
Describes how the writing center cooperates with instructors and departments across the disciplines at the University of Missouri-St. Louis.

83. Forman, J. (1980). Notes toward writing across the curriculum: Some collaborative efforts. *Journal of Basic Writing*, 2(4), 12–21.
Describes an experimental course called "The Composing Process" first offered at Goucher College (Maryland) in the fall of 1979. The sophomore-level writing course was designed to address students' writing problems outside freshman English and incorporated peer-tutoring.

84. Freisinger, R. R. (1980). Cross-disciplinary writing workshops: Theory and practice. *College English*, 42, 154–166.
Describes the language and learning theory that has shaped the author's cross-disciplinary workshops. Distinguishing language for learning from language for informing, Freisinger points out the limitations of informative writing for fostering cognitive development when stressed extensively in the schools. Participants at WAC workshops should be asked to write journals, conduct brainstorming sessions, and try out other "discovery exercises."

85. Freisinger, R. R. (1982). Cross-disciplinary writing programs: Beginnings. In T. Fulwiler & A. Young (Eds.), *Language connections: Writing and reading across the curriculum* (pp. 3–13). Urbana, IL: National Council of Teachers of English.
Presents the theoretical rationale behind the cross-disciplinary writing workshops for faculty at Michigan Technological University.

86. Fulwiler, T. (1981a). Interdisciplinary writing workshops. *CEA Critic*, 43(2), 27–32.
Describes interdisciplinary faculty writing workshops at Michigan Technological University. The workshops are designed to provide teachers with a set of general pedagogical principles about teaching writing. The article argues for a greater use of expressive writing, for emphasizing writing as a process, and for treating student writing problems as complex and varied.

87. Fulwiler, T. (1981b). Showing, not telling, at a writing workshop. *College English*, 43, 55–63.
Describes faculty workshops sponsored by the WAC program at Michigan Technological University. Workshops are designed to introduce faculty to the theory and pedagogy of WAC, and participants take part in journal writing, freewriting, and revising.

88. Fulwiler, T. (1981c). Writing across the curriculum at Michigan Tech: Theory and practice. *WPA: Writing Program Administration*, 4, 15–20.
Contends that college students will take writing much more seriously when it is expected of them in all disciplines.

89. Fulwiler, T. (1982). Teaching teachers to teach revision. In R. A. Sudol (Ed.), *Revising: New essays for teachers of writing* (pp. 100–108). Urbana, IL:

National Council of Teachers of English.
Stresses the importance that revision plays in the learning process. Presents
faculty activities emphasizing different aspects of the revision process based on
WAC workshops for faculty at Michigan Technological University.

90. Fulwiler, T. (1984). How well does writing across the curriculum work?
College English, 46, 113–125.
Based on his experience with Michigan Technological University's six-year-old
WAC program, Fulwiler discusses the lessons he and his colleagues have
learned from their endeavors. Problems included terminology, faculty resistance, attitudes toward professional "turf," translating theory into practice,
dealing with large numbers of students, establishing trust in peer review of
teaching, and "overselling." Unexpected benefits for faculty included an
increased sense of belonging to a scholarly "community," a larger volume of
writing being done by the faculty, enhanced teaching methods in general, and
more cooperative research leading to tenure and promotion.

91. Fulwiler, T. (1986). Reflections: How well does writing across the curriculum work? In A. Young & T. Fulwiler (Eds.), *Writing across the disciplines:
Research into practice* (pp. 235–246). Upper Montclair, NJ: Boynton/Cook.
As director of writing at the University of Vermont and former head of WAC
at Michigan Technological University, Fulwiler reflects on his experience as a
leader of some 40 WAC workshops at MTU and other campuses.

92. Fulwiler, T. (1988). Evaluating writing across the curriculum programs. In
S. H. McLeod (Ed.), *Strengthening programs for writing across the curriculum*
(pp. 61–75). San Francisco: Jossey-Bass.
Suggests that the complex and comprehensive nature of WAC programs
makes them difficult to evaluate. But there are certain areas in which we can
collect data, including the growth of a community of scholars; the changes in
pedagogy; the improvements in student learning; and the improvements in
student writing.

93. Fulwiler, T., & Young, A. (Eds.). (1990). *Programs that work: Models and
methods for writing across the curriculum.* Upper Montclair, NJ: Heinemann,
Boynton/Cook.
Describes successful WAC programs at 14 colleges and universities in the
United States. Chapters focus on the history and development of individual
programs, problems and solutions in implementation, and sources of funding,
and are written by teams of instructors at each institution, many of whom are
from disciplines other than English or composition. Schools discussed are
Georgetown University, UCLA, the University of Vermont, Prince George's
Community College, the University of Chicago, California State University at
Chico, Beaver College, Michigan Technological University, Robert Morris
College, the University of Massachusetts, George Mason University, the
University of Minnesota, the University of Michigan, and a consortium of
schools in the Baltimore area.

94. Gerber, J. (1977). Suggestions for a common sense reform of the English
curriculum. *College Composition and Communication, 28,* 312–313.

Contends that the primary responsibility of all college English teachers, whatever their specialties, is to teach reading and writing in every mode and at every level of competence to traditional college students and older non-traditional students as well.

95. Glick, M. D. (1988). Writing across the curriculum: A dean's perspective. *WPA: Writing Program Administration, 11*(3), 53–58.
Summarizes work underway at the University of Missouri-Columbia to adopt a comprehensive writing program with a significant WAC component.

96. Godwin, C. M. (1991). The writing consultancy project. In L. C. Stanley & J. Ambron (Eds.), *Writing across the curriculum in community colleges* (pp. 85–89). San Francisco: Jossey-Bass.
Describes the Orange County (NY) Community College Writing Consultancy Project, which involves English faculty as consultants to instructors and students in the technical and allied health programs.

97. Gordon, J. W., & Peterson, L. H. (1982). Writing at Yale: Past and present. *ADE Bulletin, 71*, 10–14.
A history of the eclectic, "scatter-shot" approach to the writing crisis taken by Yale University. The article includes descriptions of experimental freshman courses, writing-intensive courses, and tutorials.

98. Graham, J. (1981). The interdisciplinary writing program. In A. Humes (Ed.), *Moving between practice and research in writing: Proceedings of the NIE-FIPSE grantee workshop* (pp. 80–83). Los Alamitos, CA: SWRL Educational Research and Development.
Summarizes the interdisciplinary writing program at the University of Washington. Writing lab classes are taught in conjunction with content-area classes. Teachers in the writing lab and content-area classes coordinate assignments.

99. Graham, J. (1983). What works: The problems and rewards of cross-curriculum writing programs. In B. L. Smith (Ed.), *Writing across the curriculum* (pp. 16–26). Washington: American Association for Higher Education. (ERIC Document Reproduction Service No. ED 243 391)
Discusses ways of preparing non-English department faculty to teach writing. The article also considers how to set up a WAC program, how to teach writing in lecture and tutorial sections, and how to help English departments accommodate new approaches to writing instruction.

100. Graham, J. (1992). Writing components, writing adjuncts, writing links. In S. H. McLeod & M. Soven (Eds.), *Writing across the curriculum: A guide to developing programs* (pp. 110–133). Newbury Park, CA: SAGE Publications.
Analyzes the impact, advantages, and pitfalls of three types of integrated writing courses that have evolved out of WAC: core (i.e., "component"), adjunct, and linked writing courses.

101. Gray, D. J. (1988). Writing across the college curriculum. *Kappan, 69*, 729–733.

102. Griffin, C. W. (1985). Programs for writing across the curriculum: A report. *College Composition and Communication, 36,* 398–403.
Reporting on a survey of WAC programs conducted in 1984, Griffin discusses the range and diversity of WAC programs and focuses especially on writing centers, faculty workshops, and the sorts of curricular changes motivating the programs or resulting from them.

103. Hamilton-Wieler, S. (1987). Why has language and learning across the curriculum not made a greater impact? *Education Canada* [Winter], 36–41.
Argues that the paucity of WAC programs results from a "lack of a common understanding of what the concept implies in pedagogical terms."

104. Hancock, D. O. (1979). *Reading and writing programs within the disciplines.* **Fullerton, CA: University of California/ California State University Workgroup.**
A 34-page directory of innovative reading and writing skills programs at U.S. colleges and universities.

105. Haring-Smith, T. (1992). Changing students' attitudes: Writing fellows programs. In S. H. McLeod & M. Soven (Eds.), *Writing across the curriculum: A guide to developing programs* (pp. 175–188). Newbury Park, CA: SAGE Publications.
Gives the history and rationale for the Writing Fellows Program at Brown University. In this program trained undergraduate peer tutors from across the disciplines "serve as first readers for papers written in selected courses throughout the curriculum." Each fellow is assigned to work with a faculty member and students in an individual class. Haring-Smith shows how to implement, operate, and evaluate a program and avoid pitfalls.

106. Haring-Smith, T., Hawkins, N., Morrison, E., Stern, L., & Tatu, R. (1985). *A guide to writing programs: Writing centers, peer tutoring programs, and writing-across-the-curriculum.* **Glenview, IL: Scott Foresman.**
Lists WAC programs at over 100 colleges and universities.

107. Haring-Smith, T., & Stern, L. (1985). Beyond the English department: Writing across the curriculum. In T. Haring-Smith, N. Hawkins, E. Morrison, L. Stern, & R. Tatu, *A guide to writing programs: Writing centers, peer tutoring programs, and writing-across-the-curriculum* (pp. 19–27). Glenview, IL: Scott Foresman.
An introduction to a survey of WAC programs in the United States. Offers a history and synthesis of current assumptions.

108. Harris, M. (1992). The writing center and tutoring in WAC programs. In S. H. McLeod & M. Soven (Eds.), *Writing across the curriculum: A guide to developing programs* (pp. 154–174). Newbury Park, CA: SAGE Publications.
Providing a relaxed environment where students "talk writing" with their peers, a writing center can complement WAC by serving as "the hub for writing across the campus." Harris offers advice for establishing and operating a writing center and for coordinating its activities with those of the WAC program.

109. Haviland, C. P. (1985). Writing centers and writing-across-the-curriculum: An important connection. *Writing Center Journal,* **5(2)/6(1), 25–30.**
Discusses three kinds of projects, developed at Montana State University, that involve writing centers integrally in WAC: faculty-centered projects, student-centered projects, and projects centered equally on faculty and students.

110. Herrington, A. J. (1981). Writing to learn: Writing across the disciplines. *College English,* **43, 379–387.**
Describes an interdisciplinary writing project in which faculty at Johnson State College in Vermont designed courses, established goals, and created writing assignments. Presents detailed illustrations of objectives, writing tasks, and student evaluations that were developed by project participants for courses in introductory economics, psychology, U.S. history, and "Theories of Society."

111. Hesson, J. (1987). Writing across the curriculum in Appomattox. In J. Self (Ed.), *Plain talk: About learning and writing across the curriculum* **(pp. 119–122). Commonwealth of Virginia: Virginia Department of Education.**
Describes a small WAC program in the Appomattox County Public School system in central Virginia.

112. Hirsch, L., Nadal, J., & Shohet, L. (1991). Adapting language across the curriculum to diverse linguistic populations. In L. C. Stanley & J. Ambron (Eds.), *Writing across the curriculum in community colleges* **(pp. 71–77). San Francisco: Jossey-Bass.**
Shows the three different ways that Hostos Community College (NY), Miami-Dade Community College (FL), and Dawson College (Province of Quebec) have adapted their language across the curriculum programs to the needs of diverse linguistic populations.

113. Hoff, K. T. (1992, March). *WAC politics: Winning friends and influencing people.* **Paper presented at the annual meeting of the Conference on College Composition and Communication, Cincinnati, OH. (ERIC Document Reproduction Service No. ED 344 234)**
Offers seven suggestions for implementing and sustaining a WAC program.

114. Holzman, M. (1983). Articulating composition. *College English,* **45, 288–295.**
Describes a writing program and a method for incorporating the teaching of writing skills into general education courses. The article discusses twelve composition courses that were linked to general education courses, and argues that if interdepartmental programs are to be successful, there must be frequent and direct contact among administrators, chairpersons, and staff advisors.

115. Howard, R. M. (1988). *In situ* **workshops and the peer relationships of composition faculty.** *WPA: Writing Program Administration,* **12(1–2), 39–46.**
Describes a program at Colgate University in which faculty in the writing program are invited by faculty in other disciplines to provide brief, *in situ* instruction for their students. The *in situ* workshops provide a forum for "subtle, non-confrontational modification of colleagues' ideas about writing instruction and instructors."

116. Hughes-Wiener, G., & Jensen-Cekalla, S. K. (1991). Organizing a WAC evaluation project: Implications for program planning. In L. C. Stanley & J. Ambron (Eds.), *Writing across the curriculum in community colleges* (pp. 65–70). San Francisco: Jossey-Bass.
Describes the structure, operation, and benefits of the WAC evaluation project of the Minnesota Community College System.

117. Impson, B., Self, B., Dorsey, S., Hudson, L., & Johnson, L. (1991). Integrating WAC and tutoring services: Advantages to faculty, students, and writing center staff. *The Writing Lab Newsletter, 16*(2), 6–8, 11.
Five peer tutors at Southwest Missouri State University discuss the integration of WAC with the writing center at their school.

118. Jacobs, S. E. (1978). Writing across the curriculum: An update. *English Journal, 67*(8), 64–67.
Describes three books which resulted from the University of London's Writing Across the Curriculum project: *Understanding Children Writing, Understanding Children Talking,* and *Writing and Learning Across the Curriculum 11–16.*

119. Kalamaras, G. (1991, March). *Effecting institutional change through writing across the curriculum: Ideology and inner dialogue.* Paper presented at the annual meeting of the Conference on College Composition and Communication, Boston, MA. (ERIC Document Reproduction Service No. ED 332 220)
Narrates his experiences as a writing consultant to a biology department and reflects on a consultant's role in effecting institutional and curricular change.

120. Kiniry, M., & Strenski, E. (1985). Sequencing expository writing: A recursive approach. *College Composition and Communication, 36,* 191–202.
The authors propose a system for sequencing assignments in composition courses to prepare students for academic writing. The system draws from a wide range of academic disciplines, including biology, nuclear science, psychology, history, economics, and art.

121. Kirsch, G. (1988). Writing across the curriculum: The program at Third College, University of California, San Diego. *WPA: Writing Program Administration, 12*(1–2), 47–55.
Describes an alternative to the two typical kinds of WAC programs: the integration of writing into discipline-specific courses and the WAC program housed in and taught by the English department. The program, instituted in 1985 at the University of California at San Diego, focuses on the lower-division, general-education curriculum.

122. Knudson, R. (1978). How the English teach writing. *English Journal, 67*(8), 49–50.
Argues that American schools generally neglect writing in the content areas, while British secondary schools require writing regularly in all subjects, link reading assignments with writing beginning in the elementary grades, and place more emphasis on expressive writing than their American counterparts.

123. **Kujawa, R. M. (1986). A dean's eye view of a college writing program. In K. O'Dowd & E. Nolan (Eds.), *Learning to write, writing to learn* (pp. 13–17). Livonia, MI: Madonna College Humanities Writing Program.**
Traces the history of the WAC-based Humanities Writing Program at Madonna College in Livonia, Michigan.

124. **Kuriloff, P. C. (1992). The writing consultant: Collaboration and team teaching. In S. H. McLeod & M. Soven (Eds.), *Writing across the curriculum: A guide to developing programs* (pp. 134–153). Newbury Park, CA: SAGE Publications.**
Provides a model showing how "the writing consultant" (i.e., the director of WAC or other writing specialists on campus) and content-area teachers can collaborate effectively in course design and team teaching.

125. **Leahy, R. (1989). Writing centers and writing-for-learning. *Writing Center Journal, 10*(1), 31–37.**

126. **Lupack, B. T. (1983, October). *Writing across the curriculum: Designing an effective model*. Paper presented at the annual meeting of the Midwest Writing Center Association, Iowa City, IA. (ERIC Document Reproduction Service No. ED 238 025)**
Describes aspects of an effective WAC program and how to implement it, including a review of the literature on student literacy, assessments of need, and the encouragement of faculty in the effort. Lupack focuses on the role of assessment in WAC and includes samples of student and faculty surveys.

127. **Magnotto, J. N., & Stout, B. R. (1992). Faculty workshops. In S. H. McLeod & M. Soven (Eds.), *Writing across the curriculum: A guide to developing programs* (pp. 32–46). Newbury Park, CA: SAGE Publications.**
Shows WAC administrators how to plan, fund, and evaluate faculty workshops and make them "an integral part" of a WAC program. The authors offer detailed advice on scheduling and other practical matters and also suggest strategies for sustaining faculty interest once workshops are over.

128. **Mahala, D. (1991). Writing utopias: Writing across the curriculum and the promise of reform. *College English, 53*, 773–789.**
Asks whether WAC's success is actually based on shallow changes and the "lack of threat to the status quo." Drawing on comparisons of British and American WAC history and programs, Mahala suggests ways in which the changes encouraged by WAC can be deepened and made more permanent.

129. **Maimon, E. P. (1979, April). *Administering a cross-disciplinary writing program*. Paper presented at the annual meeting of the Conference on College Composition and Communication, Minneapolis, MN. (ERIC Document Reproduction Service No. ED 172 253)**
Outlines procedures for initiating a cross-disciplinary writing program similar to the one at Beaver College in Pennsylvania.

130. **Maimon, E. P. (1979). Writing in the total curriculum at Beaver College. *CEA Forum, 9*, 7–16.**

Describes the WAC program at Beaver College. Initially, freshmen take two semesters of cross-disciplinary composition which acquaint them with assignments from diverse fields, and require collaborative learning and writing of multiple drafts. The writing center provides peer consultation with trained tutors. "Course clusters" involve several content faculty working with one English professor who advises them concerning writing assignments and responding to writing in their courses. These essential WAC elements are supplemented with advanced writing courses, as well as an M.A. in Education with concentration in written communication.

131. Maimon, E. P. (1981a). Visions and revisions across the curriculum. *ADE Bulletin, 69,* **39–40.**
Outlines the freshman composition and WAC programs at Beaver College and links them to five theoretical principles.

132. Maimon, E. P. (1981b). Writing in all the arts and sciences: Getting started and gaining momentum. *WPA: Writing Program Administration,* **4(3), 3–13.**
Discusses ways of motivating content-area faculty to use writing in their courses and gives eight suggestions for initiating and sustaining WAC among all faculty.

133. Maimon, E. P. (1982). Writing across the curriculum: Past, present, and future. In C. W. Griffin (Ed.), *Teaching writing in all disciplines* **(pp. 67–73). San Francisco: Jossey-Bass.**
Discusses the history and future prospects of the WAC movement. Maimon notes that the shift from the writing-product to the writing-process paradigm has been essential for success in WAC programs.

134. Marland, M. (1977). *Language across the curriculum.* **London: Heinemann.**
Provides information for secondary schools to plan their own language policies based on the "language across the curriculum" section of the Bullock Report. The book is divided into three parts. Part One deals with the need for a language policy. Part Two outlines the teachers' approach, students' use of language, classroom technicalities, and the school's organization. Part Three describes useful pedagogy for implementing a language policy.

135. McLeod, S. H. (1987). Defining writing across the curriculum. *WPA: Writing Program Administration,* **11(1–2), 19–24.**
Traces two philosophical roots of WAC and their various current institutional manifestations in an attempt to avoid the misunderstandings that can result when administrators and faculty have only partial definitions of WAC. The two philosophical bases are the "cognitive" (which emphasizes writing as a mode of thinking and learning) and the "rhetorical" (which emphasizes the contextual and social constraints of writing). Institutional manifestations of WAC include "The Freshman Composition WAC Course," "The Adjunct Course," and "Upper-Division Writing Intensive Courses."

136. McLeod, S. H. (1988). Translating enthusiasm into curricular change. In S. H. McLeod (Ed.), *Strengthening programs for writing across the curriculum*

(pp. 5–12). San Francisco: Jossey-Bass.
Outlines the role that directors of WAC programs can play as agents of change.

137. McLeod, S. H. (1989). Writing across the curriculum: The second stage, and beyond. *College Composition and Communication, 40,* 337–343.
Reports the results of a massive survey of WAC programs at 2735 post-secondary institutions (see McLeod & Shirley, below). Several new directions for WAC are noted, including a growing emphasis on the relationship between writing and critical thinking and changes in the curricular expectations for students who must take "writing-intensive" courses in addition to composition.

138. McLeod, S. H. (1992). Writing across the curriculum: An introduction. In S. H. McLeod & M. Soven (Eds.), *Writing across the curriculum: A guide to developing programs* **(pp. 1–11). Newbury Park, CA: SAGE Publications.**
Defines WAC and its underlying assumptions and identifies two major approaches to WAC—one emphasizing "writing to learn" and the other stressing "learning to write." Noting the great diversity of programs possible, McLeod also cautions faculty and administrators to develop programs suited to the individual needs of their institutions.

139. McLeod, S. H., & Emery, L. (1988). When faculty write: A workshop for colleagues. *College Composition and Communication, 39,* 65–67.
Explains a project at San Diego State University in which faculty interested in writing and publishing join in a weekly workshop sponsored by the Learning Resource Center. The idea for the group originated among faculty exposed to the WAC program at San Diego State.

140. McLeod, S. H., & Shirley, S. (1988). National survey of writing across the curriculum programs. In S. H. McLeod (Ed.), *Strengthening programs for writing across the curriculum* **(pp. 103–130). San Francisco: Jossey-Bass.**
From surveys sent to all two- and four-year institutions in the United States and Canada, the authors compiled an annotated list of 427 WAC programs. The listing includes the contact name and address for each program, information on the school, the number of years the program has been in existence, and the components of the program.

141. McLeod, S. H., & Soven, M. (1991). What do you need to start—and sustain—a writing-across-the-curriculum program? *WPA: Writing Program Administration, 15(1–2),* 25–34.
Suggests ways of informing eager but potentially misguided administrators and deans about WAC, and defines several ingredients WAC programs must have if they are to succeed: time, resources, support systems, and an administrative structure.

142. Michaels, G. (1982). *Writing across the curriculum: Its implementation in school districts.* **St. Paul, MN: St. Paul Public School System.**
A discussion of WAC programs in the St. Paul public school system, with special emphasis on the processes of implementation.

143. Moore, B. S. (1981, July). *Making changes in writing programs for high school teachers across the curriculum.* Paper presented at the meeting of the National Endowment for the Humanities/Beaver College Summer Institute for Writing in the Humanities, Glenside, PA. (ERIC Document Reproduction Service No. ED 220 842)
High school teachers usually respond to student writing as a "product." One way of changing this to a concern for "process" is by conducting workshops for department chairpersons.

144. Nochimson, M. (1980). Writing instruction across the curriculum: Two programs. *Journal of Basic Writing, 2*(4), 22–35.
Outlines two funded workshops to encourage faculty to incorporate writing instruction into their courses: one at the College of New Rochelle and the other at Drew University.

145. Nold, E. W. (1979, December). *Nuts and normals: Helping them teach writing across the curriculum.* Paper presented at the annual meeting of the Modern Language Association, San Francisco, CA. (ERIC Document Reproduction Service No. ED 185 545)
Offers a writing program administrator's view of writing in Stanford University's engineering department. Nold also outlines the history of a program which provided tutors for faculty who did not want to teach writing and explains the tutor training course for this program.

146. Odell, L. (1991). On using writing. In L. C. Stanley & J. Ambron (Eds.), *Writing across the curriculum in community colleges* (pp. 15–21). San Francisco: Jossey-Bass.
Discusses "some ways in which community college faculty are beginning to use writing to teach the subject matter of vocational and technical courses."

147. O'Dowd, K. (1986). WAC programs: Moving beyond the ten-minute university. In K. O'Dowd & E. Nolan (Eds.), *Learning to write, writing to learn* (pp. 5–12). Livonia, MI: Madonna College Humanities Writing Program.
Based on her experience establishing a WAC program at Madonna College in Michigan, O'Dowd outlines questions and issues one must face before starting a WAC program. Includes 15 recommended readings for potential program directors.

148. Peterson, L. H. (1992). Writing across the curriculum and/in the freshman English program. In S. H. McLeod & M. Soven (Eds.), *Writing across the curriculum: A guide to developing programs* (pp. 58–70). Newbury Park, CA: SAGE Publications.
Noting that freshman English defines the meaning of "writing" for most college and university students, Peterson urges that the course reflect a WAC emphasis and require "students to read and write in various academic genres." She then outlines a model for such a WAC-oriented course.

149. Pfister, F. R. (1978, March). *Your best defense is a good offense: Involving other disciplines in teaching writing skills.* Paper presented at the annual meeting of the Conference on College Composition and Communication,

Denver, CO. (ERIC Document Reproduction Service No. 159 701)
Discusses English Department efforts to promote WAC at the School of the Ozarks.

150. Raimes, A. (1979, April). *Writing and learning across the curriculum: The experience of a faculty seminar.* Paper presented at the annual meeting of the Conference on College Composition and Communication, Minneapolis, MN. (ERIC Document Reproduction Service No. ED 176 327)
Discusses a semester-long faculty seminar at Hunter College involving teachers from 14 disciplines in weekly meetings focusing on writing in the subject areas.

151. Raimes, A. (1980). Writing and learning across the curriculum: The experience of a faculty seminar. *College English, 41,* 797–801.
Describes the WAC program and faculty seminars at Hunter College.

152. Rizzolo, P. (1982). Peer tutors make good teachers: A successful writing program. *Improving College and University Teaching, 30,* 115–119.
Describes how the Reading and Writing Center at Ogontz Campus of the Pennsylvania State University has used peer tutors to support the university's WAC program.

153. Robertson, L. R. (1981, July). *Stranger in a strange land, or stimulating faculty interest in writing across the curriculum.* Paper presented at the annual meeting of the Wyoming Conference on Freshman and Sophomore English, Laramie, WY. (ERIC Document Reproduction Service No. ED 211 996)
Amusing paper comparing the problem of faculty involvement in WAC with the territoriality demonstrated in primate communities.

154. Rose, M. (1979). When faculty talk about writing. *College English, 41,* 272–279.
Describes a cross-curricular writing workshop held at UCLA.

155. Rosenberg, V. M. (1984). Writing instruction: A view from across the curriculum. *Journal of General Education, 36,* 50–66.
A personal narrative about integrating writing into the teaching of the History of Ideas.

156. Rosenwasser, M. (1983, November). *Faculty renewal, basic learning skills, and student success: An overlooked relationship?* Paper presented at the Annual Conference of the Community College Humanities Association, San Francisco. (ERIC Document Reproduction Service No. ED 244 651)
Describes the growth of a WAC program at North Seattle Community College as part of a broad plan to revitalize faculty in the humanities. Includes faculty survey instruments and a report based on their results.

157. Russell, D. R. (1986). Writing across the curriculum in 1913: James Fleming Hosic on "co-operation." *English Journal, 75*(5), 34–37.
Noting that WAC is much older than many believe, Russell discusses the efforts of Hosic (the founder of the National Council of Teachers of English) to promote writing to learn and interdisciplinary "cooperation" in the teaching of

composition.   The article also describes some early 20th-century WAC programs.

158. Russell, D. R. (1987).   Writing across the curriculum and the communications movement: Some lessons from the past. *College Composition and Communication, 38,* **184–194.**
Describes the history of two programs which anticipated the current WAC movement: Colgate's Functional Writing Program (1949–1961) and Berkeley's Prose Improvement Committee (1950–1965). In tracing the development and demise of these cross-curricular programs, Russell offers three implications for the future of current WAC programs: 1) they must be part of an institution-wide plan with realistic goals; 2) they require plentiful, consistent funding; and 3) they demand years of persistence to bring about lasting transformation.

159. Russell, D. R. (1989).   The cooperation movement: Language across the curriculum and mass education, 1900–1930. *Research in the Teaching of English, 23,* **399–423.**
Traces the history of a movement to create "cooperation" in post-secondary language instruction by involving specialized fields in various activities, such as the grading of papers. Though the movement's success was short-lived, Russell claims that it "raised central issues of curricular organization and language pedagogy to which later reformers returned."

160.   Russell, D. R. (1990).   Writing across the curriculum in historical perspective: Toward a social interpretation. *College English, 52,* **52–73.**
Examines the precursors of the WAC movement and why they failed (see Russell 1986; 1987; 1989). The demise of these movements is traced to complex and continuing forms of structural resistance within the academy. Russell expresses cautious optimism about WAC's future, seeing signs that the resistance may be weakening as the university and society itself evolve in the postmodern era.

161. Russell, D. R. (1991).   *Writing in the academic disciplines, 1870–1990: A curricular history.* Carbondale, IL: Southern Illinois University Press.
Traces the development of WAC in educational movements over the past 12 decades in both schools and colleges. Many WAC-like innovations during this period enjoyed a brief life and eventually disappeared, a phenomenon the author explains historically and educationally. Russell focuses especially on the last 20 years of WAC and suggests some ways in which this more recent manifestation of writing in all disciplines can be sustained.

162. Ruszkiewicz, J. J. (1982, November). *Writing "in" and "across" the disciplines: The historical background.* Paper presented at the annual meeting of the National Council of Teachers of English, Washington, DC. (ERIC Document Reproduction Service No. ED 224 024)
Traces WAC theory to the writings of Aristotle, Cicero, Ramus, and Bacon.

163.   Sandler, K. W. (1992).   Starting a WAC program: Strategies for administrators.   In S. H. McLeod & M. Soven (Eds.), *Writing across the curriculum: A guide to developing programs* **(pp. 47–57). Newbury Park, CA:**

SAGE Publications.
An academic administrator explains how her peers can best work to foster WAC programs on their campuses. Sandler warns against forcibly implementing programs from "the top down" and stresses the importance of promoting a program tailored to the needs of the individual institution.

164. Scanlon, L. C. (1986). Recruiting and training tutors for cross-disciplinary writing programs. *Writing Center Journal, 6*(2), 37–42.
Argues that writing centers and labs should recruit and train staff from content areas across the curriculum in order better to serve the diverse discourse communities involved in WAC.

165. Scheffler, J. A. (1980). Composition with content: An interdisciplinary approach. *College Composition and Communication, 31*, 51–57.
Reports on the success of the Freshman Interdisciplinary Studies Program (FIS) which began at Temple University in 1975 with the college writing component as an integral part of the program.

166. Sedgwick, E., III. (1982, July). *Faculty development program in writing across the curriculum.* **Paper presented at the National Endowment for the Humanities/Beaver College Summer Institute for Writing in the Humanities, Glenside, PA. (ERIC Document Reproduction Service No. ED 220 852)**
Outlines a proposal for a faculty development program at Longwood College, Virginia.

167. Selfe, C. L., Gorman, M. E., & Gorman, M. E. (1986). Watching our garden grow: Longitudinal changes in student writing apprehension. In A. Young & T. Fulwiler (Eds.), *Writing across the disciplines: Research into practice* (pp. 97–108). Upper Montclair, NJ: Boynton/Cook.
To assess the longitudinal impact of Michigan Technological University's WAC program, the authors studied the first graduating class to be exposed to four full years of WAC activities. The authors describe the methodology and various difficulties of the assessment and report results that are both encouraging and ambivalent for the future of WAC.

168. Selfe, C. L., & McCulley, G. A. (1986). Student exposure to writing across the curriculum. In A. Young & T. Fulwiler (Eds.), *Writing across the disciplines: Research into practice* (pp. 86–96). Upper Montclair, NJ: Boynton/Cook.
Reports the results of a survey designed to assess the effects of Michigan Technological University's 1979–1983 faculty WAC workshops on "the average student" enrolled there.

169. Shaw, R. A. (1985). Growing support for elementary school writing instruction. *Educational Review, 42*, 16–18.
Traditional forces surrounding writing instruction at the elementary level have served to impede rather than to aid writing instruction. Shaw proposes an educational support system comprised of state and local curriculum guidelines, tests and textbooks distributed by local publishers, and dissemination of academic research.

170. **Sheridan, J. (1992). WAC and libraries: A look at the literature.** *Journal of Academic Librarianship*, **18,** 90–94.
Reviews literature on WAC and suggests ways academic libraries can use WAC "to foster new connections with their constituencies on campus."

171. **Shreve, R., & Page, B. (1987). Writing across the curriculum at J. J. Kelly.** In J. Self (Ed.), *Plain talk: About learning and writing across the curriculum* (pp. 115–117). Commonwealth of Virginia: Virginia Department of Education.
Traces the history of the WAC program at J. J. Kelly high school in Virginia.

172. **Silverthorn, L. (1984). Writing across the disciplines: A program for curricular development.** In C. H. Klaus & N. Jones (Eds.), *Courses for change in writing: A selection from the NEH/Iowa Institute* (pp. 270–280). Upper Montclair, NJ: Boynton/ Cook.
Describes a series of faculty development workshops (at the University of South Alabama) that acquaint teachers with the theory and practice of WAC. Includes sample sequences of assignments for courses in advanced composition, microbiology, respiratory therapy, and sociology.

173. **Smith, B. L. (1983). An interview with Elaine Maimon.** In B. L. Smith (Ed.), *Writing across the curriculum* (pp. 11–15). Washington: American Association for Higher Education. (ERIC Document Reproduction Service No. ED 243 391)
Maimon, a leader in the WAC movement and director of the program at Beaver College, discusses the history and background of WAC.

174. **Smith, L. Z. (1988). Why English departments should "house" writing across the curriculum.** *College English,* **50,** 390–395.
A response to Blair's (1988) argument (this section) that WAC should not be housed in departments of English but should be shared equally in a dialogic, cross-curricular program. Smith contends that English departments are accommodating new theories of discourse and criticism in which the distinctions between literature and non-literature are becoming obsolete and in which post-structural theory acknowledges that the literary canon forms part of a "web of intertextuality" across the curriculum.

175. **Soven, M. (1988). Beyond the first workshop: What else can you do to help faculty?** In S. H. McLeod (Ed.), *Strengthening programs for writing across the curriculum* (pp. 13–20). San Francisco: Jossey-Bass.
Once the first workshop is over, what can a WAC director do to keep the enthusiasm going? Soven describes how a number of colleges and universities have designed new workshops and symposia, collaborative teaching and co-authoring projects, and opportunities for student involvement in WAC.

176. **Soven, M. (1992). Conclusion: Sustaining writing across the curriculum programs.** In S. H. McLeod & M. Soven (Eds.), *Writing across the curriculum: A guide to developing programs* (pp. 189–197). Newbury Park, CA: SAGE Publications.
Explains how follow-up workshops, peer tutoring, and appropriate efforts at evaluation can invigorate and sustain WAC programs over the long term.

177. Spear, M. B., McGrath, D., & Seymour, E. (1991). Toward a new paradigm in writing across the curriculum. In L. C. Stanley & J. Ambron (Eds.), *Writing across the curriculum in community colleges* (pp. 23–29). San Francisco: Jossey-Bass.
Calls for a reassessment of WAC that addresses problems of literacy in community colleges.

178. Stokes, R., & Holborn, D. G. (1991). Reforming the curriculum through writing: A conversation with Elaine P. Maimon. *Issues in Writing, 4*, 4–18.
An interview with one of the leaders of the WAC movement.

179. Stout, B. R., & Magnotto, J. N. (1988). Writing across the curriculum at community colleges. In S. H. McLeod (Ed.), *Strengthening programs for writing across the curriculum* (pp. 21–30). San Francisco: Jossey-Bass.
A survey of WAC programs at community colleges shows that, while these programs have much in common with programs at four-year institutions, they differ in terms of curricula, student diversity, and demands on faculty time.

180. Stout, B. R., & Magnotto, J. N. (1991). Building on realities: WAC programs at community colleges. In L. C. Stanley & J. Ambron (Eds.), *Writing across the curriculum in community colleges* (pp. 9–13). San Francisco: Jossey-Bass.
Presents current data on WAC programs at 121 two-year colleges.

181. Strenski, E. (1988). Writing across the curriculum at research universities. In S. H. McLeod (Ed.), *Strengthening programs for writing across the curriculum* (pp. 31–41). San Francisco: Jossey-Bass.
Argues that it is possible to run successful WAC programs at research universities by appealing to faculty who know about the importance of writing, by making sure teaching assistants are included in WAC workshops, and by offering writing instruction for graduate students.

182. Strenski, E. (1992). Helping TAs across the curriculum teach writing: An additional use for the *TA Handbook*. *WPA: Writing Program Administration, 15*(3), 68–73.
Suggests ways of supporting and developing teaching assistants' involvement in WAC, including the *TA Handbook*, which enables faculty and TAs to share important information about WAC.

183. Swift, J. (1980). Global education: What's in it for us? *English Journal, 69*, 9, 46–50.
Describes the global education program and curriculum at Stevenson High School in Livonia, Michigan.

184. Tandy, K. A. (1988). Continuing funding, coping with less. In S. H. McLeod (Ed.), *Strengthening programs for writing across the curriculum* (pp. 55–60). San Francisco: Jossey-Bass.
Argues that directors of WAC programs must analyze the context of their programs, marshal support across campus, and work with key administrators to ensure continued internal support and funding.

185. Taylor, P. et al. (1987). Writing across the curriculum at Rocky Run, 1985–86. In J. Self (Ed.), *Plain talk: About learning and writing across the curriculum* (pp. 123–130). Commonwealth of Virginia: Virginia Department of Education.
Teachers at Rocky Run Intermediate School in Fairfax County, Virginia describe how their WAC program works in the areas of science, math, L. D., Spanish, choral music, band, modern industry and technology, shop, and physical education.

186. Thaiss, C. (1982). The Virginia Consortium of Faculty Writing Programs: A variety of practices. In C. W. Griffin (Ed.), *Teaching writing in all disciplines* (pp. 45–52). San Francisco: Jossey-Bass.
Describes how members of a WAC consortium in Virginia integrate writing and learning. Thaiss describes the efforts of teachers at a range of Virginia colleges, including those in statistics, mechanical engineering, rehabilitation counseling, nursing, psychology, architecture, history, and business.

187. Thaiss, C. (1983). Brief history of writing across the curriculum at George Mason. In C. Thaiss (Ed.), *Writing to learn: Essays and reflections on writing across the curriculum* (pp. 141–144). Dubuque, IA: Kendall Hunt.
Discusses the history of WAC at George Mason University from 1978 to 1982, beginning with conferences and seminars and concluding with an assessment of the impact WAC has had on the university and its work.

188. Thaiss, C. (1984). Language across the curriculum. *ERIC Digest.* Urbana, IL: ERIC.
Reviews the history and theory of the language-across-the-curriculum movement, which emphasizes the "inseparableness of language, thinking, and learning."

189. Thaiss, C. (1988). The future of writing across the curriculum. In S. H. McLeod (Ed.), *Strengthening programs for writing across the curriculum* (pp. 91–102). San Francisco: Jossey-Bass.
Considering trends and opportunities for WAC planners, Thaiss explores such problems as the "textbook title" syndrome (textbooks that describe themselves as cross-curricular when they are more of a hindrance to WAC); and the top-down decree, in which administrators try to establish WAC programs by fiat. Thaiss argues that the best hopes come from the critical mass of teachers now familiar with WAC who incorporate its principles into their classes.

190. Thaiss, C. (1992). WAC and general education courses. In S. H. McLeod & M. Soven (Eds.), *Writing across the curriculum: A guide to developing programs* (pp. 87–109). Newbury Park, CA: SAGE Publications.
Offers strategies for adapting WAC to the general education (as opposed to upper-division) classroom.

191. Torbe, M. (1979). *Language across the curriculum guidelines for schools.* London: Ward Bond Educational.

192. Ulisse, P. (1988). *Writing across the curriculum.* Stratford, CN: Housatonic Community College. (ERIC Document Reproduction Service No.

ED 310 828)
Sketches the history of the WAC movement, illustrates diverse models of WAC programs, and suggests strategies and techniques for incorporating writing in science, math, business, social science, and non-English humanities courses. Also suggests ways of implementing and evaluating programs.

193. **Wallace, R. (1988). The writing center's role in the writing across the curriculum program: Theory and practice.** *Writing Center Journal, 8*(2), 43–48.
Shows how writing centers can assist in implementing WAC.

194. **Walvoord, B. E. (1992). Getting started. In S. H. McLeod and M. Soven (Eds.),** *Writing across the curriculum: A guide to developing programs* **(pp. 12– 31). Newbury Park, CA: SAGE Publications.**
Addresses a range of WAC implementation issues, such as: generating faculty interest and involvement; adopting appropriate models; sequencing activities for faculty; identifying and avoiding pitfalls; obtaining resources; financing start-up costs; and restarting a WAC program after a hiatus.

195. **Ward, J. A. (1991, March).** *WAC reconsidered: Issues for the 90s.* **Paper presented at the annual meeting of the Conference on College Composition and Communication, Boston, MA. (ERIC Document Reproduction Service No. ED 333 456)**
Contends that WAC faces complex challenges in the 1990s, given "the diversity of academic discourse communities and the varied epistemological assumptions and pedagogical practices that underlie them."

196. **Weiser, M. S. (1992, March).** *Building on common ground: Overcoming resistance to WAC in the technical college.* **Paper presented at the annual meeting of the Conference on College Composition and Communication, Cincinnati, OH. (ERIC Document Reproduction Service No. ED 346 493)**
Explores tactical and political issues involved in developing WAC programs at technical colleges.

197. **Weiss, R. H. (1979). The humanity of writing: A cross-disciplinary program.** *Improving College and University Teaching, 27,* 144–147.
Summarizes the origins, structure, and results of the WAC program at West Chester State College in Pennsylvania.

198. **Weiss, R. H. (1980). Writing in the total curriculum: A program for cross-disciplinary cooperation. In T. R. Donovan & B. W. McClelland (Eds.),** *Eight approaches to teaching composition* **(pp. 133–149). Urbana, IL: National Council of Teachers of English.**
Argues that freshman composition courses should be geared to teaching various kinds of academic writing and encourages non-English instructors to assign writing.

199. **Weiss, R. H., & Peich, M. (1980). Faculty attitude change in a cross-disciplinary writing workshop.** *College Composition and Communication, 31,* 33– 41.
Describes a week-long interdisciplinary workshop for teachers at West Chester

State College. The workshop included sessions on prewriting, peer critiquing, writing assignments based on case studies, and other classroom activities.

200. Witt, S. P. (1991). Beyond writing across the curriculum: The community communication corps. In L. C. Stanley & J. Ambron (Eds.), *Writing across the curriculum in community colleges* **(pp. 91–96). San Francisco: Jossey-Bass.**
Describes a program at Pima Community College (AZ) in which educators and business people collaborate to improve students' communication skills.

201. Wittman, E. (1986). *Blue Ridge Technical College Writing Project.* **(ERIC Document Reproduction Service No. ED 269 799)**
Discusses criteria for good writing and suggests assignments to foster student writing. Wittman also lists some "do's and don'ts" for WAC programs.

202. Young, A. (1979, March). *Teaching writing across the university: The Michigan Tech experience.* **Paper presented at the annual meeting of the College English Association, Savannah, GA. (ERIC Document Reproduction Service No. ED 176 298)**
The WAC program at Michigan Technological University educates teachers from all disciplines in the processes and functions of language and provides follow-up experiences and help with pedagogical strategies. The program is guided by the assumptions that students learn to write by writing and rewriting; that students should write often; and that their writing should address different purposes and different audiences.

203. Young, A. (1986). Rebuilding community in the English Department. In A. Young & T. Fulwiler (Eds.), *Writing across the disciplines: Research into practice* **(pp. 6–20). Upper Montclair, NJ: Boynton/Cook.**
Criticizing English departments that separate the teaching of literature from the teaching of writing and reading, Young urges departments to function as a "community of scholars teaching and studying writing, reading, and literature as one subject." Such a community, grounded in current theories of reading and composition, can exert pedagogical influence on other departments and stimulate cross-disciplinary faculty collaboration on teaching and research.

204. Young, R. (1991). Designing for change in a writing-across-the-curriculum program. In V. A. Chappell, M. L. Buley-Meissner, & C. Anderson (Eds.), *Balancing acts: Essays on the teaching of writing in honor of William F. Irmscher* **(pp. 141–160). Carbondale, IL: Southern Illinois University Press.**
Working from an assumption that WAC programs have about a five-year lifespan, Young describes his attempts to create a "self-renewing" program at Carnegie-Mellon University.   The essay begins with a description of conventional ("inappropriate") program development, then proposes an alternative ("appropriate") system. Young's system is "faculty-centered rather than curriculum-centered or student-centered."

205. Zinsser, W. (1986, April 13). A bolder way to teach writing. *New York Times* **(Education Life), pp. 58–63.**
Discusses his visits with faculty participants in the WAC program at Gustavus Adolphus College in St. Peter, Minnesota.

Research Studies

206. Ackerman, J. M. (1991). Reading, writing, and knowing: The role of disciplinary knowledge in comprehension and composing. *Research in the Teaching of English, 25*, 133–178.
Examines how writers use prior knowledge in composing synthesis essays. Forty graduate students enrolled in psychology or business wrote synthesis essays; half the subjects did think-aloud protocols while composing. The authors analyzed the protocols for the importance and origin of information and for the quality of particular rhetorical strategies. Found that prior knowledge of a topic provides information useful in developing textual strategies during writing.

207. Anderson, S. J. (1986). Student essay assignment preferences: A study of sex, age and creativity variables. In K. O'Dowd & E. Nolan (Eds.), *Learning to write, writing to learn* (pp. 82–96). Livonia, MI: Madonna College Humanities Writing Program.
Reports on a study of three variables in college writing assignments—creativity, age of student, and sex of student. Subjects were 128 students at Madonna College drawn from courses in English, accounting, business communication, and American literature.

208. Anderson, W., Best, C., Black, C., Hurst, J., Miller, M., & Miller, S. (1990). Cross-curricular underlife: A collaborative report on ways with academic words. *College Composition and Communication, 41*, 11–36.
Less a research study than a report of perceptions and experiences, this article represents the joint efforts of five students and a teacher of writing. Each student shares his or her notes on how writing functioned in coursework and in their (very diverse) majors. S. Miller provides a conclusion to their observations, noting that little of her own writing course seemed useful in other academic settings which the students encountered.

209. Anson, C. M., & Beach, R. (1990, March). *Research on writing to learn: The interesting case of academic journals.* Paper presented at the annual meeting of the Conference on College Composition and Communication, Chicago, IL. (ERIC Document Reproduction Service No. ED 322 535)

Summarizes the state of research on writing to learn and outlines an agenda for much-needed investigations of the relationships between informal writing and students' learning. Includes a description of the authors' research on academic journals used in university settings.

210. **Applebee, A. N. (1981).** *Writing in the secondary school: English and the content areas.* **NCTE Research Report No. 21. Urbana, IL: National Council of Teachers of English.**
Describes a study of the writing that secondary school students are asked to do in six major subject areas and includes an annotated bibliography of sources of strategies for incorporating writing into content area instruction.

211. **Applebee, A. N. (1982). Writing and learning in school settings. In M. Nystrand (Ed.),** *What writers know: The language, process, and structure of written discourse* **(pp. 365–381). New York: Academic Press.**
Essentially a condensed version of Applebee (1981) above. Based on that research, Applebee argues that "the kinds of things students are asked to do with written language are narrow and ultimately unproductive, having negative effects not only on students' writing abilities but also on their subject-area learning."

212. **Applebee, A. N., Langer, J. A., Durst, R. K., Butler-Nalin, K., Marshall, J. D., & Newell, G. E. (1984).** *Contexts for learning to write: Studies of secondary school instruction.* **Norwood, NJ: Ablex.**
Describes and reports the results of a multi-tiered study of writing in American secondary schools, grades 9–12. Results suggest that students do not produce very much substantive writing in their classes (3% of time, both in and out of class, was spent on writing greater than a paragraph in length), and that its purposes and audiences are generally impoverished (writing as assessment, directed to teacher as examiner).

213. **Applebee, A. N., Lehr, F., & Auten, A. (1981). Learning to write in the secondary school: How and where.** *English Journal, 70*(5), 78–82.
Summarizes a study of writing in U.S. secondary schools that began in October 1979 and continued through April 1980. Finds that writing activities occupy an insignificant proportion of class time in the six subject areas observed, including English. Reports writing-related activities as heavily weighted toward mechanical and informational writing tasks, and makes three suggestions for improving student writing, including "a shift from writing *to display information* toward writing *to fulfill natural communicative functions.*"

214. **Armstrong, D. B. (1990). A teacher reflects on a high school English class: The dialogue journal's contributions to learning and to interpersonal relations (Doctoral dissertation, New York University, 1989).** *Dissertation Abstracts International, 51,* 02A.
A case study examining the benefits and difficulties of assigning dialogue journals.

215. **Bader, L. A., & Pearce, D. L. (1983). Writing across the curriculum, 7–12.** *English Education, 15,* 97–106.

Reports on a survey of writing assignments at the junior high school level. Little writing activity was seen as learning-oriented, and almost no activities in prewriting or revision were included.

216. Barnes, D., & Shemilt, D. (1974). Transmission and interpretation. *Educational Review, 15,* **97–106.**
Analyzes British secondary school teachers' implicit beliefs about classroom communication and learning. The Transmission teacher views writing primarily as a way to measure student performance against the teacher's expectations and criteria. The Interpretation teacher, in contrast, sees writing as a way for students to become agents in their own learning.

217. Beadle, M. E. (1989, March). *Evaluating writing across the curriculum: Struggles and insights.* **Paper presented at the annual meeting of the American Educational Research Association, San Francisco. (ERIC Document Reproduction Service No. ED 316 562)**
Describes the challenges and difficulties of an effort to assess the WAC program at Walsh College in Canton, Ohio. Urges future WAC instructors to make assessment of their programs a top priority.

218. Behrens, L. (1978). Writing, reading, and the rest of the faculty: A survey. *English Journal, 67*(6), **54–66.**
Reports the results of a survey, conducted at American University, to assess faculty members' views of student literacy and to describe the types and frequency of writing assigned to students in the various disciplines.

219. Bernhardt, S. A. (1985). Writing across the curriculum at one university: A survey of faculty members and students. *ADE Bulletin, 82,* **55–59.**
Together with colleagues at Southern Illinois University-Carbondale, Bernhardt designed surveys for both faculty and students to gather data on the quantity and quality of writing instruction in various disciplines. Results were more positive than anticipated: an "overwhelming" consensus emerged among students and faculty about the importance of writing.

220. Bridgeman, B., & Carlson, S. B. (1984). Survey of academic writing tasks. *Written Communication, 1,* **247–280.**
A study of the types of writing tasks faced by beginning undergraduate and graduate students at American universities. Results show that tasks varied considerably in frequency across fields, but the importance of individual tasks was determined by the nature of the field itself (e.g., descriptive skills were ranked higher in importance in engineering, computer science, and psychology than in other fields). Despite the frequency of creative and expressive forms in the elementary grades, the survey indicated that these forms were rare in college.

221. Britton, J., Burgess, T., Martin, N., McLeod, A., & Rosen, H. (1975). *The development of writing abilities (11–18).* **London: Macmillan Education.**
Conducted under the auspices of the Schools Council in Britain, this study helped shape the theoretical base of WAC. The research team examined over 2,000 student scripts in all subjects in order to "develop a dynamic theoretical

model" for the development of writing abilities. Scripts were classified according to their "sense of audience" (the writer's interpretation of her reader's expectations as they affect her writing) and "function" (the conventional or typical purpose a piece of writing is designed to serve). Audience categories included "Self," "Teacher," and "Wider Audience." Function categories included "Transactional" (language to get things done, i.e., to inform, persuade, or instruct); "Expressive" (language close to the self and often typical of tentative first drafts of new ideas); and "Poetic" (writing as a verbal construct, such as a poem or a shaped memoir). The team found that most scripts were addressed to a teacher in the role of "examiner" (a subclass of the "Teacher" audience) and were transactional in function.

The team hypothesized that writing abilities develop through a process of "differentiation," in which the writer addresses increasingly varied and public audiences and moves outward, from expressive language to varieties of transactional and poetic writing. The sample showed little differentiation, however; between the first and seventh years writing became increasingly dominated by a single subclass (the "informative") of the transactional function.

222. Carroll, J. A. (1984). Process into product: Teacher awareness of the writing process affects students' written products. In R. Beach & L. S. Bridwell (Eds.), *New Directions in Composition Research* (pp. 315–333). New York: Guilford.
Describes a study to determine whether exposure to and engagement in the writing process would significantly affect teachers' ability to help students improve their writing. Results show a significant relationship between teachers' own experiences with the writing process and the quality and improvement of their students' writing.

223. Claypool, S. H. (1980). *Teacher writing apprehension: Does it affect writing assignments across the curriculum?* Lexington, KY: University of Kentucky. (ERIC Document Reproduction Service No ED 216 387)
Results of a study show a correlation between teachers' writing apprehension and the number of writing tasks they assigned to students.

224. Clemmons, S. M. (1981). Identification of writing competencies needed by secondary students to perform assignments in science and social studies classes. (Doctoral dissertation, Florida State University, 1980). *Dissertation Abstracts International*, 41, 3037A.
A study of the optimal writing competencies required of students in science and social studies classes in Northwest Florida county secondary schools.

225. Crowhurst, M. (1989). *The role of writing in subject area learning.* (ERIC Document Reproduction Service No. ED 303 805)
Pre-service secondary teachers from diverse content areas were required to take a six-week language across the curriculum course. Crowhurst studied the effects of the course on participants' attitudes towards writing-to-learn. The teachers' attitudes improved during the course, and nearly all said they intended to integrate writing into their content area teaching.

226. Daniels, J. P. (1990). Reading and writing to learn: The effects of a literature program and summary writing strategies on achievement in and attitude toward social studies content among fourth-grade students (Doctoral dissertation, The University of Connecticut, 1989). *Dissertation Abstracts International, 50,* 11A.

227. Davis, B. H., Rooze, G. E., & Tallent Runnels, M. K. (1992). Writing-to-learn in elementary social studies. *Social Education, 56,* 393–397.
Results of a study suggest "that journal writing facilitates writing fluency and learning retention in 4th grade social studies."

228. Day, S. (1989). Producing better writers in sociology classes: A test of the writing-across-the-curriculum approach. *Teaching Sociology, 17,* 458–464.
An experiment conducted at Southwest Texas State College suggests a dubious correlation between writing and learning, and leads the author to conclude that WAC is an approach that "promises more than it can deliver."

229. Dilworth, C. (1980). Locally sponsored staff development for English teachers: A survey of methods and results. *English Education, 12,* 98–105.
Reports the results of a survey of 59 English curriculum coordinators. Dilworth discusses the amount of time spent on staff development, the kinds of activities, and types of programs for local education agencies.

230. Donlan, D. (1974). Teaching writing in the content areas: Hypotheses from a teacher survey. *Research in the Teaching of English, 8,* 250–262.
Presents the results of a survey of math, science, and social studies teachers who use writing in their courses. Donlan also reports on the percent of textbooks in each subject area that include writing assignments. Results show that 45% of science textbooks use writing assignments, compared with 5% in math and 19% in social studies. Math and science teachers also used report writing more frequently than social studies teachers, who favored exposition.

231. Donlan, D. (1976). *Textbook writing assignments in three content areas.* **(ERIC Document Reproduction Service No. ED 123 635)**
A follow-up and reiteration of findings reported in Donlan (1974).

232. Eblen, C. (1983). Writing across-the-curriculum: A survey of a university faculty's views and classroom practices. *Research in the Teaching of English, 17,* 343–348.
Reports the results of a survey of faculty at the University of Northern Iowa examining their attitudes toward student writing and toward the use of writing in their courses. Faculty stressed "communicative/ maturation/ organization" problems in student writing more than problems in edited standard English. Content areas stressed transactional writing over expressive writing by a 10–1 margin.

233. Emig, J. (1971). *The composing processes of twelfth-graders.* **Urbana, IL: National Council of Teachers of English.**
In what has become a historically ground-breaking study in the field of composition, this monograph reports the results of several case studies of

twelfth graders' composing processes. While not specifically focused on WAC, the monograph offers a concise review of the literature on writing and rhetoric and provides a detailed analysis of one student's composing processes and attitudes. Emig also makes an important distinction between reflexive and extensive writing which has influenced thinking on WAC.

234. Faigley, L., & Hansen, K. (1985). Learning to write in the social sciences. *College Composition and Communication, 36,* 140–149.
Explores the problems English teachers face when they teach an upper-division writing course within another discipline.

235. Fulwiler, T., Gorman, M. E., & Gorman, M. E. (1986). Changing faculty attitudes toward writing. In A. Young & T. Fulwiler (Eds.), *Writing across the disciplines: Research into practice* (pp. 53–67). Upper Montclair, NJ: Boynton/Cook.
Results of a survey designed to measure the effects of interdisciplinary writing workshops on faculty attitudes toward writing at Michigan Technological University.

236. Gambell, J. (1984). What high school teachers have to say about student writing and language across the curriculum. *English Journal, 73,* 42–44.
Interviewed teachers in Saskatchewan high schools for their impressions of student writing as it relates to content areas.

237. Gere, A. R. (1977). Writing and writing. *English Journal, 66(8),* 60–64.
Evaluates the results of interviews with University of Washington students majoring in 24 areas as to what kind and how much writing was required of them. Gere found that research papers and essay exam questions were the most frequently assigned writing tasks and that a tremendous variety existed within and across disciplines in the amount of writing required.

238. Gere, A. R., Schuessler, B. F., & Abbott, R. D. (1984). Measuring teachers' attitudes toward writing instruction. In R. Beach & L. S. Bridwell (Eds.), *New directions in composition research* (pp. 348–361). New York: Guilford.
Reports the construction and validation of a questionnaire to measure teacher attitudes toward writing. The survey showed two instructional patterns consistent with the paradigms identified by B. Kroll (1980), "Developmental Perspectives and the Teaching of Composition," *College English, 41,* 741–752. "Maturationists" emphasize expressive writing and focus on the process of writing, while "interventionists" emphasize the acquisition of product-oriented skills such as standard usage, sentence structure, and correct grammar.

239. Glaze, B. (1987). A teacher speaks out about research. In J. Self (Ed.), *Plain talk: About learning and writing across the curriculum* (pp. 87–99). Commonwealth of Virginia: Virginia Department of Education.
A high school teacher discusses how the work of Vygotsky, George Kelly, Polanyi, Britton, Emig, and others has shaped her classroom teaching.

240. Gorman, M. E. (1986). Mucking around. In A. Young & T. Fulwiler (Eds.), *Writing across the disciplines: Research into practice* (pp. 228–234). Upper

Montclair, NJ: Boynton/Cook.
Advises beginners on how to do empirical and statistical research on composition and WAC. Offers suggestions for further reading.

241. Gorman, M. E. (1986). Developing our research model. In A. Young & T. Fulwiler (Eds.), *Writing across the disciplines: Research into practice* (pp. 33–41). Upper Montclair, NJ: Boynton/Cook.
An anecdotal account of one faculty committee's effort to develop a method for evaluating a WAC program (at Michigan Technological University).

242. Gorman, M. E., Gorman, M. E., & Young, A. (1986). Poetic writing in psychology. In A. Young & T. Fulwiler (Eds.), *Writing across the disciplines: Research into practice* (pp. 139–159). Upper Montclair, NJ: Boynton/Cook.
Drawing on data from an introductory psychology class that included poetry and short story writing as well as more traditional writing assignments, the authors conclude that "poetic" writing [see Britton et al. (1975)] can enhance learning in classes other than English, and that a mix of poetic and other kinds of writing stimulates exploration and imagination to a greater extent than does "expressive" and/or "transactional" writing alone.

243. Greene, S. (1993). The role of task in the development of academic thinking through reading and writing in a college history course. *Research in the Teaching of English*, 27(1), 46–75.
A study examining "how two different writing tasks affected the development of students' thinking in composing from sources in a college course in European history."

244. Grossman, J. L. (1989). Journal writing and adult learning: A naturalistic inquiry (Doctoral dissertation, The Fielding Institute, 1988). *Dissertation Abstracts International*, 50, 04A.

245. Harris, J. & Hult, C. (1985). Using a survey of writing assignments to make informed curricular decisions. *WPA: Writing Program Administration*, 8(3), 7–14.
Reports the results of a survey of faculty in each of the academic departments at Texas Technological University. Results showed that the essay or theme was the most often required form of writing, followed by the essay exam and the short research paper.

246. Herrington, A. J. (1984). Writing in academic settings: A study of the rhetorical contexts for writing in two college chemical engineering courses (Doctoral dissertation, Rensselaer Polytechnic Institute, Troy, NY). *Dissertation Abstracts International*, 45 (1–2), 104–A.
A case study examining the purposes that writing serves for learning in two college chemical engineering courses. One course was a lab section and the other a process design class. Results showed that students and teachers perceive the two contexts as different communities, with varying issues, writer and reader roles, and purposes. Herrington suggests implications for understanding various academic contexts as sites for writing and learning.

247. Herrington, A. J. (1985). Writing in academic settings: A study of the contexts for writing in two college chemical engineering courses. *Research in the Teaching of English, 19,* 331–359.
Investigated two college chemical engineering courses as disciplinary communities. Findings showed that the two courses "represented distinct communities where different issues were addressed, different lines of reasoning used, different writer and audience roles assumed, and different social purposes served by writing." Also see Herrington (1984) above.

248. Herrington, A. J. (1988). Teaching, writing, and learning: A naturalistic study of writing in an undergraduate literature course. In D. A. Jolliffe (Ed.), *Advances in writing research, vol. 2: Writing in academic disciplines* (pp. 133–166). Norwood, NJ: Ablex.
Examines the functions writing serves for learning in an undergraduate literature class, the ways functions influence the professor's manner of conducting the class, and the effects of functions and the professor's manner of teaching on students' writing and learning.

249. Herrington, A. J. (1992). Assignment and response: Teaching with writing across the disciplines. In S. P. Witte, N. Nakadate, & R. D. Cherry (Eds.), *A rhetoric of doing: Essays on written discourse in honor of James L. Kinneavy* (pp. 244–260). Carbondale, IL: Southern Illinois University Press.
Drawing on the WAC practices of teachers in a variety of academic fields (including economics, anthropology, and chemical engineering), Herrington aims to "provide reference points for teachers to reflect on their own pedagogical practices." The essay focuses on the design of writing assignments, how the writing process is integrated into coursework, and teachers' responses to students' writing. The brief case studies illustrate the power of WAC in improving students' writing and learning.

250. Herrington, A. J., & Cadman, D. (1991). Peer review and revising in an anthropology course: Lessons for learning. *College Composition and Communication, 42,* 184–199.
Demonstrates the value of peer review in classes across the curriculum. Examines the exchanges of two students in an anthropology course as they discuss their writing. Revision and peer review turn students from passive learners into agents of their own thinking and language development.

251. Hirsch, L. R., & King, B. (1983, April). *The relative effectiveness of writing assignments in an elementary algebra course for college students.* **Paper presented at the annual meeting of the American Educational Research Association, Montreal, Quebec.** (ERIC Document Reproduction Service No. ED 232 872)
In a study of students in four sections of an elementary algebra course at Rutgers University, the authors found "that writing assignments employed without teacher engagement were no more effective than traditional mathematics assignments."

252. Hughes, G. F., & Martin, G. R. (1992, April). *The relationship between instructional writing experience and the quality of student writing: Results* *from a longitudinal study in the Minnesota Community College System.* **Paper presented at the annual meeting of the American Educational Research Association, San Francisco, CA.** (ERIC Document Reproduction Service No. ED 345 276)

A study shows that students who experienced instructional writing across the curriculum improved as writers over the course of the academic year. A related study suggests "that the *quality* of writing assignments is likely to be more important than the *number* of writing assignments students are given."

253. Hughes-Wiener, G., & Martin, G. (1989, October). *Results of instructional research in a writing across the curriculum staff development program.* **Paper presented at the annual meeting of the American Educational Research Association, San Francisco.**

A study of the WAC project in the Minnesota Community College system attributes improved writing and subject-matter learning to faculty involvement in WAC.

254. Huot, B. (1992). Finding out what they are writing: A method, rationale and sample for writing-across-the-curriculum research. *WPA: Writing Program Administration, 15*(3), 31–40.

Describes a method for studying writing in various disciplines across any campus. Illustrates the method by describing how it worked in a School of Social Work on the author's campus.

255. Jolliffe, D. A., & Brier, E. M. (1988). Studying writers' knowledge in academic disciplines. In D. A. Jolliffe (Ed.), *Advances in writing research, vol. 2: Writing in academic disciplines* **(pp. 35–87). Norwood, NJ: Ablex.**

Demonstrates a research methodology for investigating dimensions of writers' knowledge that affect writing ability in academic fields.

256. Kalmbach, J. R. (1986a). The laboratory reports of engineering students: A case study. In A. Young & T. Fulwiler (Eds.), *Writing across the disciplines: Research into practice* **(pp. 176–183). Upper Montclair, NJ: Boynton/Cook.**

Kalmbach collected five engineering students' portfolios containing all the writing they had done in classes at Michigan Technological University. In a ranking of their academic activities, the students rated lab experiments as the most important but writing and written lab reports as least important. Kalmbach concludes that this discrepancy occurred because report writing was "isolated from any sort of meaningful problem-solving context" and suggests ways to make the writing of lab reports more meaningful to students.

257. Kalmbach, J. R. (1986b). The politics of research. In A. Young & T. Fulwiler (Eds.), *Writing across the disciplines: Research into practice* **(pp. 217–227). Upper Montclair, NJ: Boynton/Cook.**

Describes how research on writing and WAC can be politicized, with pointless or damaging results, by its opponents and proponents.

258. Kalmbach, J. R., & Gorman, M. E. (1986). Surveying classroom practices: How teachers teach writing. In A. Young & T. Fulwiler (Eds.), *Writing across*

the disciplines: Research into practice (pp. 68–85). Upper Montclair, NJ: Boynton/Cook.
A survey of faculty participants in the first five weeks of Michigan Technological University's WAC workshops shows that changes in attitude caused by the workshops resulted in changes in classroom activities and assignments.

259. Klinger, G. C. (1977). A campus view of writing. *College Composition and Communication, 31*, 153–158.
Describes the results of a questionnaire on writing attitudes sent to 2,700 college teachers nationwide with a 16% response rate. Results suggest that it is possible to gain the support of the entire university to improve student writing.

260. Konopak, B. C., Martin, S. H., & Martin, M. A. (1990). Using a writing strategy to enhance sixth-grade students' comprehension of content material. *Journal of Reading Behavior, 22*, 19–37.
In a world history course, sixth-graders in an experimental group performed writing tasks in addition to their ordinary classwork, while those in the control group did not. Results of a written post-test indicate that the experimental group "generated significantly higher quality ideas than the control group" and also significantly improved as writers.

261. Langer, J. A., & Applebee, A. N. (1987). *How writing shapes thinking: A study of teaching and learning.* Urbana, IL: National Council of Teachers of English. (ERIC Document Reproduction Service No. ED 286 205)
A study of writing assignments in the secondary school curriculum and their effect on learning. Chapters 1–3 describe the project and methods and the teachers, students, and instructional techniques studied. Chapter 4 describes effective writing activities used in content area classrooms. Chapter 5 discusses "the redefinition of teaching and learning that occurred in the classrooms where writing worked best to foster academic learning." Chapters 6–8 examine the kinds of thinking and learning encouraged by different types of writing. Chapter 9 presents theoretical and practical implications.

262. MacVaugh, P. Q. (1990). Writing to learn: A phenomenological study of the use of journals to facilitate learning in the content areas (Doctoral dissertation, Boston University, 1990). *Dissertation Abstracts International, 51*, 04A.

263. Maimon, E. P., & Nodine, B. (1978, December). *Measuring behavior and attitudes in the teaching of writing among faculties in various disciplines.* Paper presented at the annual meeting of the Modern Language Association, New York. (ERIC Document Reproduction Service No. ED 167 999)
Reports on a survey intended to measure faculty perceptions of student writing prior to initiating a WAC program at Beaver College.

264. Mallett, M., & Newsome, B. (1977). *Talking, writing, and learning 8–13.* London: Evans/Methuen.
Reports results of a two-year study of British students (ages 8–13) in six school environments that emphasize the potential of talking and writing for learning.

265. Mallonee, B., & Breihan, J. R. (1985). Responding to students' drafts: Interdisciplinary consensus. *College Composition and Communication, 65,* **213–231.**
A report of a four-year project in cross-curricular writing at Loyola College in Baltimore. The authors organized a network of cross-curricular seminars, workshops, and surveys involving 5 composition instructors and 14 other instructors, each from a different discipline. Results of this collaboration suggest four points of consensus about how to respond to students' drafts.

266. Marshall, J. D. (1984). Process and product: Case studies of writing in two content areas. In A. N. Applebee, J. A. Langer, R. K. Durst, K. Butler-Nalin, J. D. Marshall, & G. E. Newell, *Contexts for learning to write: Studies of secondary school instruction* **(pp. 149–168). Norwood, NJ: Ablex.**
Compares the uses of writing in a social science and a biology classroom in one secondary school.

267. Marshall, J. D. (1987). The effects of writing on students' understanding of literary texts. *Research in the Teaching of English, 21,* **30–63.**
In an experiment involving 80 high school students of American Literature, students who performed personal and formal analytic writing tasks scored significantly higher on posttests of reading comprehension than did students who engaged in only "restricted" writing tasks.

268. Martin, N. (1973). *Information to understanding.* **London: Schools Council Project Writing Across the Curriculum, 11–13.**
Examines learning and language instruction in different school subjects. Finds that writing is not used to its full potential in various subject areas.

269. Martin, N., Medway, P., & Smith, H. (1984). From information to understanding: What children do with new ideas. In N. Martin (Ed.), *Writing across the curriculum pamphlets* **(pp. 4–33). Upper Montclair, NJ: Boynton/Cook.**
Illustrates how children use talk and writing to restructure their thinking and to "understand the new ideas they [meet] in lessons." Emphasizes the importance of expressive language as defined by Britton et. al (1975) to learning.

270. McCarthy, L. P. (1985). *A stranger in strange lands: A college student writing across the curriculum.* **Unpublished doctoral dissertation, University of Pennsylvania.**
Studies the writing experiences of three students at Loyola College over a three-year period. McCarthy describes ethnographic observations, interviews, composing-aloud protocols, and text analyses of one student in freshman composition, poetry, and cell-biology courses. The student's success was influenced by the stated requirements and instructions, as well as by unarticulated social expectations concerning writing contexts.

271. McCarthy, L. P. (1987). A stranger in strange lands: A college student writing across the curriculum. *Research in the Teaching of English, 21,* **233–265.**
Summarizes the author's 1985 study (above) of one college student's experiences writing in three courses during his freshman and sophomore

years. The study supports a view of writing as tied to the conventions, roles, and processes of specific discourse communities.

272. McCarthy, L. P., & Fishman, S. M. (1991). Boundary conversations: Conflicting ways of knowing in philosophy and interdisciplinary research. *Research in the Teaching of English, 25,* 419–468.
A naturalistic study comparing the learning processes of undergraduates in a philosophy course with the collaborative learning experiences of the authors themselves. The authors suggest the benefits of working from multiple epistemologies even within specific learning contexts.

273. McCarthy, L. P., & Walvoord, B. F. (1988). Models for collaborative research in writing across the curriculum. In S. H. McLeod (Ed.), *Strengthening programs for writing across the curriculum.* (pp. 77–89). San Francisco: Jossey-Bass.
In collaborative research projects, teachers from two or more disciplines cooperate to understand better their students' thinking and writing. The authors describe three models for collaborative research in WAC: the focused pair, the reciprocal pair, and the chief researcher/many collaborators model.

274. McCulley, G. A. (1986). Research in writing across the curriculum: Beginnings. In A. Young & T. Fulwiler (Eds.), *Writing across the disciplines: Research into practice* (pp. 42–48). Upper Montclair, NJ: Boynton/Cook.
Calls for more empirical studies of WAC, primarily to discover the uses and roles of writing to communicate; to understand how writing can foster learning in different subject areas; and to identify and develop appropriate rhetorical concerns across the curriculum.

275. McCulley, G. A., & Soper, J. A. (1986). Assessing the writing skills of engineering students: 1978–1983. In A. Young & T. Fulwiler (Eds.), *Writing across the disciplines: Research into practice* (pp. 109–135). Upper Montclair, NJ: Boynton/Cook.
Chronicles the goals and complexities of a five-year effort to evaluate the writing of senior engineering students at Michigan Technological University.

276. McGinley, W. J. (1990). The role of reading and writing in the acquisition of knowledge: A study of college students' self-directed engagement in reading and writing to learn (Doctoral dissertation, University of Illinois at Urbana-Champaign, 1989). *Dissertation Abstracts International, 50,* 10A.

277. McTeague, F., Payne, R., Graham, A., & Murray, J. (1980). *An investigation of secondary student writing across the curriculum and some suggestions for school language policies.* Toronto: York Borough Board of Education. (ERIC Document Reproduction Service No. ED 182 770)
The writing of 117 students in every grade and subject in a Canadian secondary school was studied over a nine-day period, including amounts, purposes, and audiences. Based on the results, the authors suggest the need for extra audience response, greater variety of tasks for learning and thinking, and a view of writing as a process.

278. Messina, S., & White, D. (1992, April). *Classroom research: Writing assessment in paired and separate history and English classes.* Paper presented at the conference of the College Reading and Learning Association Conference, San Francisco, CA. (ERIC Document Reproduction Service No. ED 343 636)
A study conducted at Solano Community College in California shows that students who took an integrated course combining history and English composition improved more, both as writers and as students of history, than did their counterparts (in control groups) who studied composition and history in separate classes or who took history and no composition.

279. Miller, L. D., & England, D. A. (1989). Writing to learn algebra. *School Science and Mathematics, 89,* 299–312.
Miller and England describe a collaboration between three secondary math teachers and two university faculty (the authors) to determine how writing-to-learn can be used to teach and learn algebra. Results suggest that in-class writing helped students learn and assisted teachers toward a better understanding of their students' affective and instructional needs.

280. Newell, G. (1984). Learning from writing in two content areas: A case study/protocol analysis. *Research in the Teaching of English, 18,* 265–287.
Describes a study of the effects of three school writing tasks (notetaking, answering study questions, and writing essays) on three measures of learning (concept application, recall, and gain in passage-specific knowledge). Results showed gains in passage-specific knowledge for essay writing. Essay writing also enabled students to integrate information from their readings into their knowledge of a topic. Notetaking and answering study questions remained isolated and detached from other skills.

281. Newkirk, T. & Atwell, N. (Eds.). (1988). *Understanding writing: Ways of observing, learning, and teaching* (2nd ed.). Portsmouth, NH: Heinemann.
Discusses language skills instruction K–8 from the perspective of elementary school teachers who participate as observers/researchers in their own classrooms. Articles address a range of theoretical and practical concerns, including collaborative learning, writing/reading relationships, assessment, and the use of textbooks.

282. Nocerino, M. A. (1987). How do we know? In J. Self (Ed.), *Plain talk: About learning and writing across the curriculum* (pp. 159–162). Commonwealth of Virginia: Virginia Department of Education.
Outlines some aspects of evaluating WAC programs and concludes that "Effective classroom and school-based evaluation techniques do help teachers better understand when and what students are learning."

283. Odell, L., Goswami, D. & Quick, D. (1983). Writing outside the English composition class: Implications for teaching and for learning. In R. W. Bailey & R. M. Fosheim (Eds.), *Literacy for life: The demand for reading and writing* (pp. 175–196). New York: Modern Language Association.
A study comparing the writing and surrounding contexts of five students, with extensive coursework in economics and political science, and five legislative

analysts employed by a state legislature who held positions to which the undergraduate subjects might aspire. The study compared in detail the subjects' contexts for writing. Results showed marked differences in the assumptions and processes underlying each context. The authors recommend that educators use the results of research on writing in nonacademic settings to inform their pedagogical practices.

284. Parker, R. P. (1985). Surveying writing practices across the curriculum: Models and findings. *NASSP Bulletin, 69*(478), 34–40.
A comparative analysis of four WAC research projects designed to study the uses, types, and effectiveness of writing in high schools in New Jersey, Australia, and Canada. Discusses research design, measurement, and utility of the research.

285. Pearce, D. L. (1984). Writing in content-area classrooms. *Reading World,* 23, 234–241.
Based on interviews with 70 high school teachers, this study attempts to determine the amount and nature of writing used across the curriculum in high school classes. Results show writing is not limited to English classes, but it is seldom used to help students acquire and critically learn course concepts.

286. Pearce, D. L., & Davison, D. M. (1988). Teacher use of writing in the junior high mathematics classroom. *School Science and Mathematics, 88*(1), 6–15.
The authors studied the amount, kinds, and uses of writing in junior high mathematics classrooms. Results indicated that: "more teachers used writing tasks that were mechanical and passive in nature...than any other kinds of writing activities" and that "individual teachers did not use a variety of writing activities in their classes"; the most frequent types of writing involved mere mechanical transcription of information; students nearly always wrote for the teacher rather than peers in the classroom; and exercises "which incorporated instructional support (i.e., prewriting and revision) were rare to non-existent."

287. Penrose, A. M. (1989). *Strategic differences in composing: Consequences for learning through writing* **(Technical Report No. 31). Center for the Study of Writing. (ERIC Document Reproduction Service No. ED 310 402)**
Attempts, among other things, to measure the effects of individual differences on learning through writing.

288. Penrose, A. M. (1992). To write or not to write: Effects of task and task interpretation on learning through writing. *Written Communication, 9,* 465–500.
A study of 40 college freshmen suggests "that task interpretation and the nature of the material to be learned are important variables in the relationship between writing and learning."

289. Peters, L. (1983). Writing across the curriculum: Across the U.S. In C. Thaiss (Ed.), *Writing to learn: Essays and reflections on writing across the curriculum* (pp. 9–24). Dubuque, IA: Kendall Hunt.
Reports the results of a 1982 survey of 122 American colleges and universities.

290. Petty, W. T., & Finn, P. J. (1981). Classroom teachers' reports on teaching written composition. In S. Haley-James (Ed.), *Perspectives on writing in grades 1–8* (pp. 19–33). Urbana, IL: National Council of Teachers of English.
Based on responses to two widely distributed questionnaires, Petty and Finn discuss the frequency of writing in the classroom, materials used, emphases of composition, and instructional problems.

291. Philips, J. F. (1990). The effects of writing to learn instructional strategies on writing apprehension and academic self-concept (Doctoral dissertation, West Virginia University, 1989). *Dissertation Abstracts International, 50,* 10A.

292. Pittendrigh, A. S., & Jobes, P. C. (1984). Teaching across the curriculum: Critical communication in the sociology classroom. *Teaching Sociology, 11,* 281–296.
Reports on a sociology class experiment using the principle of "retroduction." A highly structured approach to writing was seen as best incorporating this model, which stresses planning, writing, and revision.

293. Prior, P. (1991). Contextualizing writing and response in a graduate seminar. *Written Communication, 8,* 267–310.
Reports an ethnographic study of the nature of writing and response in a graduate-level seminar in a college of education at a large university. Prior examines the students' expectations, assumptions, and knowldege as well as the professor's responses and evaluations of the students and their writing.

294. Procter, M. (1992, March). *The university as context for writing: How undergraduates see it.* Paper presented at the annual meeting of the Conference on College Composition and Communication, Cincinnati, OH. (ERIC Document Reproduction Service No. ED 346 783)
A survey of undergraduates at the University of Toronto, which has an active WAC program, suggests a disturbing "gap of attitude and understanding between the institution and the students" regarding the educational value and functions of writing.

295. Rebele, J. E. (1985). An examination of accounting students' perceptions of the importance of communication skills in public accounting. *Issues in Accounting Education,* 41–50.
Though accounting practitioners see writing skills as extremely important in their profession, this study shows that accounting students view writing skills as "a relatively unimportant determinant of success in a public accounting firm." Rebele suggests changing student attitudes by incorporating more writing into accounting courses.

296. Rose, B. J. (1989). Using expressive writing to support the learning of mathematics (Doctoral dissertation, The University of Rochester, 1989). *Dissertation Abstracts International, 50,* 04A.

297. Rymer, J. (1988). Scientific composing processes: How eminent scientists write journal articles. In D. A. Jolliffe (Ed.), *Advances in writing research, vol.*

2: Writing in academic disciplines (pp. 211–250). Norwood, NJ: Ablex.
Rymer interviewed and collected protocols from nine biochemists as they wrote journal articles. She finds that scientists typically discover new ideas and information as they write, even though scientific writing is stereotypically viewed as mere recapitulation of previously defined knowledge.

298. Scharton, M. (1983). Composition at Illinois State University: A preliminary assessment. *Illinois English Bulletin, 71,* 11–22.
Reports the results of a questionnaire in which faculty at Illinois State University were asked to assess the quality of their students' writing. While over 85% of respondents were "dissatisfied" with students' writing, results showed that teachers "make [writing] assignments at all levels, for diverse purposes, and with confidence that they are using a powerful instrument for teaching and learning."

299. Schumacher, G. M., & Nash, J. G. (1991). Conceptualizing and measuring knowledge change due to writing. *Research in the Teaching of English, 25,* 67–95.
Proposes reconceptualizing the way researchers study the impact of writing on learning. The new approach involves changing "how we select writing tasks in writing-to-learn investigations and how we assess the changes due to writing."

300. Schwartz, M. (1984). Response to student writing: A college-wide perspective. *College English, 46,* 55–62.
By eliciting responses from faculty across the curriculum to three sets of paired passages, Schwartz shows how different disciplines have different rhetorical values.

301. Selfe, C. L., & Arbabi, F. (1983). Writing to learn: Engineering student journals. *Engineering Education, 74*(3), 86–90.
See Selfe & Arbabi (1986).

302. Selfe, C. L., & Arbabi, F. (1986). Writing to learn: Engineering student journals. In A. Young & T. Fulwiler (Eds.), *Writing across the disciplines: Research into practice* (pp. 184–191). Upper Montclair, NJ: Boynton/Cook. Reprinted from *Engineering Education,* 1983, 74 (3), 86–90.
Based on a study of two sections of a civil engineering class—one that included journal writing and one that did not—the authors contend that journal writing offers a time-efficient means of improving student performance on writing assignments, problem-solving, and other classroom activities and of better acquainting instructors with students' needs, opinions, and attitudes.

303. Selfe, C. L., Petersen, B. T., & Nahrgang, C. L. (1986). Journal writing in mathematics. In A. Young & T. Fulwiler (Eds.), *Writing across the disciplines: Research into practice* (pp. 192–207). Upper Montclair, NJ: Boynton/Cook.
Reports mixed results from an experiment designed to measure the effects of journal writing on learning, knowledge, and attitudes about writing in a college mathematics class.

304. Simpson, M. L. (1989, March). *A comprehensive study strategy using student writing as a means of learning content area concepts.* **Paper presented at the annual meeting of the American Educational Research Association, San Francisco. (ERIC Document Reproduction Service No. ED 305 631)**
From experiments, Simpson concludes that the independent study strategy PORPE ("Predict, Organize, Rehearse, Practice, Evaluate") provides content area teachers with a comprehensive study strategy for helping students prepare for essay and multiple choice exams.

305. Singer, D. & Walvoord, B. F. (1984). Process-oriented writing instruction in a case-method class. In J. A. Pearce II & R. B. Robinson, Jr. (Eds.), *Proceedings of the Academy of Management* **(pp. 121–125). Boston: Academy of Management.**
Describes a study in which three different modes of writing instruction were tested in three otherwise identical sections of a business management class. The study suggested that intervention at the draft stage improved students' writing and their mastery of course content.

306. Stempien, M. (1990). An analysis of writing-to-learn in the context of a survey of mathematics course for students in the liberal arts (Doctoral dissertation, State University of New York at Buffalo, 1990). *Dissertation Abstracts International, 51,* **08A.**

307. Stevens, R. S., III (1985). Writing and learning: What the students say. In A. R. Gere (Ed.), *Roots in the sawdust: Writing to learn across the disciplines* **(pp. 211–221). Urbana, IL: National Council of Teachers of English.**
Summarizes the results of interviews in which 80 high school students were asked their opinions on writing. Concludes that students are capable of recognizing links between writing and learning and can undertake greater challenges than are assumed in courses that simply teach to "the basics."

308. Stewart, M. F., & Hayden L. L. (1983). Teachers' writing assessments across the high school curriculum. *Research in the Teaching of English, 17,* **113–125.**
Examines differences in the quality ratings which 20 teachers in each of three senior high school curricular areas gave to samples of written arguments by college freshmen. Results show a high level of rating consistency across the curriculum and a general agreement regarding certain variables that might predict the ratings.

309. Stout, D. E., Sumutka, A. R., & Wygal, D. E. (1991). Experiential evidence on the use of writing assignments in upper-level accounting courses. *Advances in Accounting, 9,* **125–141.**
Reports an accounting instructor's experiences using informal and formal writing assignments in two upper-level accounting courses. The study suggests that the impact of writing assignments on student learning and course/instructor evaluations is affected by contextual factors (i.e., students in a night class registered a greater impact than students in a day class).

310. Swanson-Owens, D. (1986). Identifying natural sources of resistance: A case study of implementing writing across the curriculum. *Research in the*

Teaching of English, 20, 69–97.
Reports on a case study with two goals: to identify and analyze the resistance to
implementing WAC programs in schools; and to suggest a practical pedagogical
model for teachers interested in implementing WAC programs.

311. Swilky, J. (1991, March). *Cross-curricular writing instruction: Can writing
instructors resist institutional resistance?* **Paper presented at the annual
meeting of the Conference on College Composition and Communication,
Boston, MA. (ERIC Document Reproduction Service No. ED 331 066)**
A case study of two instructors explores sources of faculty resistance to WAC
and implies ways that WAC leaders can better address such resistance.

312. Tierney, R. (1981). Using expressive writing to teach biology. In A. M.
Wotring & R. Tierney, *Two studies of writing in high school science.* Berkeley,
CA: Bay Area Writing Project. Reprinted in M. Myers (1985), *The teacher-re-
searcher: How to study writing in the classroom* (pp. 149–166). Urbana, IL:
National Council of Teachers of English.
See Wotring & Tierney (1981), this section.

313. Tighe, M. A. (1991). *Teaching composition across the curriculum in
Southeastern Alabama and Suffolk County, England.* (ERIC Document
Reproduction Service No. ED 331 094).
In a comparative analysis of British and American teachers, Tighe found that
both groups relied heavily on transactional writing and focused—as the
assumed audience of their assignments—on the teacher.

314. Tighe, M. A. & Koziol, S. M., Jr. (1982). Practices in the teaching of writing
by teachers of English, social studies, and science. *English Education, 14,* 76–85.
Reports on a survey of English, social studies, and science teachers (7–12) in
Western Pennsylvania schools. Results show the need for staff workshops,
more expressive writing in all areas, more emphasis on prewriting, and
different formats for evaluative feedback.

315. Trimmer, J. F. (1985). Faculty development and the teaching of writing.
WPA: Writing Program Administration, 9(1–2), 11–30.
Reports the results of two questionnaires. The first focused on competency
testing and other politically sensitive issues. The second focused on writing
programs designed to acquaint faculty with research on the teaching of writing;
problems that have prevented senior faculty from acknowledging the value of
research on the teaching of writing; and how literature and composition will be
connected in the future. Results are used to define three faculty attitudes
towards writing which Trimmer labels the "rhetoric of cynicism," the
"rhetoric of conflict," and the "rhetoric of complacency."

316. Walvoord, B. F., & McCarthy, L. P. (1991). *Thinking and writing in
college: A naturalistic study of students in four disciplines.* Urbana, IL:
National Council of Teachers of English.
Examines the role of writing assignments in Business Administration, History,
Psychology, and Biology, with special focus on how students interpreted and
responded to assignments and how faculty read students' papers. The authors

employed multiple research strategies, including interviews, writing logs, and conversations with the teachers.

317. Wason-Ellam, L. (1987, March). *Writing as a tool for learning: Math journals in grade one.* **Paper presented at the annual meeting of the National Council of Teachers of English Spring Conference, Louisville, KY. (ERIC Document Reproduction Service No. ED 285 194)**
A study of pupils doing "hands-on" mathematics in a first-grade classroom. Rather than simply transcribing information in the language of teachers or textbooks, students used journals expressively to self-question, organize information, assimilate and accomodate new knowledge, and make guesses. Results indicate that journals helped to personalize students' knowledge.

318. Webb, T. A. (1990). Student and faculty response to writing to learn at the college level (Doctoral dissertation, Michigan State University, 1990). *Dissertation Abstracts International, 51,* **05A.**
Concludes that the teacher's manner of presenting writing and WAC can significantly affect how students respond.

319. Weiss, R. H., & Walters, S. A. (1979, November). *Research on writing and learning: Some effects of learning-centered writing in five subject areas.* **Paper presented at the annual meeting of the National Council of Teachers of English, San Francisco, CA. (ERIC Document Reproduction Service No. ED 191 073)**
Reports a study involving college freshmen and teachers in the areas of history, psychology, physical sciences, reading theory and practice, and statistics. The study was conducted to test the following four hypotheses: 1) more subject-area writing will produce better writing; 2) more subject-area writing will reduce writing apprehension; 3) the frequency and amount of learner-centered writing about a subject will increase learning of that subject; and 4) concepts students write about will be clearer to them than the concepts they do not write about. The findings supported the third and fourth, but not the first and second, hypotheses.

320. Weiss, R. H., & Walters, S. A. (1980). *Writing to learn.* **Paper presented at the annual meeting of the American Educational Research Association, Boston. (ERIC Document Reproduction Service No. ED 191 056)**
Describes a study conducted to assess the effects of writing in content-area courses on (1) student learning; (2) writing performance; and (3) writing apprehension. [See Weiss & Walters (1979)]

321. West, G. K., & Byrd, P. (1982). Technical writing required of graduate engineering students. *Journal of Technical Writing and Communication,* **12(1), 1–6.**
Describes a survey in which engineering faculty were asked to rank, in order of frequency, the types of writing assignments they gave to graduate students. Results showed that faculty "assigned examinations, quantitative problems, and reports most frequently, that they assigned homework and papers (term and publication) less frequently, and that they assigned progress reports and

proposals least frequently." The authors suggest that the content of technical writing classes be altered to prepare students more fully for the kinds of writing emphasized in graduate engineering courses.

322. White, B. F. (1990). Writing before reading: Its effects upon discussion and understanding of text (Doctoral dissertation, University of Wisconsin-Madison, 1990). *Dissertation Abstracts International, 51,* 03A.
In experiments, students' understanding of short stories improved when reading was preceded by autobiographical writing.

323. Williamson, M. M. (1984). The functions of writing in three college undergraduate curricula (Doctoral dissertation, State University of New York at Buffalo). *Dissertation Abstracts International, 45,* 775A.
Williamson examined similarities and differences of writing functions in undergraduate sociology, biology, and English classes as perceived by teachers in the fields. The key finding was that conformity to register and discourse formats was seen as a prerequisite to success in biology and sociology. Students may not be aware of these tacit expectations. As expected, note-taking constituted the bulk of writing done in the disciplines studied.

324. Williamson, M. M. (1988). A model for investigating the functions of written language in different disciplines. In D. A. Jolliffe (Ed.), *Advances in writing research, vol. 2: Writing in academic disciplines* **(pp. 89–132). Norwood, NJ: Ablex.**
Contends that the concept of register can help to explain the functions—linguistic, social, and intellectual—that writing serves in three undergraduate curricula. Williamson demonstrates a qualitative research methodology used in a study of writing in English, biology, and sociology departments.

325. Wotring, A. M., & Tierney, R. (1981). *Two studies of writing in high school science.* **Berkeley: Bay Area Writing Project. (ERIC Document Reproduction Service No. ED 238 725)**
Wotring had students in a high school chemistry class write expressively in "thinkbooks." While thinkbooks helped some students with course content, most seemed unable to accept "writing to think" (as opposed to writing to memorize or transcribe ideas) as a legitimate kind of writing. In the other part of the monograph, Tierney describes an experiment to test whether students who do expressive writing in biology learn better than students who merely do traditional assignments. Students who did expressive writing performed better than others on recall tests but about the same on multiple-choice tests.

326. Yates, J. M. (1983). *Research implications for writing in the content areas.* **Washington, DC: National Education Association.**
A volume intended for K–12 teachers. Part One traces the theoretical and historical roots of WAC and characterizes WAC as a movement in which students learn "by doing." Part Two tells how to integrate writing, reading, and speaking into any content-area course. Part Three describes language activities explored by teachers in English, history/social science, foreign languages/bilingual education, and science/math.

327. Zemelman, S. (1977). How college teachers encourage students' writing. *Research in the Teaching of English, 11,* 227–234.
Reports the results of a study of faculty views and methods in WAC at Livingston College of Rutgers University.

Theory and Rationale

328. Anson, C. M. (1987). The classroom and the "real world" as contexts: Reexamining the goals of writing instruction. *Journal of the Midwest Modern Language Association,* 20(1), 1–16.
Suggests that many of our professional and curricular discrepancies can be explained by the clash of two ideological extremes, one of which assumes that writing instruction should indoctrinate students into an academic culture, and the other that a content-neutral, skills-based pedagogy will help students "survive" in all writing contexts, especially those beyond school. Anson advocates a pedagogy based on the development of strategies for writing in many discourse communities.

329. Bailey, R. W. (1983). Writing across the curriculum: The British approach. In P. L. Stock (Ed.), *Fforum: Essays on theory and practice in the teaching of writing* (pp. 24–32). Upper Montclair, NJ: Boynton/Cook.
Discusses the theoretical rationale for the British approach to WAC.

330. Baker, S. (1983). Writing as learning. In P. L. Stock (Ed.), *Fforum: Essays on theory and practice in the teaching of writing* (pp. 224–227). Upper Montclair, NJ: Boynton/Cook.
Defines *The Practical Stylist* as a cross-curricular treatment of writing.

331. Barnes, D., Britton, J., & Rosen, H. (1971). *Language, the learner, and the school* **(rev. ed.). Harmondsworth, England: Penguin Books.**
In a collection of essays, Barnes examines teacher behavior and interaction with students in the secondary classroom; Britton examines writing as a way of learning; and Rosen discusses a document on language policy across the curriculum and the rationale behind it. All three authors emphasize the importance of integrating writing, speaking, and reading, and recommend policies for language across the curriculum.

332. Bartholomae, D. (1985). Inventing the university. In M. Rose (Ed.), *When a writer can't write* (pp. 134–165). New York: Guilford.
A discussion of the problems students face becoming enculturated into an academic community of language users. Bartholomae argues that each time a student writes in an academic context, she must "invent" the branch of the

university in which she is located.   Much of the essay turns around the author's examination of 500 student essays written during a placement exam.

333. Baum, J. (1975). Interdisciplinary studies, the latest experimental rage.
College Composition and Communication, 26, 30–33.
Advocates interdisciplinary writing courses.

334. Bazerman, C. (1980). A relationship between reading and writing: The conversational model. *College English, 41,* 656–661.
Outlines strategies for encouraging students to become more active readers and writers.   A conversational model (for the interplay of reading and writing) "points to the fact that writing occurs within the context of previous writing and advances the total sum of the discourse."   Bazerman construes each piece of writing as "a contribution to an ongoing, written conversation."

335. Bazerman, C. (1981). What written knowledge does: Three examples of academic discourse. *Philosophy of the Social Sciences, 11,* 361–387.
Examines three texts—one in molecular biology, one in sociology, and one in literary criticism—from four perspectives: the object under study, the literature of the field, the anticipated audience, and the author's own self. Bazerman shows how statements of knowledge are embodied in the language of each discipline and how these differ along clear epistemological lines in the three essays.

336. Beach, R., & Bridwell, L. (1984). Learning through writing: A rationale for writing across the curriculum. In A. D. Pellegrini & T. D. Yawkey (Eds.), *The development of oral and written language in social contexts* (pp. 183–198). **Norwood, NJ: Ablex.**
In a review of WAC theory and research, the authors provide a rationale for integrating writing into all instructional contexts. They also discuss the importance of considering the conventions of context and audience during the writing process and of learning to evaluate information critically.

337. Bechtel, J. (1985). A new view of writing. In J. Bechtel (Ed.), *Improving writing and learning* (pp. 11–29). **Boston: Allyn and Bacon.**
Summarizes the principles behind WAC and writing-to-learn.

338. Bizzell, P. (1982a). Cognition, convention, and certainty: What we need to know about writing. *Pre/Text, 3,* 213–243.
A critique of the dominant cognitive perspective toward the study of writing, which neglects the social functions of communication. Bizzell suggests that contemporary models of writing analyze the "hows" of writing but not its "whys."   She offers an alternative social perspective based on the work of Soviet linguist Vygotsky. She further argues that people cannot write unless they can define their goals "in terms of the community's interpretive conventions."

339. Bizzell, P. (1982b). College composition: Initiation into the academic community. *Curriculum Inquiry, 12,* 191–207.
In a review of two WAC textbooks, Bizzell examines the history of

composition studies and the various attempts to define the discipline's role in initiating students into academic discourse. A constructivist, Bizzell critiques cognitivist and "individualistic" approaches for discounting the function of social context in literacy development.

340. Bizzell, P. (1984, March). *What happens when basic writers come to college?* Paper presented at the annual meeting of the Conference on College Composition and Communication, New York, NY.
Following the work of William Perry, Jr., Bizzell sees the major problem of the basic writer in the academic setting as one of a conflict of "world view" and a clash of discourse conventions. Thus, basic writers must become "bicultural" in order to succeed, since the academic "world view" tends to be hegemonic. Bizzell warns of the socio-political problems involved in such a transition.

341. Bizzell, P. (1987). Literacy in culture and cognition. In T. Enos (Ed.), *A sourcebook for basic writing teachers* (pp. 125–137). New York: Random House.
A socio-political overview of the types and functions of literacy and how they relate to the basic writer. The discourse of academic literacy is debunked as the only literacy leading to cognitive growth and metalinguistic awareness. Bizzell promotes a theory of "multiple literacy" in the academic setting.

342. Bloom, L. Z. (1992, March). *The composition curriculum: A paradigm of possibilities.* Paper presented at the annual meeting of the Conference on College Composition and Communication, Cincinnati, OH. (ERIC Document Reproduction Service No. ED 345 266)
Argues that the process paradigm of composition, which largely displaced the current-traditional paradigm, must itself be supplanted as curricula respond to continuing political, pedagogical, social, and other changes.

343. Brandt, D. (1986). Toward an understanding of context in composition. *Written Communication, 3,* 139–157.
Argues that the study of writing has largely ignored the role of social context. Writing is a "social enterprise...best understood in relationship to the social event that [the writer] is in the process of accomplishing."

344. Britton, J. (1971). What's the use? A schematic account of language functions. *Educational Review, 23,* 205–219.
An early discussion of Britton's three language functions (transactional, expressive, and poetic). Britton argues that research is needed to verify the scheme but believes that it offers one approach to the consideration of "language across the curriculum."

345. Britton, J. (1972a). *Language and learning.* Harmondsworth, England: Penguin.
Develops "the theory that we use language as a means of organizing a representation of the world—each for himself—and that the representation so created constitutes the world we operate in, the basis of all the predictions by which we set the course of our lives." Britton also discusses "expressive" language as the foundation for all other types of discourse.

346. Britton, J. (1972b). Writing to learn and learning to write. In *The humanity of English*. Urbana, IL: National Council of Teachers of English.
Argues for the importance of learning about any subject through the act of writing.

347. Britton, J. (1982). *Prospect and retrospect: Selected essays of James Britton*. Upper Montclair, NJ: Boynton/Cook.
Collected essays tracing the development of Britton's model of language and its relation to the subjective and objective components of learning. Of key interest is the essay "Writing to Learn and Learning to Write," his most detailed account of language functions.

348. Britton, J. (1983). Language and learning across the curriculum. In P. L. Stock (Ed.), *Fforum: Essays on theory and practice in the teaching of writing* (pp. 221–224). Upper Montclair, NJ: Boynton/Cook.
Reiterates his humanistic analysis of the role of writing in the learning process. Programs in WAC should not stress a concern for language so much as a concern for the "quality of learning."

349. Britton, J. et al. (1974). *Keeping options open—Writing in the humanities*. London University and Schools Council. (ERIC Document Reproduction Service No. ED 177 550)
Discusses a WAC project involving 14- to 16-year-old students in the humanities. Includes examples of writing, with focus on first-hand experience, function, and audience.

350. Clark, W. (1984). *Writing to learn in all subjects*. Urbana, IL: NCTE/SLATE Steering Committee on Social and Political Concerns. (ERIC Document Reproduction Service No. ED 263 618)
After summarizing the rationale for WAC, Clark suggests ideas for developing district-wide WAC programs and presents five strategies for incorporating writing into content-area classrooms.

351. Clifford, J. (1991). The neopragmatic scene of theory and practice in composition. *Rhetoric Review, 10*(1), 100–107.

352. Comprone, J. J. (1988). Reading Oliver Sacks in a writing-across-the-curriculum course. *Journal of Advanced Composition, 8,* 158–166.
Applies to the work of Oliver Sacks the theory that a writer must always be torn between the need to adhere to the "field-specific" conventions of his or her discipline and the desire to communicate with a larger audience beyond the discipline itself. Sacks' writing is "squarely set in the middle of this field-specific/field-universal tension in contemporary academic discourse." Comprone suggests several ways in which such discourse—also exemplified in such writers as Stephen Jay Gould, Richard Selzer, and Lewis Thomas—can be used for reading and writing in cross-disciplinary writing courses.

353. Comprone, J. J. (1991, March). *Writing across the disciplines: Where do we go from here?* Paper presented at the annual meeting of the Conference on College Composition and Communication, Boston, MA. (ERIC Document

Reproduction Service No. ED 331 053)
Attempts to redefine WAC within the context of literacy theory.

354. Connery, B. A. (1988). Using journals in the cross-curricular course: Restoring process. *Journal of Advanced Composition, 8,* 97–104.
Argues that, in many preprofessional and cross-curricular writing courses, attention to the process of writing is often subverted by too limited a focus on the forms and conventions of the writing in the discipline. Connery advocates using journals to create an intellectual environment that restores process and learning to the act of writing.

355. D'Arcy, P. (1977, January 28). Going back inside. *The Times Educational Supplement* (London), p. 43.
Notes that WAC requires strong commitment from teachers and describes factors which discourage its implementation.

356. D'Arcy, P. (1984). Keeping options open: Writing in the humanities. In N. Martin (Ed.), *Writing across the curriculum pamphlets* (pp. 86–113). Upper Montclair, NJ: Boynton/Cook.
Argues that students may write better and learn more when they compose in function categories other than the teacher as "examiner" [see Britton et al. (1975)].

357. Dowst, K. (1980). The epistemic approach: Writing, knowing, and learning. In T. R. Donovan & B. W. McClelland (Eds.), *Eight approaches to teaching composition* (pp. 65-85). Urbana, IL: National Council of Teachers of English.
Views language itself as a way of knowing, and hence writing as a way of composing one's reality.

358. Elbow, P. (1991a). Reflections on academic discourse: How it relates to freshmen and colleagues. *College English, 53*(2), 135–155.
Argues against teaching "academic discourse" (of the kind written across academic institutions) in freshman writing courses. Instead, freshmen should write papers that "render experience rather than explain it." Contends that is difficult to teach academic discourse because it is neither unitary nor consistent, and because it takes so many forms and manifestations.

359. Elbow, P. (1991b). Some thoughts on *Expressive Discourse***: A review essay.** *Journal of Advanced Composition, 11,* 83–93.
Replies to Jeanette Harris's *Expressive Discourse,* which critiques Elbow, James Britton, and other so-called "rhetorical expressionists."

360. Emig, J. (1977). Writing as a mode of learning. *College Composition and Communication, 28,* 122–128.
Argues that writing represents a "unique mode of learning—not merely valuable, not merely special, but unique." Writing provides a powerful means of feedback and of making connections between analysis and synthesis, verbal language and abstract formulations.

361. Emig, J. (1983). *The web of meaning: Essays on writing, teaching, learning, and thinking.* Ed. D. Goswami & M. Butler. Upper Montclair, NJ: Boynton/Cook.
An anthology of Emig's writings from 1963–1982. In such chapters as "Writing as a Mode of Learning" (1977) and "The Tacit Tradition: The Inevitability of a Multi-Disciplinary Approach to Writing" (1979), Emig examines some of the theoretical issues central to WAC.

362. Executive Committee of the National Council of Teachers of English. (1983). Essentials of English: A document of reflection and dialogue. *English Journal, 72,* 51–53.
Posits the relevance of language arts to thinking and learning generally and crystallizes major principles behind WAC.

363. Fader, D. (1966). *Hooked on books.* New York: Medallion Books.
Argues that reading and writing should be a part of every classroom in all curricular areas. Many examples of strategies for different classes are included.

364. Falke, A. (1982). What every educator should know about reading research. In T. Fulwiler & A. Young (Eds.), *Language connections: Reading and writing across the curriculum* (pp. 123–138). Urbana, IL: National Council of Teachers of English.
Defining reading comprehension as the ability to reconstruct the author's main thesis and supporting ideas, Falke attempts to "acquaint teachers with the fundamentals of reading research in order that they may more confidently and effectively guide their students' learning."

365. Fillion, B. (1979). Language across the curriculum. *McGill Journal of Education, 14,* 47–60.
Describes the educational and political context in which language across the curriculum gained momentum in Canada.

366. Fletcher, S. L. (1981, December). *Gracing our work: Generating theory from writing across the curriculum.* Paper presented at the annual meeting of the Modern Language Association, New York, NY. (ERIC Document Reproduction Service No. ED 218 644)
Proposes a unifying theory of WAC based on the classical metaphor of the Three Graces.

367. Fulwiler, T. (1979). Journal-writing across the curriculum. In *Classroom practices in teaching English 1979–1980: How to handle the paper load* (pp. 15–22). Urbana, IL: National Council of Teachers of English.
Summarizes Britton's research and emphasizes the value of expressive writing for increasing fluency, improving learning, and promoting cognitive growth.

368. Fulwiler, T. (1982). Writing: An act of cognition. In C. W. Griffin (Ed.), *Teaching writing in all disciplines* (pp. 15–26). San Francisco: Jossey-Bass.
Citing work by Vygotsky, Britton, Emig, and others, Fulwiler reviews theories about thought, language, and learning that have inspired WAC. He argues

that writing-to-be-evaluated inhibits learning and shares ways of incorporating writing-to-learn into every classroom.

369. Fulwiler, T. (1986). The argument for writing across the curriculum. In A. Young & T. Fulwiler (Eds.), *Writing across the disciplines: Research into practice* (pp. 21–32). Urbana, IL: National Council of Teachers of English.
Fulwiler draws on recent composition theory and his own experience as a leader of interdisciplinary writing workshops to argue for the importance of writing in all areas. He closes with 20 suggestions for developing and evaluating writing assignments in any discipline.

370. Gates, R. L. (1988). Causality, community, and the canons of reasoning: Classical rhetoric and writing across the curriculum. *Journal of Advanced Composition, 8,* 137–145.
Claims that the classical concepts of *aita* (the foundation of scientific thinking) and *kairos* (the foundation of rhetoric) can provide a theory that relates social and scientific thought to discourse and moves beyond the grounding of WAC in the personal knowledge-making espoused by Britton and others.

371. Gere, A. R. (1985). Introduction. In A. R. Gere (Ed.), *Roots in the sawdust: Writing to learn across the disciplines* (pp. 1–8). Urbana, IL: National Council of Teachers of English.
An introduction to a collection of essays on writing-to-learn by 15 secondary teachers. Gere analyzes the principles behind writing-to-learn and its value in developing higher levels of cognitive thinking.

372. Hairston, M. (1982a). The winds of change: Thomas Kuhn and the revolution in the teaching of writing. *College Composition and Communication, 33,* 76–88.
Invokes the concepts of "paradigm" and "paradigm shift," as developed by Thomas Kuhn in *The Structure of Scientific Revolutions,* to explain a massive paradigm shift that is occurring in the teaching of writing. The decades-old paradigm is the current-traditional paradigm, which neglects invention, views composing as a linear process, emphasizes the written product rather than the writing process, equates "teaching editing" with "teaching writing," and posits writing as "a mysterious creative activity" which can't be taught. The "emerging paradigm" studies how writers write, focuses on writing as a process, addresses invention, views the writing process as recursive rather than linear, and emphasizes writing as a way of learning as well as communicating.

373. Hairston, M. (1982b). The winds of change: Thomas Kuhn and the revolution in the teaching of writing. In B. L. Smith (Ed.), *Writing across the curriculum* (pp. 4–10). Washington: American Association for Higher Education. (ERIC Document Reproduction Service No. ED 243 391)
An abridged version of Hairston (1982a).

374. Haley-James, S. (1982). Helping students learn through writing. *Language Arts, 59,* 726–731.
Discusses three dimensions of WAC theory: the linkage between writing and

learning; the types and occasions of writing that have proven meaningful; and the pedagogical uses of writing in various content areas.

375. Halliday, M. A. K. (1973). *Explorations in the functions of language.* **New York: Elsevier.**
Explores the purposes for which language is used and how these are achieved through speaking, listening, writing and reading. Chapter One discusses early childhood language development. In the second chapter, the developmental functions of language are linked to a more refined functional theory for adult language. Chapter Three discusses the function of language in creating socially significant meanings. General principles for "socio-semantics" are developed in the fourth chapter, which argues that meaning is related to both the internal structures and social contexts of language. The final chapter relates this functional theory of language to the wider background of semiotics by applying it to an analysis of William Golding's *The Inheritors.*

376. Hansen, K. (1988). Rhetoric and epistemology in the social sciences: A contrast of two representative texts. In D. A. Jolliffe (Ed.), *Advances in writing research, vol. 2: Writing in academic disciplines* **(pp. 167–210). Norwood, NJ: Ablex.**
Examines writing in the social sciences from the perspective of rhetorical theory.

377. Harris, J. (1990). *Expressive discourse.* **Carbondale, IL: Southern Illinois University Press.**
Attacks the concept of "expressive discourse" as "virtually meaningless" and argues that the term should be abandoned. Expressive discourse is "poorly defined and...it is probably poorly defined because it is not a real category" (49). Harris proposes alternative terms and categories "that are commonly accepted or that are sufficiently descriptive to be used with some precision and accuracy" (49).

378. Hedley, J., & Parker, J. E. (1991). Writing across the curriculum: The vantage of the liberal arts. *ADE Bulletin, 98,* **22–28.**
Critiques models of WAC which emphasize socializing undergraduates "into particular knowledge communities." Such models reflect the institutional bias of large research universities, "where faculty horizons tend to be strictly disciplinary or departmental." Particularly in liberal arts colleges, WAC should emphasize "inquiry" rather than the learning of specialized discourse conventions.

379. Herrington, A. J. (1981). Writing to learn: Writing across the disciplines. *College English, 43,* **379–387.**
Argues that teachers in all disciplines should be using writing in their courses.

380. Herrington, A. J. (1985). Classrooms as forums for reasoning and writing. *College Composition and Communication, 36,* **404–413.**
Discusses two different ways in which writing and learning are linked in scholarship on WAC: (1) the perspective of a school community, in which writing becomes a means to engage in the process of thinking; and (2) the

perspective of a particular disciplinary community, in which writing becomes a medium for learning social and intellectual conventions of that discipline. Herrington urges that teachers combine these two perspectives to integrate writing into content courses and offers specific questions as a heuristic to provide a basis for designing writing assignments that reflect such a blend.

381. Hillocks, G., Jr. (1982). Inquiry and the composing process: Theory and research. *College English, 44,* **659–673.**
Discusses eight major strategies of inquiry for analytical writing: observation, generalization, description, comparison, contrast, definition, hypothesis, and test. Linking these strategies to stages of cognitive development, Hillocks argues that they are more apt to improve writing abilities than imitating prose models.

382. Holland, R. M., Jr. (1988). Discovering the forms of academic discourse. In L. Z. Smith (Ed.), *Audits of meaning: A festschrift in honor of Ann E. Berthoff* **(pp. 71–79). Portsmouth, NH: Boynton/Cook.**
Argues that the value, functions and forms of discourse in various academic disciplines ought to guide the way that teachers "invite new scholars to write *as* scholars, whatever their academic discipline." Holland explores the idea of "form" in discourse, then provides a sequence of writing assignments adaptable for teaching the forms of academic discourse in most of the conventional disciplines.

383. Hollenbeck, A. (1983). Mentorships and learning to write: Reflections on process. In C. Thaiss (Ed.), *Writing to learn: Essays and reflections on writing across the curriculum* **(pp. 31–37). Dubuque, IA: Kendall Hunt.**
Applies Levinson's five concepts of mentors to the teaching of writing. Hollenbeck narrates his own experience with writing mentors and discusses the role of the true mentor in developing writing abilities.

384. Irmscher, W. F. (1979). Writing as a way of learning and developing. *College English, 30,* **240–244.**
Offers several definitions of "writing," with special emphasis on writing as a way of learning that is basic to all disciplines.

385. Jolliffe, D. A. (1985). Audience, subject, form, and ways of speaking: Writers' knowledge in the disciplines (Doctoral dissertation, University of Texas at Austin, 1984). *Dissertation Abstracts International, 46,* **367A.**
Examines the inconsistencies and irregularities in the implementation of WAC programs. Jolliffe focuses on whether WAC programs should teach general writing skills or teach the specific type of writing performed in each subject area. He argues the latter, and unifies it under a consistent theory which he labels disciplinary enculturation—a theory of how learning proceeds in the content areas.

386. Karlson, R. (1983). The teaching of writing: Applications of Lozanov. In C. Thaiss (Ed.), *Writing to learn: Essays and reflections on writing across the curriculum* **(pp. 38–45). Dubuque, IA: Kendall Hunt.**
Applies the Lozanov Learning Method to the teaching of writing.

387. Kinneavy, J. L. (1971). *A theory of discourse.* **Engelwood Cliffs, NJ: Prentice-Hall.**
Proposes a text-centered theory of discourse based on the ostensible purposes underlying writers' texts. Beginning with a history of discourse, Kinneavy then identifies four basic "aims" governing the characteristics or conventions of differents kinds of texts. Each of these aims—"expressive," "persuasive," "referential," and "literary"—has as its focus a different element in the rhetorical triangle—respectively, the writer, the reader, the "reality" being presented, or the text.

388. Kinneavy, J. L. (1983). Writing across the curriculum. In *Profession '83: Selected articles from the Bulletins of the ADE and the ADFL* **(pp. 13–20). New York: Modern Language Association.**
Distinguishes two kinds of WAC programs: those in which courses are taught in a centralized department (such as English), and those in which faculty in various disciplines are trained to teach writing in their own courses. Kinneavy calls for a synthesis of both approaches, echoing the context of Western rhetorical tradition and current educational writing theory.

389. Knoblauch, C. H., & Brannon, L. (1983). Writing as learning through the curriculum. *College English, 45,* **465–474.**
The authors find that most high school and college WAC programs are unsound because they reduce writing to a prescribed format for displaying learning. Knoblauch and Brannon argue that learning is a process of making meaning and that writing is a heuristic for discovering and articulating such meaning. The authors also stress that, in writing in content courses, the expertise of the English teacher is subordinate to that of the content teacher, since only the teacher of a particular discipline knows enough about the learning processes characteristic of that field to respond in a manner that establishes intellectual dialogue and stimulates conceptual growth.

390. Kuriloff, P. C. (1991). Writing across the curriculum and the future of freshman English: A dialogue between literature and composition. *ADE Bulletin, 98,* **34–39.**
Imagines a dialogue between two characters named "Literature" and "Composition" as a way of dramatizing the significant differences between the two and their relationship with WAC. Kuriloff then suggests ways of bringing literature and composition closer together and of enhancing their connections with the rest of the curriculum through a program of textual studies such as that proposed by Robert Scholes in *Textual Power.*

391. Lightfoot, M., & Martin, N. (Eds.). (1988). *The word for teaching is learning: Essays for James Britton.* **London: Heinemann.**
Essays addressing the work of one of WAC's most influential researcher-theorists. Most of the essays are by British and Commonwealth educators.

392. Madigan, C. (1985). Improving writing assignments with communication theory. *College Composition and Communication, 36,* **183–190.**
Offers an adaptation of the discourse paradigm developed by Roman Jakobson.

393. Maimon, E. P. (1980). Cinderella to Hercules: Demythologizing writing across the curriculum. *Journal of Basic Writing, 2,* 3–11.
Argues that a WAC program "cannot be introduced by a lone Hercules" and exposes other myths potentially damaging to WAC.

394. Maimon, E. P. (1983). Maps and genres: Exploring connections in the arts and sciences. In W. B. Horner (Ed.), *Composition and literature: Bridging the gap* **(pp. 110–125). Chicago: University of Chicago Press.**
Argues for extending the literary theory of genre to other disciplines in the arts and sciences as a means of helping English faculty to understand the thinking processes of writers in other fields. If students learn the various concepts of genre, audience, and situation when entering the university, they will be better prepared to write in different genres in content courses.

395. Maimon, E. P. (1988). Collaborative learning and writing across the curriculum. *WPA: Writing Program Administration, 9*(3), 9–15.
Argues that, wherever WAC has been successfully implemented, collaborative learning plays a central role.

396. Maimon, E. P. (1991, March). *Errors and expectations in writing across the curriculum: Diversity, equity, and the ideology of writing across the curriculum.* **Paper presented at the annual meeting of the Conference on College Composition and Communication, Boston, MA. (ERIC Document Reproduction Service No. ED 331 092)**
Contends that WAC's major contribution to education is that it is "a wedge into a reform pedagogy," a vehicle for reinvigorating teacher-student relations and education generally.

397. Martin, N. (1976). Language across the curriculum: A paradox and its potential for change. *Educational Review, 28,* 206–219.
Discusses major problems concerning the teaching, development, and study of language.

398. Martin, N., D'Arcy, P., Newton, B., & Parker, R. (1976). *Writing and learning across the curriculum, 11–16.* **London: Ward Lock.**
Invoking the model of writing developed by Britton et al. (1975), the authors encourage teachers to expand the audience for school writing to include audiences other than the "teacher-as-examiner." They also advise that students use language in diverse environments and not simply to learn correct usage.

399. Martin, N., Medway, P., Smith, H., & D'Arcy, P. (1984). Why write? In N. Martin (Ed.), *Writing across the curriculum pamphlets* **(pp. 34–59). Upper Montclair, NJ: Boynton/Cook.**
This collection of five papers focuses on purpose and audience and how they influence changes in writing. The authors discuss various kinds of writing, with examples from the writing of children in early secondary schools.

400. Mayher, J. S., & Lester, N. B. (1983). Putting learning first in writing to learn. *Language Arts, 60,* 717–722.

Criticizes the methods of learning in typical American school settings, which involve the passive reception of information. The authors suggest that a more active way of learning should be widely introduced, involving the key role of writing as a means of discovery.

401. Mayher, J. S., Lester, N. B., & Pradl, G. M. (1983). *Learning to write/Writing to learn* **. Upper Montclair, NJ: Boynton/Cook.**
An outgrowth of the 1980 New York University-CBS Sunrise Semester Course of the same title, this book is aimed at helping teachers at all grade levels and in all content areas "run writer- and learner-centered classrooms." Chapters address writing as a process of constructing meaning; the composing process; connections between writing and cognitive development; "Writing to Learn Across the Curriculum"; response and evaluation; and other topics. Each chapter is followed by writing-to-learn activities.

402. Medway, P. (1984). From talking to writing. In N. Martin (Ed.), *Writing across the curriculum pamphlets* **(pp. 60–85). Upper Montclair, NJ: Boynton/Cook.**
Stresses the importance of expressive talk and argues that writing is involved in the processes of reflecting on and reformulating ideas.

403. Moffett, J. (1968). *Teaching the universe of discourse.* **New York: Houghton Mifflin.**
Moffett's pedagogical theory of discourse calls for a radical reformation of school curricula and has greatly influenced the write-to-learn movement as well as WAC more generally. He attacks traditional, content-dominated distinctions between disciplines for obscuring what is common to all—the symbolization of experience through language. The symbol system of language can be learned only through *use* and not by being studied as an object. Students should be given opportunities to manipulate discourse "in every realistic way it can be used." For example, to have students work with the discourse of drama is not simply to have them study dramas as objects, but to have them dramatize through such activities as soliloquy, dialogue, and monologue.

Chapter One outlines discourse as something to be used and manipulated rather than studied. Chapter Two outlines the varieties of discourse, which constitute "a hierarchy of levels of abstraction" determined by changing referential relations between speaker/writer and subject and shifting rhetorical relations between speaker/writer and listener/reader. The chapter models a curriculum based on theories of cognitive development and aimed at helping students to develop fluency with discourse along all levels of the hierarchy. Chapters Three and Four discuss functions and applications of "drama" and "narrative" within a discourse-based curriculum. Chapter Five criticizes pedagogies that focus on grammar and the sentence. Chapter Six argues that students "learn to write by writing." Chapter Seven presents conclusions and implications.

404. North, S. M. (1985). Journal writing across the curriculum: A reconsideration. *Freshman English News,* **14(2).**
Identifies two major problems with the resurgence of journals: (1) journal

writing is seen as inherently expressive; and (2) WAC programs tend to assign universal properties to the relationship between language and knowledge regardless of context. North proposes three models for classroom power structures: non-negotiable (teacher-controlled), negotiable, and private (student-controlled). He argues that most classes mix the models and concludes that journal writing must be defined pluralistically, according to discourse conventions.

405. Odell, L. (1980). The process of writing and the process of learning. *College Composition and Communication, 31,* **42–50.**
Argues that writing requires complex conceptual activities which vary from one context to another. He illustrates the specific conceptual demands in four writing assignments and suggests that writing teachers and content-area teachers collaborate to generate a range of heuristic procedures for helping students respond to writing assignments.

406. Parker, R. P. (1982). Language, schools, and the growth of mind. *CEA Critic, 44*(2), **6–13.**
Examines the role that society, culture, language and the classroom play in the development of intellect.

407. Parker, R. P., & Goodkin, V. (1987). *The consequences of writing—enhancing learning in the disciplines.* **Upper Montclair, NJ: Boynton/Cook.**
Rebutting the assumption that knowledge is foundational and can be "transmitted" from one person to another, the authors argue that knowledge is socially constructed through symbolization (particularly writing activities) and that teachers across the disciplines can best promote learning by involving students in a spectrum of language activities—formal and informal, imaginative and analytic. Chapters one thorugh three articulate the history and rationale for this constructivist theory of knowledge and explore its implications for WAC and classroom teaching. Chapter four presents case studies of students and teachers in five content areas (Entomology, Clinical Nursing, Psychology of Human Relations, Psychology of Women, and Mathematics) who have applied constructivist approaches in their classes.

408. Perelman, L. (1986). The context of classroom writing. *College English, 48,* **471–479.**
Compares the context of classroom writing with other discourse situations. Academic discourse not only has to be read within the framework of an academic discipline; it also must "possess the ability to convince others within the specific conventions of that discipline."

409. Petersen, B. T. (1982). In search of meaning: Readers and expressive language. In T. Fulwiler & A. Young (Eds.), *Language connections: Reading and writing across the curriculum* (pp. 107–122). Urbana, IL: National Council of Teachers of English.
Calls for all academic subjects to adopt a comprehensive concept of language in the classroom. Petersen insists that all students should respond orally to both the text and their own writings on the text, and he recommends that those writings proceed from the personally expressive (journals, diaries, and

response notebooks) to more formal expository forms such as essays and research papers.

410. Petrosky, A. (1982). From story to essay: Reading and writing. *College Composition and Communication, 33,* **19–36.**
Argues against methodology that treats reading, response, and composition as separate forms of discourse. Petrosky calls for a synthesis of all three, arguing that writing is the best way for readers to make meaning for themselves because writing about reading provides a "process of discovery rooted in inferential thinking."

411. Press, H. B. (1979). Basic motivation for basic skills: The interdependent approach to interdisciplinary writing. *College English, 41,* **310–313.**
Argues for interdisciplinary cooperation in the teaching of writing.

412. Rose, M. (1985). The language of exclusion: Writing instruction at the university. *College English, 47,* **341–359.**
Indicts the public and the American university system for perpetuating the myth of exclusionary language, which is riveted on error and which posits writing as a skill or tool rather than a discipline. Rose defines language as a cognitive discipline which has been shortchanged in college curricula and urges that writing be incorporated into the heart of the college curriculum.

413. Rosen, L. (1978). An interview with James Britton, Tony Burgess, and Harold Rosen. *English Journal, 67*(8), **50–58.**
The interviewees discuss writing, functions of writing, and the findings and implications of their research at the University of London.

414. Russell, D. R. (1993). Vygotsky, Dewey, and externalism: Beyond the student/discipline dichotomy. *Journal of Advanced Composition, 13,* **173–197.**
Argues "that by denying the conceptual split between student and subject matter, scheme and content, Dewey and Vygotsky not only critique certain Romantic notions of student-centered pedagogy but in doing so also challenge the very idea of general composition courses in higher education and thus lead us to a radical critique of the very institutional base on which composition studies in the United States rests."

415. Savage, G. (1992, March). *Beyond evangelism: Ideology and social responsibility in WAC.* **Paper presented at the annual meeting of the Conference on College Composition and Communication, Cincinnati, OH. (ERIC Document Reproduction Service No. ED 346 478)**
Discusses the frankly ideological and political role that WAC proponents must play if WAC "is to escape being the handmaiden to the so-called content disciplines."

416. Self, J. (1987). Getting the whole picture. In J. Self (Ed.), *Plain talk: About learning and writing across the curriculum* **(pp. 1–6). Commonwealth of Virginia: Virginia Department of Education.**
Analyzes the "traditional" views of faculty and administrators toward writing and describes the way that these views can distort the assumptions of WAC.

417. Shafer, R. E. (1981). A British proposal for improving literacy. *Educational Forum, 46,* **81–96.**
Investigates the theoretical background and recommendations of the London Writing Across the Curriculum Project. Buber, Sapir, Dewey, Cassirer, Langer, Polanyi, Vygotsky and Piaget are seen as direct or indirect influences on Britton's categorizations of discourse into functional and audience-specific types, as well as his study of the links between speech and writing and between the spectator and participant roles.

418. Shuman, R. B. (1984). School-wide writing instruction. *English Journal,* **73, 54–73.**
Asserts the pragmatic value of "expressive" writing in the content areas, stressing the tenets of Vygotsky, Britton, and Applebee. Teachers must be shown that journal-keeping enhances learning. Offers practical considerations for the implementation of school-wide programs at the high school level.

419. Slevin, J. F. (1988). Genre theory, academic discourse, and writing within disciplines. In L. Z. Smith (Ed.), *Audits of meaning: A festschrift in honor of Ann E. Berthoff* **(pp. 3–16). Portsmouth, NH: Boynton/Cook.**
Explores the nature of university-wide writing programs in light of genre theory and recent trends in post-structuralist criticism with an aim toward "enriching our understanding of [these programs'] purposes."

420. Smith, B. L. (1983). Writing across the curriculum: What's at stake? In B. L. Smith (Ed.), *Writing across the curriculum* **(pp. 1–3). Washington: American Association for Higher Education. (ERIC Document Reproduction Service No. ED 243 391)**
Reviews WAC theory, focussing especially on the declining emphasis on writing in high schools and colleges.

421. Tchudi, S. N. (1986). The hidden agendas in writing across the curriculum. *English Journal, 75*(7), **22–25.**
Advocates the idea of an interdisciplinary English, in which instructors no longer see themselves "as teachers of British and American literature, writing, and language," but as teachers of learning.

422. Tchudi, S. N. (1992). The interdisciplinary island: Whole language, holistic learning and teacher education. *Holistic Education Review, 5*(1), **30–36.**

423. Tirrell, M. K., Pradl, G. M., Warnock, J., & Britton, J. (1990). Re-presenting James Britton: A symposium. *College Composition and Communication, 41,* **166–186.**
Collects revised versions of papers originally presented, at the 1988 Convention of the National Council of Teachers of English, in celebration of James Britton's 80th birthday. The authors assess Britton's impact on "English studies generally and...composition particularly."

424. Troutman, B. I. (1977). An interdisciplinary approach to curriculum and instruction: From purpose to method. *Clearing House, 50,* **200–201.**
A general discussion of the value of interdisciplinary education.

425. Tschumy, R. D. (1982). Writing across the curriculum: What's in a name? *NASSP Bulletin, 66,* 63–70.
Examines the implications of WAC theory at the high school level.

426. Van Nostrand, A. D. (1979). Writing and the generation of knowledge. *Social Education, 43,* 178–180.
A concise discussion of some relationships between thinking, writing, and learning—with brief reference to classwork in American history.

427. Wallace, R. (1986). Writing across the curriculum. *NASSP Bulletin, 70,* 108–109.
Argues for a content-specific approach in teaching writing.

428. Walshe, R. D. (1987). The learning power of writing. *English Journal, 76(6),* 22–27.
Suggests that the traditional classroom should be turned into the write-to-learn classroom.

429. Walzer, A. E. (1985). Articles from the "California Divorce Project": A case study of the concept of audience. *College Composition and Communication, 36,* 150–159.
Criticizing current methodology in the teaching of audience, Walzer urges a conception of audience as the "conventions of the discourse of a particular rhetorical or interpretive community." Writers in the social sciences, for example, should target their audience as fellow workers in social science. Walzer calls for redesigned composition courses emphasizing narrowly defined, specific audiences.

430. Williams, J. T. (1978). *"Learning to write, or writing to learn?" A critical analysis and evaluation of the Schools Council Project of Written Language of 11- to 18-year-olds and its development project, "Writing Across the Curriculum."* **Atlantic Highland, NJ: Humanities Press.**
Provides background and a critique of the work reported in Britton et al. (1975) and Martin et al. (1976). Williams first traces the history of the Schools Council Projects and examines their underlying hypotheses. She then offers a critical evaluation of the projects for future educational and language research.

431. Young, A. (1982). The poetic function of language. In T. Fulwiler & A. Young (Eds.), *Language connections: Writing and reading across the curriculum* **(pp. 77–98). Urbana, IL: National Council of Teachers of English.**
Creative writing is rarely included in content-area instruction, let alone standard composition courses. Young argues that the poetic function [see Britton et al. (1975)] allows a deep, personalized perspective on experience that facilitates understanding in a way expressive and transactional writing cannot. Includes examples and exercises.

432. Zinsser, W. (1988). *Writing to learn.* **New York: Harper & Row.**
A largely anecdotal and personal account of the importance of writing to learning.

PART TWO: PEDAGOGY

General Pedagogy

433. Anderson, J. (1992/1993). Journal writing: The promise and the reality. *Journal of Reading, 36,* **304–309.**
Explores problems connected with assigning course journals, including grading; "overuse"; monotonous use (e.g., where students use the journal for one type of writing only, such as summary-writing); use of the journal "to express blatant bigotry and prejudice"; and others. Anderson urges teachers "to monitor [their] instruction in journal writing and to improve it constantly to fit the needs of students."

434. Anderson, J. R., Eisenberg, N., Holland, J., Wiener, H. S., & Rivera-Kron, C. (1983). *Integrated skills reinforcement: Reading, writing, speaking, and listening across the curriculum.* **New York: Longman.**
Written by teachers for teachers, this text outlines "a holistic approach for helping students use all the modes of language for exploring and mastering course content." The book is in five parts: "Strategies for Assessing Students' Communication Skills in Relation to Content Courses"; "Strategies for Helping Students Write for Content Courses"; "Strategies for Encouraging Students' Effective Use of Oral and Listening Skills in Content Courses"; "Strategies for Helping Students Read Successfully in Content Courses"; and "Integrating Language Skills for Content Mastery."

435. Atwell, N. (Ed.). (1990a). *Coming to know: Writing to learn in the intermediate grades.* **Portsmouth, NH: Heinemann.**
Teachers of grades three through six show how they use write-to-learn activities to teach math, reading, science, and social studies. Essays address the following subjects: "Researching and Reporting"; "The Power of Learning Logs"; "Reading and Writing"; and "Teaching and Learning." See 1990 entries for: Thompson (2); Blake; Chard; Vaughan; Farnsworth; Wheeler; Haney; Greenleaf; Atwell (3); and Maxim.

436. Atwell, N. (1990b). Genres for report writing. In N. Atwell (Ed.), *Coming to know: Writing to learn in the intermediate grades* **(pp. 163–166). Portsmouth, NH: Heinemann.**
Lists and describes 30 different forms of writing (e.g., journals, scripts, poetry, animal stories, etc.) that children can use to report information.

437. Atwell, N. (1990c). Prompts for learning log entries. In N. Atwell (Ed.), *Coming to know: Writing to learn in the intermediate grades* (pp. 167–184). Portsmouth, NH: Heinemann.
Lists prompts for enabling elementary students to "make constructive, imaginative use of learning logs" in all subject areas.

438. Atwell, N. (1990d). Resources for writing and reading to learn. In N. Atwell (Ed.), *Coming to know: Writing to learn in the intermediate grades* (pp. 217–233). Portsmouth, NH: Heinemann.
Lists over 100 resources, primarily for use at the elementary grade-level.

439. Barr, M., D'Arcy, P., & Healy, M. K. (Eds.). (1982). *What's going on? Language/ learning episodes in British and American classrooms, grades 4–13.* Upper Montclair, NJ: Boynton/Cook.
Thirteen U.S. and British teachers describe how they have used language and writing to enhance classroom instruction.

440. Bean, J. C., Drenk, D., & Lee, F. D. (1982). Microtheme strategies for developing cognitive skills. In C. W. Griffin (Ed.), *Teaching writing in all disciplines* (pp. 27–38). San Francisco: Jossey-Bass.
A finance, English, and physics teacher suggest microthemes (short essay assignments) to help students improve their writing and learn course content.

441. Bechtel, J. (1985). *Improving writing and learning: A handbook for teachers in every class.* Boston: Allyn & Bacon.
This handbook is intended primarily for teachers and students at the high school and introductory college levels. Following sections on rationale and expressive writing, Bechtel offers chapters on assessment, record-keeping tasks (e.g., notetaking, questioning, and process logs), research papers, essay tests, and creative writing (its value and application to classes other than English). The final chapter suggests models for school-wide writing programs.

442. Bent, V. H. (1987). Student fear and writing: Writing across the curriculum can help. In J. Self (Ed.), *Plain talk: About learning and writing across the curriculum* (pp. 145–148). Commonwealth of Virginia: Virginia Department of Education.
Discusses how WAC can help curb student anxieties about writing.

443. Berkenkotter, C. (1982). Writing and problem-solving. In T. Fulwiler & A. Young (Eds.), *Language connections: Writing and reading across the curriculum* (pp. 33–44). Urbana, IL: National Council of Teachers of English.
Discusses how a problem-solving approach to writing can help students in composition courses and in other disciplines, such as physics and math.

444. Berthoff, A. E. (1981). A curious triangle and the double-entry notebook: Or, how theory can help us teach reading and writing. In *The making of meaning: Metaphors, models, and maxims for writing teachers* (pp. 41–47). Montclair, NJ: Boynton/Cook.
Explains the double-entry or dialectical notebook as a device for teaching students that "how we construe is how we construct." [See also Berthoff (1987)]

445. Berthoff, A. E. (1987). Dialectical notebooks and the audit of meaning. In T. Fulwiler (Ed.), *The journal book* (pp. 11–18). Portsmouth, NH: Heinemann.
Introduces the dialectical notebook as a vehicle for enacting an "audit of meaning." The dialectical notebook "is a double-entry journal with the two pages facing one another in dialogue. On one side are observations, sketches, noted impressions, passages copied out, jottings on reading or other responses; on the facing page are notes on these notes, responses to these responses...." The structure of such notebooks represents and facilitates the process of thinking itself, which consists of "looking and looking again" in a kind of inner dialogue.

446. Blake, M. (1990). Learning logs in the upper elementary grades. In N. Atwell (Ed.), *Coming to know: Writing to learn in the intermediate grades* (pp. 53–60). Portsmouth, NH: Heinemann.
Shows how students can use learning logs for mapping, webbing, predicting, listing, tapping prior knowledge, and brainstorming. Illustrates with examples from student logs in science and social studies.

447. Blumenthal, S. (1981). Writing in content areas. In M. F. Hayes et al. (Eds.), *Teachers and Writers: Articles from the Ohio Writing Project* (pp. 47–49). Oxford, OH: Summer Institute, Miami University.

448. Boutwell, M. A. (1983). Reading and writing process: A reciprocal agreement. *Language Arts, 60*, 723–730.
In a case study, Boutwell describes how a third-grader reads and writes actively, shuttling "back and forth from writing to reading, rewriting to rereading." Reading and writing work together, inextricably, to enhance learning.

449. Brand, A. G. (1992). Drafting essay assignments: What the disciplines can learn from direct writing assessment. *Issues in Writing, 4*, 156–174.

450. Brewster, M. (1988). Ten ways to revise tired learning logs. *English Journal, 77*, 57.
To assure creative use of logs, Brewster suggests six ways to vary styles of expression and provide a different point of view, and four ways to vary log structure and provide an attractive vehicle for ideas.

451. Brosmer, M. (1981). Journal-keeping: Classroom and lifetime activity. In M. F. Hayes et al. (Eds.), *Teachers and writers: Articles from the Ohio Writing Project* (pp. 103–107). Oxford, OH: Summer Institute, Miami University.

452. Brostoff, A. (1979). Good assignments lead to good writing. *Social Education, 43*, 184–186.
Describes ways of building writing assignments across the curriculum that encourage students to learn and to produce more effective texts.

453. Burnham, C. C. (1992). Crumbling metaphors: Integrating heart and brain through structured journals. *College Composition and Communication, 43*, 508–515.
Presents "structured journals" as a means of integrating "what in the lives of

many students have become seemingly unrelated activities—thinking and feeling—and unconnected realms—the public and the private." Integration is achieved by keeping two sequenced journals: a "Personal Development Journal," which stresses expressive writing; and a "Learning Log," which emphasizes such "higher-level" cognitive activities as abstracting, summarizing, classifying, and formulating.

454. Caulfield, P. (1986). Tagmemic invention: Discovery across the curriculum. In K. O'Dowd, & E. Nolan (Eds.), *Learning to write, writing to learn* (pp. 64–71). Livonia, MI: Madonna College Humanities Writing Program.
Explains how the heuristic developed by Kenneth Pike (often known as "tagmemic invention") can be adapted to courses across the curriculum. Caulfield illustrates the flexibility of tagmemic theory by showing how it can be used in psychology, art, and physics.

455. Chard, N. (1990). How learning logs change teaching. In N. Atwell (Ed.), *Coming to know: Writing to learn in the intermediate grades* (pp. 61–68). Portsmouth, NH: Heinemann.
Summarizes how students' learning logs help her decide what to teach, "gain...students' cooperation, fine-tune methods, and develop new ways of teaching."

456. Christiansen, L. (Ed.). (1983). *A guide to journal writing*. Madison, WI: University of Wisconsin, School of Education, Wisconsin Writing Project. (ERIC Document Reproduction Service No ED 249 519)
Discusses the philosophy and value of journal writing and answers some of the major questions teachers have about it. Appended are bibliographies of published journals, fictional and nonfictional, and of writings about journals.

457. Connors, M. (1981). Writing as a learning process. In M. F. Hayes et al. (Eds.), *Teachers and writers: Articles from the Ohio Writing Proejct* (pp. 31–34). Oxford, OH: Summer Institute, Miami University.

458. Cordeiro, P. (1990). Problem-based thematic instruction. *Language Arts, 67*, 26–33.
The author borrows the pedagogical techniques of Dorothy Heathcote to intensify learning in her elementary classrooms. While learning in traditional classrooms often occurs in a "decontextualized" or "abstract-academic" atmosphere, Cordeiro's students use such activities as drama, simulation, and role-play to create authentic and meaningful contexts for writing, reading, and learning.

459. Couch, R. (1989). Dealing with objections to writing across the curriculum. *Teaching English in the Two-Year College, 16*, 193–196.
Discusses the problems associated with convincing faculty in other disciplines of the importance of writing to learning.

460. Cunningham, P. M., & Cunningham, J. W. (1987). Content area reading-writing lessons. *Reading Teacher, 40*, 506–512.
Shows how reading-writing lessons in relation to content help students to learn how to extract and organize information.

461. D'Arcy, P. (1987). Writing to learn. In T. Fulwiler (Ed.), *The journal book* (pp. 41–46). Portsmouth, NH: Heinemann.
Narrates her own initial and evolving commitment to the principles of writing-to-learn and to the assigning of journals in her classes.

462. Diamond, I. M., Haugen, N. S., & Kean, J. M. (1980). *Interdisciplinary writing: A guide to writing across the curriculum.* Madison: University of Wisconsin/Wisconsin Writing Project. (ERIC Document Reproduction Service No. ED 193 655)
Recommends activities that teachers of all subjects can use to help students write.

463. Dittmer, A. (1986). Guidelines for writing assignments in the content areas. *English Journal, 75*, 59–63.
Suggests guidelines for designing writing assignments in math, physics, accounting, social studies, biology, and other subjects.

464. Dodd, A. W. (1987). A writing log helps teachers help students. *Teaching English in the Two-Year College, 14*, 27–31.
Describes her use of writing logs in a basic writing class.

465. Draper, V. (1979). *Formative writing: Writing to assist learning in all subjects.* Curriculum Publication 3, University of California. Berkeley, CA: Bay Area Publications. (ERIC Document Reproduction Service No. ED 184 115)
Discusses the nature of "formative" writing (which involves free expression through the use of journal techniques, freewriting, question-asking, and other strategies) and offers examples of formative writing assignments along with samples of student writing.

466. Elbow, P., & Clarke, J. (1987). Desert island discourse: The benefits of ignoring audience. In T. Fulwiler (Ed.), *The journal book* (pp. 19–32). Portsmouth, NH: Heinemann.
Elbow and Clarke argue the benefits of ignoring audience in the preliminary stages of the writing process. "The value of learning to ignore audience while writing…is the value of learning to cultivate the private dimension: the value of writing to make meaning to oneself, not just to others."

467. Farnsworth, L. (1990). In the schema of things. In N. Atwell (Ed.), *Coming to know: Writing to learn in the intermediate grades* (pp. 77–85). Portsmouth, NH: Heinemann.
Describes write-to-learn activities (diagramming, time lines, mapping, and others) that help improve learning among elementary-level special education students.

468. Fillion, B. (1983). Let me see you learn. *Language Arts, 60*, 702–710.
Examines the implications of several theoretical principles important to WAC.

469. Flynn, E. A. (1982). Reconciling readers and texts. In T. Fulwiler & A. Young (Eds.), *Language connections: Writing and reading across the curriculum* (pp. 139–152). Urbana, IL: National Council of Teachers of English.

Flynn suggests that most reading problems are not caused by laziness or lack of self-discipline, but by inappropriate textbooks, weak teacher-prescribed reading activities, and the failure of teachers to integrate reading and writing well in their courses. She offers several strategies to remedy these problems.

470. Freisinger, D., & Burkland, J. (1982). Talking about writing: The role of the writing lab. In T. Fulwiler & A. Young (Eds.), *Language connections: Writing and reading across the curriculum* (pp. 167–178). Urbana, IL: National Council of Teachers of English.
Provides a practical training manual for tutors who work in writing labs serving students in WAC programs.

471. Fulwiler, T. (1980). Journals across the disciplines. *English Journal, 69*(9), 14–19.
Contends that "assigning journals increases writing fluency, facilitates learning and promotes cognitive growth, regardless of class size or disciplinary specialization." Fulwiler describes ways that journals have been used by professors of geography, American government, music, metallurgy, drama, literature, and composition and describes eight practical techniques to integrate academic and personal knowledge across the curriculum.

472. Fulwiler, T. (1982). The personal connection: Journal writing across the curriculum. In T. Fulwiler & A. Young (Eds.), *Language connections: Writing and reading across the curriculum* (pp. 15–32). Urbana, IL: National Council of Teachers of English.
Argues that journal writing is excellent for interdisciplinary learning because it is demanding and encourages imaginative/speculative thinking. Fulwiler suggests ways to introduce journals to faculty members. He also illustrates several types of journal assignments and suggests methods for reading and evaluation.

473. Fulwiler, T. (1985a). Writing and learning, grade three. *Language Arts, 62,* 55–59.
Discusses four samples of classroom journal writing by a third grader to show how journals can improve writing and learning across the curriculum among students of all ages.

474. Fulwiler, T. (1985b). Writing is everybody's business. *National Forum, 65,* 21–24.
Links flaws in student writing to flaws in school curricula, which too often stress "the superficial and correct at the expense of the analytical and speculative." Curricula must devote more attention to writing-to-learn, as opposed to writing-to-be-tested, to give students a larger stake in their school work.

475. Fulwiler, T. (1986, Aug. 10). Write on! Practice makes perfect. *Washington Post* (Education Review), n.p.
Asserts that "the quality of student writing reflects the quality of the curriculum as much as the quality of the writer's mind." Fulwiler suggests informal writing, multiple drafting, and group conferencing as ways of increasing student interest in writing.

476. Fulwiler, T. (1987a). Introduction: Guidelines for using journals in school settings. In T. Fulwiler (Ed.), *The journal book* **(pp. 1–8). Portsmouth, NH: Heinemann.**
Provides a rationale for assigning journals in classrooms, particularly in courses across the disciplines. Also includes, in its entirety, an NCTE document, "Guidelines for Using Journals in School Settings."

477. Fulwiler, T. (Ed.). (1987b). *The journal book.* **Portsmouth, NH: Heinemann.**
A collection of essays addressing the theory and practical use of journals in classrooms across the curriculum. Sections include: "The Language of Speculation"; "Journals and the Teaching of English"; "Journals and the Arts and Humanities"; and "Journals and the Quantitative Disciplines." See 1987 entries for: Fulwiler (2); Berthoff; Elbow and Clarke; Summerfield; D'Arcy; Staton; Medway; Stillman; Lowenstein; Belanoff; Gatlin; Lindberg; Dickerson; Summerfield; Burnham; Atwell; Tashlik; Davala; Nathan; Fulwiler & Fulwiler; McGonegal; Reif & Davis; Steffens; Mulholland; Sweterlitsch; Thaiss; Larson & Merrion; Ambrose; Kent; North; Halberg; Graybeal; Sandler; Grumbacher; Jensen; Meese; Schubert; BeMiller; Allen & Fauth; Brodsky & Meagher; Baltensperger; and Hickman.

478. Fulwiler, T. (1987c). *Teaching with writing: An interdisciplinary workshop approach.* **Upper Montclair, NJ: Boynton/Cook.**
Outlines the process and experience of a WAC workshop aimed at high school and college teachers in all disciplines.

479. Fulwiler, T., & Jones, R. (1982). Assigning and evaluating transactional writing. In T. Fulwiler & A. Young (Eds.), *Language connections: Writing and reading across the curriculum* **(pp. 45–56). Urbana, IL: National Council of Teachers of English.**
Drawing on writing process theory, Fulwiler and Jones suggest practical ways to assign and evaluate transactional writing, the writing most common in courses across the disciplines. How teachers assign and evaluate such writing is important because it significantly affects student learning.

480. Ganz, A. (1983). Writing as a problem-solving experience. *Language Arts,* **60, 737–739.**
Contends that the writing process can help students work through life crises. Illustrates with the example of one of her second-grade students.

481. Giordano, G. (1978, October). *A modular lesson for writing research papers in content area classes.* **Paper presented at the meeting of the College Reading Association, Washington, DC. (ERIC Document Reproduction Service No. ED 176 219)**
Urging that instructors in fields other than English assign research papers, Giordano outlines a modular research assignment for high school students and college freshmen.

482. Glaze, B. (1987). Learning logs. In J. Self (Ed.), *Plain talk: About learning and writing across the curriculum* **(pp. 149–154). Commonwealth of Virginia:**

Virginia Department of Education.
Advocates the use of learning logs in the classroom and lists numerous ideas and prompts for writing in such logs. Also discusses evaluation.

483. Grattan, M. C., & Robbins, S. P. (1983). Content area models: A key to student writing improvement in writing center programs. *Teaching English in the Two-Year College, 49,* 117–121.
Contends that discipline-specific writing models—such as outlines, diagrams, and facsimiles—can help with writing instruction in content areas. Different models work best for different content areas: letters for business classes, surveys for sociology classes, etc.

484. Graves, D. H. (1978). *Balance the basics: Let them write.* **New York: Ford Foundation.**
Though writing is central to education, this brief report concludes that the American educational system emphasizes reading (i.e., passive learning, the "receiving" of messages) to the virtual neglect of writing (i.e., active learning, the "sending" of messages). To right this imbalance Graves advocates a process-centered approach to writing instruction and illustrates how it has been used in various schools "where writing and expression are valued."

485. Graves, R. L. (1981). Using writing models from across the curriculum. *English Quarterly, 14,* 31–40.
Argues that models of good writing do not intimidate students and that teachers of writing should expand their concept of good writing to include ordinary sources such as newspapers, magazines, song lyrics, letters, advertisements, and brochures.

486. Griffin, C. W. (1982). Final synthesis: But what do I do tomorrow? In C. W. Griffin (Ed.), *Teaching writing in all disciplines* **(pp. 83–88). San Francisco: Jossey-Bass.**
Urges teachers to continue assigning plenty of transactional writing but adds a strong endorsement of expressive writing. Griffin also suggests that a WAC program must begin from the bottom up, with faculty, in order to succeed.

487. Griffin, C. W. (1983). A process of critical thinking: Using writing to teach many disciplines. *Improving College and University Teaching, 31* (3), 121–128.
Shows how recent theory about writing to learn can reshape writing instruction across the curriculum in three major areas: a) assignment-making; b) teacher intervention in the students' writing process; and c) teacher assessment of student writing.

488. Haley-James, S. (1982). Helping students learn through writing. *Language Arts, 59,* 726–731.
Discusses ways that teachers can use writing to teach subject matter.

489. Heathcote, D. (1983). Learning, knowing, and languaging in drama: An interview with Dorothy Heathcote. *Language Arts, 60,* 695–701.
As a self-interview, Heathcote's essay enacts its own premise—that dramatic form stimulates thinking and learning.

490. Hennings, D. G. (1982). *Teaching communication and reading skills in the content areas.* **Bloomington, IN: Phi Delta Kappa.**
Argues that instruction for language and thinking skills should enable children to communicate about content from subject areas. The book addresses comprehension and study skills, vocabulary development, and writing skills. Each section includes practical teaching strategies that emphasize student involvement.

491. Hill, M. (1991). Writing summaries promotes thinking and learning across the curriculum—But why are they so difficult to write? *Journal of Reading, 34,* **536–539.**
Suggests ways of fostering effective summary writing among students in science, social studies, and other subjects. Hill observes that students' ability to summarize is affected by developmental factors and thus calls for a developmental approach to teaching summary writing.

492. Howie, S. H. (1984). *A guidebook for teaching writing in the content areas.* **Rockleigh, NJ: Allyn & Bacon.**
Provides a practical guide for the content area teacher to begin using writing in her classroom. Each chapter discusses an aspect of writing and gives teaching objectives, sample writing activities, and a brief annotated bibliography of sources on that subject.

493. Ingham, Z. (Ed.) (1986). *Writing across the curriculum sample assignments, 1986–1987.* **Tucson, AZ: Pima Community College. (ERIC Document Reproduction Service No. ED 296 743)**
Shares 50 sample writing assignments—including short papers, formal papers, and interactive learning logs—for classes across the disciplines.

494. Jenkinson, E. B. (1988). Learning to write/writing to learn. *Phi Delta Kappan, 69,* **712–717.**

495. Jobst, J. (1982). Audience and purpose in writing. In T. Fulwiler & A. Young (Eds.) *Language connections: Writing and reading across the curriculum* **(pp. 57–76). Urbana, IL: National Council of Teachers of English.**
Criticizes techniques for teaching the concept of audience to students across the academic disciplines. Jobst recommends that teachers in all fields assign writing and that they simulate specific audiences for students. Two broad categories of audience-simulation activities are suggested—"Audience in the Classroom" and "Audiences Beyond the Classroom."

496. Juell, P. (1985). The course journal. In A. R. Gere (Ed.), *Roots in the sawdust: Writing to learn across the disciplines* **(pp. 187–201). Urbana, IL: National Council of Teachers of English.**
A two-part report on the use of journals in subject-area courses. Part One states the objectives and defines the rationale for using journals, while Part Two describes numerous journal-writing strategies.

497. Kalmbach, J., & Powers, W. (1982). Shaping experience: Narration and understanding. In T. Fulwiler & A. Young (Eds.), *Language connections: Writing*

and reading across the curriculum (pp. 99–106). Urbana, IL: National Council of Teachers of English.
Advocates the use of narrative writing assignments in all academic disciplines.

498. Kirby, D., & Liner, T., with R. Vinz (1988). *Inside out: Developmental strategies for teaching writing* **(2nd ed.). Upper Montclair, NJ: Boynton/Cook.**
Outlines problems with traditional writing instruction and suggests ways of creating a classroom atmosphere conducive to writing. The authors discuss in detail the use of journals and poetry in the writing class. Chapters also address the quality of student writing, response to student writing, voice, audience, writing about literature, grading, and the use of other media in the writing class.

499. Kreeft, J. (1984). Dialogue writing—Bridge from talk to essay writing. *Language Arts, 61,* **141–150.**
Argues that dialogue journals [see Staton (1987)] "provide a natural means by which children can move from a skill they already know (face-to-face oral communication) to a new skill (unilateral sense-making in writing)."

500. Kuriloff, P. C. (1991). Reaffirming the writing conference: A tool for writing teachers across the curriculum. *Journal of Teaching Writing, 10*(1), 45–57.

501. Laipson, H. K. (1991). Discipline-specific assignments: Primary resources for writing across the curriculum. In L. C. Stanley & J. Ambron (Eds.), *Writing across the curriculum in community colleges* **(pp. 51–55). San Francisco: Jossey-Bass.**
Describes learn-to-write assignments developed by community college instructors of hotel and restaurant management, respiratory therapy, nursing, secretarial studies, and accounting.

502. Langer, J. A. (1986). Learning through writing: Study skills in the content areas. *Journal of Reading, 29,* **400–406.**
Describes a study designed to examine the interaction of writing and learning. Subjects were six students living in an upper middle class suburban community in the San Francisco Bay area.

503. Larson, R. (1983). *Writing in the academic and professional disciplines.* **New York: Herbert Lehman College.**
A guide for content faculty who are incorporating writing into their courses. Includes reflections on WAC, a list of short writing activities, questions teachers should ask themselves about writing assignments, questions to elicit student written response to what they read, suggestions concerning written comments on student papers, and commentary on a sample student essay.

504. LeFevre, K. B., & Dickerson, M. J. (1981). *Until I see what I say: Teaching writing in all disciplines.* **Burlington, VT: University of Vermont, IDC Publications.**
Provides a guide for teachers seeking new ways of using writing in the classroom. Chapters 1 and 2 discuss the rationale and need for frequent writing classes in content areas. Chapters 3–7 focus directly on issues related to the

actual use of writing in the classroom: choosing topics, making writing assignments, strategies for generating ideas, helping students develop rhetorical plans, and revising prose. The final two chapters discuss responding to student writing and theories of the composing process.

505. Lehr, F. (1980). ERIC/RCS report: *Writing as learning in the content areas.* **English Journal, 69(8), 23–25.**
Offers strategies for using writing to improve both composing skills and learning, particularly in the areas of social studies, science, mathematics, and career education.

506. Lewis, R. (1983). Marking myself marking papers. In C. Thaiss (Ed.), *Writing to learn: Essays and reflections on writing across the curriculum* **(pp. 127–134). Dubuque, IA: Kendall Hunt.**
Interested in what he and other teachers "do" when they grade writing, Lewis reflectively observes himself evaluating a set of freshman essays.

507. Lidrbauch, J. (1981). Handling the paper load. In M. F. Hayes et al. (Eds.), *Teachers and writers: Articles from the Ohio Writing Project* **(pp. 68–72). Oxford, OH: Summer Institute, Miami University.**

508. Lindberg, G. (1987). The journal conference: From dialectic to dialogue. In T. Fulwiler (Ed.), *The journal book* **(pp. 119–128). Portsmouth, NH: Heinemann.**
Suggests ways to keep a reading journal and to monitor journal conferences. Argues that students can learn better by sharing their journals with others.

509. Lowenstein, S. (1987). A brief history of journal keeping. In T. Fulwiler (Ed.), *The journal book* **(pp. 87–97). Portsmouth, NH: Heinemann.**
Traces the evolution of journals from ancient China and medieval Japan to post-Renaissance Europe, America, and modern times. Lowenstein also reviews the personal and cultural transmutations of such common journal forms as the travel diary, the spiritual diary, and the personal journal.

510. Lutzker, M. (1988). *Research projects for college students: What to write across the curriculum.* **Westport, CT: Greenwood.**
A college librarian offers advice to teachers across the disciplines on "designing writing assignments that are directly tied to library-based research." Chapters provide practical suggestions on such topics as: assigning and structuring assignments; working with library staff; addressing issues of documentation style; assigning alternatives to the traditional research paper; and helping students to use primary and secondary sources.

511. MacAllister, J. (1982). Responding to student writing. In C. W. Griffin (Ed.), *Teaching writing in all disciplines* **(pp. 59–66). San Francisco: Jossey-Bass.**
Argues that content area teachers must reject various popular myths about response and suggests several strategies for responding effectively.

512. Maher, J. (1986). No short cut to the playground: A student looks at journaling. In K. O'Dowd & E. Nolan (Eds.), *Learning to write, writing to learn* **(pp.**

51–56). Livonia, MI: Madonna College Humanities Writing Program.
An English major at Madonna College describes a survey in which she asked 100 of her peers about their experience with journals. An overwhelming majority claimed that journals had significantly enhanced their learning.

513. Maimon, E. P. (1979). Talking to strangers. *College Composition and Communication, 30,* 364–369.
Argues that writing is similar to "talking to strangers" for many freshman composition students. Such students are "uninitiated into the rites" of written discourse in the majority of academic disciplines. Maimon outlines a variety of methods for improving writing instruction, including collaborative learning, multiple drafting, and completing writing assignments involving risk.

514. Maxim, D. (1990). Bury yourself in books: Childrens' literature for content-area study. In N. Atwell (Ed.), *Coming to know: Writing to learn in the intermediate grades* (pp. 185–215). Portsmouth, NH: Heinemann.
Lists books in over 30 subject areas.

515. Mayher, J. S., & Lester, N. B. (1983). Putting learning first in writing to learn. *Language Arts, 60,* 717–722.
Discusses the meaning of learning in the typical American school setting and suggests a construct of learning whereby learners "engage in the material on the basis of their previous experience and make it their own."

516. McCleary, W. J. (1985). A case approach for teaching academic writing. *College Composition and Communication, 36,* 203–212.
McCleary defines (with examples) a case approach for academic writing, provides the theoretical background for casebook rhetoric, offers advice for implementing the approach, and shows how to write a case assignment.

517. McClure, A. A., & Zitlow, C. S. (1991). Not just the facts: Aesthetic response in elementary content area studies. *Language Arts, 68,* 27–33.
Urges teachers to pay heightened attention to children's aesthetic/emotional responses to science, social studies, and mathematics, and suggests practical techniques for doing so.

518. McGinley, W., & Madigan, D. (1990). The research "story": A forum for integrating reading, writing, and learning. *Language Arts, 67,* 474–483.
Noting that research papers often intimidate students, McGinley and Madigan suggest that teachers facilitate the research process by having students write the "stories" of their research efforts. Such stories give students a personal stake in their own learning while also introducing them "to the *process* of inquiry and the role that reading, writing, and talking play in this process."

519. Medway, P. (1987). Logs for learning: Writing in one English school. In T. Fulwiler (Ed.), *The journal book* (pp. 64–76). Portsmouth, NH: Heinemann.
Discusses how learning logs promote active learning by stimulating students to pose questions, to connect new information with prior experience, and to synthesize and integrate knowledge over broad areas.

520. **Medway, P., & Goodson, I. (1984). Cooperative learning. In N. Martin (Ed.), *Writing across the curriculum pamphlets* (pp. 132–138). Upper Montclair, NJ: Boynton/Cook.**
Calls for a "cooperative" teacher-student relationship in which the teacher's knowledge "can be challenged and reinterpreted in ways that reveal new meanings for both student and teacher."

521. **Metcalf, J. (1983). Written expression—motor expression. Addendum: Please, coach, you're getting ink on my sweat socks. In C. Thaiss (Ed.), *Writing to learn: Essays and reflections on writing across the curriculum* (pp. 27–30). Dubuque, IA: Kendall Hunt.**
A physical education teacher compares written expression to motor expression, and discusses gains in proficiency relative to the expenditure of effort.

522. **Moffett, J. (1981). *Active voice: A writing program across the curriculum.* Montclair, NJ: Boynton/Cook.**
Provides a flexible guide for teachers to develop writing programs for elementary, secondary, and collegiate classes. Moffett gives an overview of the development and philosophy of his program, reviews briefly the importance of sequencing, and introduces classroom processes for pre-writing, mid-writing, and post-writing. See Moffett (1968) for a theoretical foundation for this text.

523. **Morgan, C. G. (1987a). Initiating writing-to-learn practices. In J. Self (Ed.), *Plain talk: About learning and writing across the curriculum* (pp. 141–143). Commonwealth of Virginia: Virginia Department of Education.**
Gives tips to teachers desiring to use write-to-learn activities in their classes.

524. **Morgan, C. G. (1987b). The writing/learning connection for L.D. students. In J. Self (Ed.), *Plain talk: About learning and writing across the curriculum* (pp. 60–68). Commonwealth of Virginia: Virginia Department of Education.**
Describes the rationale for using writing to learn with learning-disabled students at the high school level, and provides specific strategies for doing so.

525. **Moss, A., & Holder, C. (1988). *Improving student writing: A guidebook for faculty in all disciplines.* Dubuque, IA: Kendall-Hunt.**
Offers "practical methods and ideas" for promoting writing-to-learn and improving student writing. Chapters include: "Assigning Writing"; "Assignments That Work" (with sample assignments from six disciplines); "Essay Examinations"; "Strategies for Helping Students"; "Integrating Reading and Writing"; and "Evaluating Student Writing."

526. **Myers, J. W. (1984). *Writing to learn across the curriculum.* Fastback No. 209. Bloomington, IN: Phi Delta Kappa Educational Foundation.**
Suggests how writing can be used in the language arts, the social sciences, the sciences, mathematics, the industrial arts, business and vocational studies, health and physical education, art and music, and home economics.

527. **Neubert, G. A., & McNelis, S. J. (1986). Improving writing in the disciplines. *Educational Leadership, 43*(7), 54–58.**
Discusses the theory and practice of writing response groups.

528. Newman, J. M. (1988). Sharing journals: Conversational mirrors for seeing ourselves as learners, writers and teachers. *English Education*, 20, 134–156.
Analyzes what happens when teachers keep journals. The author responds to the journals to help teachers develop ideas about writing and learning.

529. Nolan, E. (1986). Writing and the senior seminar: Empowering students for entry into the scholarly community. In K. O'Dowd & E. Nolan (Eds.), *Learning to write, writing to learn* (pp. 19–26). Livonia, MI: Madonna College Humanities Writing Program.
Describes how writing can become an educational force in a senior seminar in the humanities. Since the seminar capitalizes on the humanities as hermeneutics and knowledge as social artifact, it provides an excellent site for clarifying the goals of writing for the humanist.

530. Odell, L. (1980). Teaching writing by teaching the process of discovery: An interdisciplinary enterprise. In L. W. Gregg & E. R. Steinberg (Eds.), *Cognitive processes in writing* (pp. 139–154). Hillsdale, NJ: Erlbaum.
Suggests how instructors can use writing to teach students strategies for thinking.

531. Parsons, L. (1989). *Response journals*. Portsmouth, NH: Heinemann.
A practical guidebook for assigning and evaluating response journals, with focus on literature and the humanities.

532. Pierce, E. (1983). Reinforced learning through written case studies. In C. Thaiss (Ed.), *Writing to learn: Essays and reflections on writing across the curriculum* (pp. 64–71). Dubuque, IA: Kendall Hunt.
Discusses how written case studies can encourage movement from simple to complex thinking. The author relates the case study process (as developed in the discipline of Finance) to the concept of writing to learn.

533. Pradl, G. M., & Mayher, J. S. (1985). Reinvigorating learning through writing. *Educational Leadership*, 42, 4–8.
Argues that journal writing helps students to learn and to personalize their learning.

534. Preston, J. (1982). *Writing across the curriculum. Some questions & answers & a series of 11 writing projects for instructors of the general education core courses: Energy and the Natural Environment, Humanities, Individual in Transition, and Social Environment*. Miami, FL: Miami-Dade Community College. (ERIC Document Reproduction Service No. ED 256 414)

535. Rainer, T. (1979). *The new diary*. New York: St. Martin's Press.
Emphasizing the diary as the only form of writing untouched by formal and external restraints, Rainer presents and explores methods of using diaries for "transforming personal problems," "discovering joy," "overcoming writer's blocks," and meeting other personal and creative needs. Examples from over 100 diaries suggest that diary writing can be an important means of exploration and thinking, and thus relevant to WAC.

536. Reed, S. D. (1988). Logs: Keeping an open mind. *English Journal, 77,* 52–56.
Explains why students should keep reading logs in the classroom.

537. Ronald, K. (1987). The politics of teaching professional writing. *Journal of Advanced Composition, 7,* 23–30.
Explores the complexities and contradictions of teaching professional writing courses. Topics discussed are: the "rhetorical maze of several levels of audiences" through which students must run; the political ramifications of English departments charged with teaching students how to write more effectively in every conceivable field; the dilemma of whether to focus on subject matter or discursive forms and conventions; and whether expressive writing has a place in the professional writing course.

538. Sanders, A. (1985). Learning logs: A communication strategy for all subject areas. *Educational Leadership, 42,* 7.
Describes an instructional strategy in which students make entries in their learning logs in the last five minutes of each period, responding to the teacher's questions.

539. Sax, R. (1986). Flashlights in a haunted house: Freewriting in the composition classroom. In K. O'Dowd & E. Nolan (Eds.), *Learning to write, writing to learn* (pp. 46–50). Livonia, MI: Madonna College Humanities Writing Program.
Assesses the limitations and advantages of freewriting as a means of helping students write.

540. Schiff, P. (1982). Responding to writing: Peer critiques, teacher-student conferences, and essay evaluation. In T. Fulwiler & A. Young (Eds.), *Language connections: Writing and reading across the curriculum* (pp. 153–166). Urbana, IL: National Council of Teachers of English.
Emphasizes peer critiquing and teacher-student conferencing as ways of providing feedback on students' early writing drafts.

541. Schlawin, S. A. (Ed.). (1980). *Writing right across the curriculum, K–12.* Poughkeepsie, NY: Dutchess County Board of Cooperative Educational Services. (ERIC Document Reproduction Service No. ED 199 700)
Devised by participants in a summer workshop focusing on writing in the content areas, this guide describes activities for improving writing skills at all grade levels.

542. Self, J. (1987). The picture of writing to learn. In *Plain talk: About learning and writing across the curriculum* (pp. 9–20). Commonwealth of Virginia: Virginia Department of Education.
Shows how WAC can transform the activity of learning across the curriculum. Suggests 16 specific writing-to-learn strategies.

543. Shine, M. (1983). Motivating university students to write and publish. In C. Thaiss (Ed.), *Writing to learn: Essays and reflections on writing across the curriculum* (pp. 135–139). Dubuque, IA: Kendall Hunt.

Shares a classroom exercise that motivates students to write for conferences and journals.

544. Simmons, J. M. (Ed.). (1983). *The shortest distance to learning: A guidebook to writing across the curriculum.* **Los Angeles, CA: Office of Academic Interinstitutional Programs, Los Angeles Community College District. (ERIC Document Reproduction Service No. ED 241 073)**
A teacher guide stressing the integration of writing skills into content teaching through the use of learning logs, model assignments, and essay questions.

545. Soven, M., & Sullivan, W. (1990). Demystifying the academy: Can exploratory writing help? *Freshman English News, 19,* 13–16.
Argues that expressive writing can play an important role in enculturating students into the world of academic discourse.

546. Stanley, L. C. (1991). Writing-to-learn assignments: The journal and the microtheme. In L. C. Stanley & J. Ambron (Eds.), *Writing across the curriculum in community colleges* (pp. 45–50). San Francisco: Jossey-Bass.
Shows how to adapt journal and microtheme writing to courses in math, botany, electrical technology, and college-life.

547. Staton, J. (1980). Writing and counseling: Using a dialogue journal. *Language Arts, 57,* 514–518.
Narrates how a sixth-grade teacher writes dialogue journals [see Staton (1987)] with her students as a means of helping them with learning and personal problems.

548. Staton, J. (1987). The power of responding in dialogue journals. In T. Fulwiler (Ed.), *The journal book* (pp. 47–63). Portsmouth, NH: Heinemann.
Defines the dialogue journal as a journal kept jointly by student and teacher, in which both write interactively in a form of conversation. Staton then gives a history of dialogue journals in elementary classrooms, describes how various teachers have used them, and provides a guide for using dialogue journals with elementary students.

549. Steinacker, D. (Ed.). (1984). *Writing: Don't leave it in the English classroom—Activities to enhance teaching in all areas.* **San Jose, CA: English Department, San Jose State University, South Bay Writing Project. (ERIC Document Reproduction Service No. ED 260 410)**
Contains five sections, each devoted to a different type of cross-curricular writing activity (journals, letters, newspaper stories, personal narratives, and poetry). Each section suggests writing activities of that particular type for classes in art, home economics, industrial arts, mathematics, physical education, science, and social studies, and includes samples of student writing from each discipline.

550. Stillman, P. (1987). "Of myself, for myself." In T. Fulwiler (Ed.), *The journal book* (pp. 77–86). Portsmouth, NH: Heinemann.
A teacher and professional writer offers his personal testimonial to the benefits of journal keeping.

551. Storlie, E. F., & Barwise, M. (1985). *Asking good questions, getting good writing.* Minneapolis, MN: Minneapolis Community College.
This teacher's handbook on WAC includes chapters on getting more writing from students; asking questions that demand thinking and writing; using informal and nontraditional writing assignments; and saving time when responding to or evaluating writing assignments.

552. Strickland, H. (1987). Publishing. In J. Self (Ed.), *Plain talk: About learning and writing across the curriculum* (pp. 155–156). Commonwealth of Virginia: Virginia Department of Education.
Discusses the rewards of publishing for teachers and for students.

553. Styles, K., & Cavanaugh, G. (1980). Language across the curriculum: The art of questioning and responding. *English Journal, 69,* 24–27.
A descriptive analysis of language use in all disciplines to improve thinking. Emphasizing oral language, the authors examine different types of questions asked and kinds of thinking they encourage.

554. Summerfield, G. (1987). Not in utopia: Reflections on journal-writing. In T. Fulwiler (Ed.), *The journal book* (pp. 33–40). Portsmouth, NH: Heinemann.
Reviewing the published journals of Amelia Earhart, Francis Kilvert and others, Summerfield contends that all writing, even the most ostensibly private (e.g., journal writing) is a social act.

555. Talbot, B. (1990). Writing for learning in school: Is it possible? *Language Arts, 67,* 47–56.
Warns against turning writing-to-learn into "something students must do," because obligatory writing-to-learn may constrain students as much as have more traditional writing assignments.

556. Tchudi, S. N. (1984). *Writing in the content areas: The NEA Inservice Training Program.* West Haven, CT: National Education Associaion.
A training program to help teachers in all disciplines and at all levels to integrate writing into their courses. The package includes various media (audiotapes, filmstrips, etc.) as well as prototypes of handouts which can be copied and distributed.

557. Tchudi, S. N. (1986). *Teaching writing in the content areas: College level.* Washington, D. C.: National Education Association.
Chapters One through Five of this monograph review recent theory and research on writing to learn and suggest specific strategies that content area instructors can use to assign and evaluate writing in their classes. Chapters Six and Seven discuss methods for developing and coordinating a campus WAC program and include historical reviews of five WAC programs—at Michigan Technological University, University of North Carolina at Wilmington, State University College of New York at Fredonia, University of Michigan, and Montana State University.

558. Tchudi, S. N., Tchudi, S. J., Huerta, M. C., & Yates, J. (1983). *Teaching writing in the content areas* (3 vols). Washington, DC: National Education

Association.
A comprehensive rationale and plan for implementing WAC programs. Although each volume focuses on a specific level (elementary, middle school/junior high, and senior high), all share the same design. Part One of each volume presents a primer for developing content-area writing lessons; Part Two offers model teaching units in the content areas; and Part Three suggests methods for evaluation and additional ideas for content-area writing.

559. Thaiss, C. (1983). *Learning better, learning more: In the home and across the curriculum.* **(The talking and writing series, K–12: Successful classroom practices.) Washington, DC: Dingle Associates. (ERIC Document Reproduction Service No. ED 233 383)**
Describes five settings where writing and speaking are used to help students learn course content: a home setting, a fifth-grade history class, a high school science class, a ninth-grade math class, and a high school social studies class. Thaiss analyzes the theory, pedagogy, and activities at work in each setting and suggests further ideas for classroom activities and for additional reading.

560. Thaiss, C. (1986). *Language across the curriculum in the elementary grades.* **Urbana, IL: ERIC.**
Takes readers inside five elementary classes where teachers make the language arts of speaking, listening, writing, and reading central to their courses.

561. Thompson, A. (1990). Thinking and writing in learning logs. In N. Atwell (Ed.), *Coming to know: Writing to learn in the intermediate grades* **(pp. 35–51). Portsmouth, NH: Heinemann.**
Illustrates how third-graders use learning logs for seven broad purposes: to focus, gather, remember, organize, predict and elaborate, integrate, and evaluate.

562. Tollefson, S. (1988). *Encouraging student writing: A guide for instructors.* **Berkeley: University of California, Office of Educational Development.**
A pamphlet designed to help college faculty integrate writing into their courses across the curriculum.

563. Trede, M. (1992). Queen for a day. *Gifted Child Today, 15*(2), 30–33.
An excerpt from the author's book, *Rock Writing,* which emphasizes "that writing taught in language arts is the 'rock' or foundation of writing skills in all academic areas."

564. Vaughan, C. L. (1990). Knitting writing: The double-entry journal. In N. Atwell (Ed.), *Coming to know: Writing to learn in the intermediate grades* **(pp. 69–75). Portsmouth, NH: Heinemann.**
Shows how double-entry journals [see Berthoff (1987)] serve "as knitting needles or nails to help children connect new strands of learning to what they already know." Illustrates with examples of journals from science and social studies.

565. Walley, C. W. (1991). Diaries, logs and journals in the elementary classroom. *Childhood Education, 67*(3), 149–154.

Addresses problems teachers face in assigning diaries, logs, and journals; summarizes the benefits of each type of writing; and suggests ways of making each activity more interesting for students and teachers.

566. Walpole, J. R. (1981). Content writing. *Teaching English in the Two-Year College, 7,* 103–106.
Proposes exercises for summarization in content areas and argues against the importance of expressive writing in favor of traditional composition skills.

567. Walvoord, B. F. (1985). Freshmen, "focus," and writing across the curriculum. *Freshman English News, 14* (2), 13–17.
Discusses the problem of teaching students to transfer skills of "focus"—e.g., developing a limited, specific thesis—to writing outside the composition class. Illustrates with an example of a student writing in a history class, and discusses studies of focus in the writing of students in management, biology, and economics courses.

568. Walvoord, B. F. (1986). *Helping students write well: A guide for teachers in all disciplines* **(2nd ed.). New York: Modern Language Association.**
A condensed handbook for instructors in all fields who are committed to strengthening student writing. Major emphasis is on the writing process.

569. Weiner, W. F. (1986). When the process of writing becomes a tool for learning. *English Journal, 75,* 73–75.
Describes how the author used writing to help students learn in the Gifted and Talented section of a sophomore English course.

570. Wells, M. C. (1992/1993). At the junction of reading and writing: How dialogue journals contribute to students' reading development. *Journal of Reading, 36,* 294–302.
Wells studied the year-long dialogue journal writing of eight eighth-graders to measure the effects of dialogue journals [see Staton (1987)] on reading development. Results suggest that the journals helped students forge connections between what they read and what they know. In addition, journals helped them develop a stronger sense of audience (students wrote dialogue "letters" for classroom peers as well as for the instructor).

571. West, J. K. (1985). Thirty aides in every classroom. In A. R. Gere (Ed.), *Roots in the sawdust: Writing to learn across the disciplines* **(pp. 175–186). Urbana, IL: National Council of Teachers of English.**
Discusses how peer- and self-evaluation and other write-to-learn activities can help students become "aides" in their own education while also helping instructors to learn more about their students.

572. Wheeler, N. S. (1990). Showing the way: Using journal writing to develop learning and teaching strategies. In N. Atwell (Ed.), *Coming to know: Writing to learn in the intermediate grades* **(pp. 129–138). Portsmouth, NH: Heinemann.**
Describes how journal writing benefitted a learning-disabled child.

573. Winston, L., & Low, D. (1990). Devin's daybook. *Language Arts, 67,* **35–46.**
Winston describes the remarkably extensive daybook of Devin Low, a third-grader and co-author of her article. She concludes that, though Devin was unusual, "all children can learn to write given time, ownership [of their material], and response."

574. Wolfe, D., & Reising, R. (1983). *Writing for learning in the content areas.* **Portland, ME: J. Weston Walch.**
This text for secondary school teachers emphasizes the role that writing can play in learning course content. Chapter 1 explains how writing can be used to enhance thinking and learning in any discipline. Chapters 2–6, each of which is devoted to a different disciplinary area (English, social studies, math/science, business, and vocational education), suggest writing activities to achieve instructional tasks within each area. Chapters also discuss writing evaluation and other issues, and include several reproducible pages of writing activities for students. Chapter 7 further discusses writing assessment in the content areas and provides ten sample assessment forms for classroom use.

The Arts and Humanities

575. Ambrose, J. (1987). Music journals. In T. Fulwiler (Ed.), *The journal book* (pp. 261–268). Portsmouth, NH: Heinemann.
Argues that journals in music classes help students to monitor reactions to specific pieces and performances and provide good practice in writing about music.

576. Ameigh, T. M. (1993). Learn the language of music through journals. *Music Educators Journal, 79*(5), 30–32.
Shares several journal writing activities to help students become more articulate about their responses to music.

577. Arkle, S. (1985). Better writers, better thinkers. In A. R. Gere (Ed.), *Roots in the sawdust: Writing to learn across the disciplines* (pp. 148–161). Urbana, IL: National Council of Teachers of English.
Explains how he uses writing-to-learn techniques in a twelfth grade literature class to help students understand content. Arkle encourages students to write essays that derive from their personal connection with the material rather than from the instructor's lectures.

578. Atwell, N. (1987). Building a dining room table: Dialogue journals about reading. In T. Fulwiler (Ed.), *The journal book* (pp. 157–170). Portsmouth, NH: Heinemann.
Shows how she creates a relaxed, conversational environment for reading and discussing literature in her eighth grade classes. Students choose their own reading rather than following a prescribed reading list. Atwell uses dialogue journals [see Staton (1987)] to engage students in sustained and collaborative discussion of the works they read.

579. Bailey, G., & Ross, G. (1983). Overcoming declining literacy with personalized, programmed instruction. *Teaching Philosophy, 6*(2), 139–145.
Describes the structure and focus of a special philosophy course designed to allow marginally admissible students to increase their academic skills and prepare for mainstream university instruction.

580. Bauso, J. A. (1988). Incorporating reading logs into a literature course. *Teaching English in the Two-Year College,* [Dec.], 255–261.
Argues that reading logs can make students more active readers of texts. Suggests numerous kinds of writing to do in logs and discusses how to use and share logs in class.

581. Beaty, D., & Schoenewolf, C. R. (1973). A marriage of English and music. *Music Educator's Journal, 59*(7), 64–65.
Describes a university program in which the music department joined with the freshman composition division of the English department to offer special composition sections tailored for music majors.

582. Belanoff, P. (1987). The role of journals in the interpretive community. In T. Fulwiler (Ed.), *The journal book* **(pp. 101–110). Portsmouth, NH: Heinemann.**
Describes how journals can free students to write for themselves and each other instead of simply for teachers. Through journal writing and sharing, students can realize that literary interpretation is not the prerogative of professors alone; that they, also, are empowered members of interpretive communities.

583. Berger, J. (1984). Writing to learn in philosophy. *Teaching Philosophy, 7,* 217–222.
Summarizes the recent emphases in writing pedagogy on revision, audience, and purpose and suggests writing activities to teach philosophy: one-paragraph assignments, paragraph revision, and writing to generate discussion.

584. Beyer, B. K. (1979). Prewriting and rewriting to learn. *Social Education, 43,* 187–189, 197.
Shares prewriting and revising activities for social studies classes.

585. Beyer, B. K. (1980). Using writing to learn in history. *History Teacher, 13*(2), 167–178.
Suggests that writing can help develop "historical-mindedness" and provides six detailed guidelines for using writing for learning in secondary and college classrooms.

586. Beyer, B. K., & Brostoff, A. (1979a). The time it takes: Managing/ evaluating writing in social studies. *Social Education, 43,* 194–197.
Suggests how social studies teachers can meet the double time demands of teaching course content and teaching writing.

587. Beyer, B. K., & Brostoff, A. (1979b). Writing to learn in social studies. *Social Education, 43,* 176–177.
Argues that writing in the social studies class can help students to think as well as to grasp course content.

588. Bosley, D. S., & Jacobs, J. (1992). Collaborative writing: A philosopher's guide. *Teaching Philosophy, 15,* 17–32.
Offers a rationale and methods for assigning students to write collaboratively

in the philosophy class. The authors illustrate the collaborative approach with a description of their "Philosophy of the Arts" course and conclude with a summary of benefits and drawbacks to the approach.

589. Bozyk, D. (1986). Conversational writing: The value of informal letter writing in the college history course. In K. O'Dowd & E. Nolan (Eds.), *Learning to write, writing to learn* (pp. 39–45). Livonia, MI: Madonna College Humanities Writing Program.
As an antidote to student anxiety over writing formal papers, Bozyk advocates informal letter writing. In addition to enhancing learning, letter writing gives students confidence, practice, and skills to compose in the more formal contexts required of working historians.

590. Breihan, J. R. (1986). Prewriting in college history courses. *Perspectives: American Historical Association Newsletter, 24,* 20–21.
Suggests several kinds of prewriting exercises, including class notes, journals, simple analyses, narratives, and summaries.

591. Brostoff, A., & Beyer, B. K. (1980). An approach to integrating writing into a history course. *Journal of Basic Writing, 2(4),* 36–52.
Describes a model developed by two faculty members, one in writing and one in history, who designed, taught, and evaluated an African history course in which writing played a central role. Includes an appendix of 12 exercises.

592. Brozick, J. R. (1978). New perspectives on composition: A review of the literature. *Journal of Aesthetic Education, 12(3),* 83–92.
Offers teachers in the humanities an overview of changing views in the teaching of composition and their foundation in theories of language and cognition.

593. Burnham, C. C. (1987). Reinvigorating a tradition: The personal development journal. In T. Fulwiler (Ed.), *The journal book* (pp. 148–156). Portsmouth, NH: Heinemann.
Emphasizes the journal as a means of promoting personal and psychological growth in the composition class. Burnham relates journals to William Perry, Jr.'s model of cognitive development and uses assignments incorporating the techniques of "Intensive Journal" writing developed by depth psychologist Ira Progoff.

594. Clark, W. H. (1976). On teaching composition. *Journal of Aesthetic Education, 10(3–4),* 107–114.
Argues that, to improve the writing ability of college graduates, we must increase the breadth of their exposure to writing.

595. Collett, M. J. (1991). Read between the lines: Music as a basis for learning. *Music Educators Journal, 78(3),* 42–45.
Describes a program that helps at-risk students learn and develop self-esteem through a combination of music, reading, journal writing, and other language activities.

596. Cookston, D. (1982). "This guy can really write." In M. Barr, P. D'Arcy, & M. K. Healy (Eds.), *What's going on? Language/learning episodes in British and American classrooms, grades 4–13* (pp. 196–217). Upper Montclair, NJ: Boynton/Cook.
Discusses her use of reading logs in a high school literature class.

597. Cooter, R. B., Jr., & Chilcoat, G. W. (1990). Content-focused melodrama: Dramatic renderings of historical text. *Journal of Reading, 34,* 274–277.

598. Coppenger, M. (1979). Written dialogue: An alternative to the term paper. *Teaching Philosophy, 3,* 197–202.
As an alternative to traditional term papers in philosophy, Coppenger proposes a dialogic process of writing and responding. The student submits a single-page argument in reaction to one of fifty philosophical questions. The teacher then responds by asking questions or making comments that stimulate further written argument.

599. Culpin, C. B. (1984). Language, learning and thinking skills in history. *Teaching History, 39,* 24–28.
A British school administrator discusses how he investigated current practices in history teaching with an eye to improving the integration of language, thinking and learning in various English schools.

600. Cunningham, F. J. (1985). Writing philosophy: Sequential essays and objective tests. *College Composition and Communication, 36,* 166–172.
Contends that traditional term papers and final exams in philosophy are artificial and describes how he combines "fill in the blank" tests with writing assignments that focus on the students' writing process.

601. Cushner, K. (1992). Creating cross-cultural understanding through internationally cooperative story writing. *Social Education, 56,* 43–46.
Describes a program in which American elementary-level students write stories cooperatively with children from other countries and cultures. The program improves cross-cultural understanding while also exercising students' writing skills.

602. Daniel, S. H. (1979). Preparations for a research paper in philosophy. *Teaching Philosophy, 3,* 185–188.
Shares a form for students to complete as they do philosophy research in the library. The form helps familiarize students with the research process.

603. Davala, V. (1987). Respecting opinions: Learning logs in middle school English. In T. Fulwiler (Ed.), *The journal book* (pp. 179–186). Portsmouth, NH: Heinemann.
Argues that logs can help student learning.

604. Deckert, A. J., Hummer, C. C., Reed, S. D., Brewster, M., Heath, G., & Stover, K. (1988). Journals, logs, and freewriting. *English Journal, 77*(2), 47–62.
A series of five short essays addressing the uses, benefits, and limitations of journals, logs, and freewriting.

605. Dickerson, M. J. (1987). Exploring the inner landscape: The journal in the writing class. In T. Fulwiler (Ed.), *The journal book* (pp. 129–136). Portsmouth, NH: Heinemann.
Identifies the journal as a vehicle for encouraging "that inner synthesis of self and the world necessary for creative learning to take place."

606. Dimmitt, J. P., & Van Cleaf, D. W. (1992). Integrating writing and social studies: Alternatives to the formal research paper. *Social Education, 56,* 382–384.
Arguing that the formal research paper is an inappropriate assignment for middle school students, the authors suggest a number of alternatives, such as oral history projects, dialogue diaries, letters, monologues, position papers, and other assignments that prepare students for more formal research.

607. DiYani, R. (1980). Sound and sense: Writing about music. *Journal of Basic Writing, 2,* 62–71.
Explains how a course in writing about music can be advantageous both to students and to teachers. Suggests a number of writing assignments.

608. Dolgin, A. (1981). Teach social studies through writing. *The Social Studies, 72,* 8–10.
Arguing that writing should be viewed as a problem solving process, Dolgin offers suggestions for assessing students' writing and an instructional strategy for teaching social studies through writing.

609. Faulconer, J. E., Williams, R. N., & Packard, D. J. (1988). Using critical reasoning to teach writing. *Teaching Philosophy, 11,* 229–244.
The authors describe their effort to create a philosophy syllabus "which would neither teach writing and add to that critical reasoning nor teach reasoning and add to it writing, but which would teach reasoning and writing as essential to each other, as aspects of one whole."

610. Fishman, S. M. (1985). Writing-to-learn in philosophy: A before and after story. *Teaching Philosophy, 8,* 331–334.
Describes his philosophy before and after he began using writing-to-learn in his philosophy courses. While some writers have stressed the *writing* side of writing to learn, Fishman focuses on the *learning* side.

611. Fishman, S. M. (1989). Writing and philosophy. *Teaching Philosophy, 12,* 361–374.
Explains how and why he has students freewrite in introductory philosophy courses.

612. Flynn, E. A. (1986). Composing responses to literary texts: A process approach. In A. Young & T. Fulwiler (Eds.), *Writing across the disciplines: Research into practice* (pp. 208–214). Urbana, IL: National Council of Teachers of English.
Relates process theories of writing to the process of reading and interpreting literary texts.

613. Forsman, S. (1985). Writing to learn means learning to think. In A. R. Gere (Ed.), *Roots in the sawdust: Writing to learn across the disciplines* **(pp. 162–174). Urbana, IL: National Council of Teachers of English.**
Examines connections between writing and thinking by examining the tasks students accomplish in her high school literature classes. Forsman discusses strategies for using writing to develop critical thinking and reviews student evaluations of these.

614. Freeman, D. E., & Freeman, Y. S. (1991). "Doing" social studies: Whole language lessons to promote social action. *Social Education, 55,* **29–32, 66.**
Outlines a program to involve students (including international students) as critical readers and transformers of their communities.

615. Freeman, E. B. (1986). Writing and social studies instruction: Implications of research. *Social Studies Teacher, 8*(1), **1, 4, 8.**
Lists and describes numerous writing activities to improve learning, stimulate critical thinking, and forge connections between students and the communities in which they live. Aimed primarily at middle school teachers and students.

616. Fulwiler, L. (1987). What's a horny? Or, writing and counseling in the middle school. In T. Fulwiler (Ed.), *The journal book* **(pp. 299–305). Portsmouth, NH: Heinemann.**
A school counselor shows how she uses writing in individual and small group counseling and in classroom presentations. Students write in journals to learn, to understand themselves, and to develop healthier interpersonal communications.

617. Fulwiler, T., & Fulwiler, M. (1987). Writing and learning, grade three; *And* **still writing and learning, grade ten. In T. Fulwiler (Ed.),** *The journal book* **(pp. 193–200). Portsmouth, NH: Heinemann.**
Toby Fulwiler and his daughter collaborate to discuss her development as a journal writer from elementary school to high school.

618. Garver, E. (1983). How to develop ideas: The contribution philosophy can make to improve literacy. *Teaching Philosophy, 6,* **97–102.**
Argues that philosophy instructors can promote literacy by showing students how to develop ideas. Moving between abstract and concrete ideas and principles, the philosophy teacher can help students develop ideas through practical reasoning.

619. Gatlin, L. (1987). Losing control and liking it: Journals in Victorian literature. In T. Fulwiler (Ed.), *The journal book* **(pp. 111–118). Portsmouth, NH: Heinemann.**
Describes his experiences with journals in Victorian literature classes. Journals transform his class structure in exciting and problematic ways.

620. Gaudiani, C. (1981). *Teaching composition in the foreign language curriculum.* **Washington, D. C.: Center for Applied Linguistics. (ERIC Document Reproduction Service No. ED 209 961)**
Offers "a text-editing approach" to teaching writing in foreign language classes.

621. Gilles, C. (1989). Reading, writing, and talking: Using literature study groups. *English Journal, 78*(1), 138–141.
In literature study groups, students are asked to read the book they have chosen, keep a log, and relate the book to their own experiences.

622. Giroux, H. A. (1978). Writing and critical thinking in the social studies. *Curriculum Inquiry, 8,* 291–310.
Argues that writing and critical thinking are linked dialectically and illustrates how writing may be used to think critically on any given social studies subject.

623. Giroux, H. A. (1979). Teaching content and thinking through writing. *Social Education, 43,* 190–193.
Outlines an approach used (in an American history class) to demonstrate that writing in a subject is synonymous with learning it.

624. Golden, C. (1986). Composition: Writing and the visual arts. *Journal of Aesthetic Education, 20*(3), 59–68.
Discusses her use of visual art to teach composition students about revision. Golden's assignments focus on parallels between the genesis of a painting and that of a written manuscript; on analogies between the painter's sketches and the writer's verbal map or outline; on the painter's early studies and the writer's drafts; and so on.

625. Gorovitz, S. (1979). Taped commentary on student writing. *Teaching Philosophy, 3,* 189–195.
Describes a method of providing taped commentary on student rough drafts in a course on distributive justice and public policy. Includes a sample draft with written commentary and a transcription of the instructor's taped response.

626. Graves, D. H. (1989). When children respond to fiction. *Language Arts, 66,* 776–783.
Describes a research project in which students and teachers write letters to each other about the books they read. The letters improve learning, foster community and understanding among students and teachers, and provide an important means of evaluating children's growth as readers of fiction.

627. Graybeal, J. (1987). The team journal. In T. Fulwiler (Ed.), *The journal book* (pp. 306–311). Portsmouth, NH: Heinemann.
In an introductory religion course, students organized into teams keep collaborative journals. In addition to the benefits of individual journals, team journals have advantages which derive from writing for an audience of peers.

628. Greenleaf, C. (1990). Taking charge of curriculum. In N. Atwell (Ed.), *Coming to know: Writing to learn in the intermediate grades* (pp. 149–159). Portsmouth, NH: Heinemann.
Describes an effort to develop a third-grade curriculum "that integrates writing and literature with content-area studies and the fine arts."

629. Gunn, A. S. (1979). Writing philosophical essays: Guidance notes for students. *Teaching Philosophy, 3,* 203–211.

Offers notes distributed to students to help them write essays in philosophy. The notes consist of general remarks about writing in philosophy, definitions of a philosophical essay, how to understand the question, being clear and precise, giving your own opinions, and using facts and sources.

630. Halberg, F. (1987). Journal writing as person making. In T. Fulwiler (Ed.), *The journal book* **(pp. 289–298). Portsmouth, NH: Heinemann.**
Describes his integration of psychologist Ira Progoff's "Intensive Journal" method into two mid-level philosophy courses. The "Intensive Journal" is a vehicle for self-building and self-definition.

631. Hancock, M. R. (1992). Literature response journals: Insights beyond the printed page. *Language Arts, 69,* **36–42.**
Analyzes a sixth-grader's literature response journal to show how journals promote intellectual risk-taking and enhance thought, writing quality, and students' emotional participation in literature.

632. Herman, W. E. (1986). Psychological poetry: Learning through creative expression. In K. O'Dowd & E. Nolan (Eds.), *Learning to write, writing to learn* **(pp. 75–81). Livonia, MI: Madonna College Humanities Writing Program.**
Describes how he incorporates poetry writing into psychology classes.

633. Holsinger, D. (1983). Writing to learn history. In C. Thaiss (Ed.) *Writing to learn: Essays and reflections on writing across the curriculum* **(pp. 49–55). Dubuque, IA: Kendall Hunt.**
Shares suggestions for using writing exercises in history courses.

634. Jacobs, E. (1983). Improving the literature class as we've improved the writing class. In C. Thaiss (Ed.), *Writing to learn: Essays and reflections on writing across the curriculum* **(pp. 56–62). Dubuque, IA: Kendall Hunt.**
Describes how interpretation groups, peer evaluation of student drafts, and pre-reading of in-class writing exercises enhanced the involvement of students in a short-subject literature course.

635. Keightley, D. (1979). Improving student skills in a history lecture course. *History Teacher, 12,* **171–179.**
Describes how he integrated writing into a lecture course on Chinese civilization. Keightley concludes that writing activities improve contact between students, books, and teachers and provide a more enduring learning experience.

636. Keim, M. C. (1991). Creative alternatives to the term paper. *College Teaching, 39,* **105–107.**
Illustrates four alternatives to traditional term papers: abstracts and book reviews, group papers and projects, thought papers, and take-home finals.

637. Kent, O. T. (1987). Student journals and the goals of philosophy. In T. Fulwiler (Ed.), *The journal book* **(pp. 269–277). Portsmouth, NH: Heinemann.**
Describes how he incorporated journals into his philosophy class and used them as the sole means for determining students' grades.

638. Kentleton, J. (1981). The importance of the essay. *Teaching History, 29,* 25–27.
Advocates the use of the traditional essay in writing about history.

639. Kiernan, H. (1992). Teaching civic identity and civic writing. *Social Education, 56,* 9–12.
Describes an interdisciplinary program, undertaken at the Southern Regional School District in Manahawkin, NJ, to involve students in innovative research and writing about their own communities.

640. Klein, I. (1990). Teaching in a liberal arts college: How foreign language courses contribute to "writing across the curriculum" programs. *Modern Language Journal, 74,* 28–35.
Uses her experience at Loyola College (Maryland) to discuss how foreign language teachers participate in WAC. Identifies a need for closer cooperation among foreign language, English, and composition departments.

641. Kneeshaw, S. (1992). KISSing in the history classroom: Simple writing activities that work. *The Social Studies, 83,* 176–179.
Suggests three "short and simple" composing activities to improve student learning and writing without unduly burdening the instructor with paperwork. The activities are journal-writing, microthemes, and pretest writing exercises.

642. Koeller, S. (1992). Social studies research writing: Raising voices. *Social Education, 56,* 379–382.
Outlines an alternative approach to teaching research writing in secondary social studies classes. The approach teaches "new perspectives, critical thinking, imagination, and [social] concern."

643. Larson, C. M., & Merrion, M. (1987). Documenting the aesthetic experience: The music journal. In T. Fulwiler (Ed.), *The journal book* (pp. 254–260). Portsmouth, NH: Heinemann.
Shows how to incorporate journals into elementary and junior high music classes.

644. Lindberg, G. (1987). The journal conference: From dialectic to dialogue. In T. Fulwiler (Ed.), *The journal book* (pp. 119–128). Portsmouth, NH: Heinemann.
Describes his use of "dialectical notebooks" [see Berthoff (1987)] in literature classes and his method of responding to the journals in one-to-one conferences. Journal writing and conferencing expose students to the open-ended, dialectical nature of literary interpretation.

645. Mahoney, M. (1979). Essay writing in political education. *Teaching Political Science, 7,* 51–72.
Argues that improvement of often ineffective and ungrammatical student writing can be achieved in conjunction with the substantive purposes of a political science course.

646. Marik, R. (1985). Teaching special education history using writing-to-learn strategies. In A. R. Gere (Ed.), *Roots in the sawdust: Writing to learn across the disciplines* (pp. 72–91). Urbana, IL: National Council of Teachers of English.
Discusses experiences using writing-to-learn strategies in a special education class in history.

647. McConachie, S. (1987). Writing to learn English: Students make it work. In J. Self (Ed.), *Plain talk: About learning and writing across the curriculum* (pp. 77–84). Commonwealth of Virginia: Virginia Department of Education.
An English teacher shares strategies for engaging students through writing, including journal-writes, reflecting on oral and written responses to literature, and writing about learning in composition.

648. McGonegal, P. (1987). Fifth grade journals: Results and surprises. In T. Fulwiler (Ed.), *The journal book* (pp. 201–209). Portsmouth, NH: Heinemann.
Describes the results of a variety of brief in-class writing activities.

649. McLeod, J. R. (1992). Creative writing in the social studies. *Social Education, 56,* 398.
Outlines several creative assignments (e.g., writing historical fiction) that "encourage students to learn about the people, culture, government, and resources" of other lands for purposes "other than study for a test."

650. McMahan, C. (1985). Writing across the *English* curriculum: Using journals in literature class. *Teaching English in the Two-Year College, 12,* 269–271.
While teachers across the disciplines are incorporating more writing into their classes, McMahan notes that instructors of literature within English departments often resist including writing. McMahan traces this resistance to the paperload these instructors already encounter as composition teachers and suggests a variety of journal writing activites they can use to improve student learning without simultaneously increasing paperload or distracting from course content.

651. Miller, E., Clegg, L. B., & Vanderhoof, B. (1992). Creating postcards from the famous for social studies classes. *Journal of Reading, 36,* 134–135.
After reading a biography, students write "'imaginary postcards' with messages as they might have been written by the subject of the biography and sent to appropriate contemporaries or across time to those who faced a similar problem in a different period."

652. Moore, L. E., & Peterson, L. H. (1986). Convention as connection: Linking the composition course to the English and college curriculum. *College Composition and Communication, 37,* 466–477, 488, 506.
Offers a model for a freshman composition course "that is compatible both with the aims of writing across the curriculum and with the English department's sense of its traditional concerns."

653. Morocco, G., & Soven, M. (1990). Writing across the curriculum in the foreign language class: Developing a new pedagogy. *Hispania, 73,* 845–849.

Suggests ways of employing writing as a mode of learning and of expression in foreign language classes.

654. Mulholland, B. M. (1987). It's not just the writing. In T. Fulwiler (Ed.), *The journal book* (pp. 227–238). Portsmouth, NH: Heinemann.
In Mulholland's eleventh grade American Civilization class, students learn by sharing, reading, listening, and speaking as well as by writing.

655. Nathan, R. (1987). I have a loose tooth and other unphotographable events: Tales from a first grade journal. In T. Fulwiler (Ed.), *The journal book* (pp. 187–192). Portsmouth, NH: Heinemann.
Argues that, through acts of writing and drawing, a student "teaches *herself* about language, life, and...the interaction of the two."

656. Naumann, J. A., Jr. (1991). Letter writing: Creative vehicle to higher-level thinking. *Social Education, 55*, 198.
Assuming roles of individuals from history, students research the lives and times of these individuals and prepare writings in the form of letters rather than traditional research papers.

657. Newton, B. (1984). A language for life—or school? In N. Martin (Ed.), *Writing across the curriculum pamphlets* (pp. 125–131). Upper Montclair, NJ: Boynton/Cook.
Geography students discuss the importance of language in education.

658. Newton, E. V. (1991). Developing metacognitive awareness: The response journal in college composition. *Journal of Reading, 34*, 476–478.
Uses the example of a freshman writing class to show how keeping a response journal "can be a powerful metacognitive tool."

659. North, S. M. (1987). The philosophical journal: Three case studies. In T. Fulwiler (Ed.), *The journal book* (pp. 278–288). Portsmouth, NH: Heinemann.
Describes case studies of three students in a writing-intensive philosophy course where journal writing is central. The studies showed that the students used and learned from their journals in highly individual ways.

660. Page, B. (1987). From passive receivers to active learners in English. In J. Self (Ed.), *Plain talk: About learning and writing across the curriculum* (pp. 37–50). Commonwealth of Virginia: Virginia Department of Education.
A high school English teacher describes her use of WAC strategies, including journal writing, the metaphorical question, the formula poem, and the "admit slip" (in which students "admit" anonymously to their real feelings, questions, or processes regarding the course or its contents).

661. Pearse, S. (1985). Writing to learn: The nurse log classroom. In A. R. Gere (Ed.), *Roots in the sawdust: Writing to learn across the disciplines* (pp. 9–30). Urbana, IL: National Council of Teachers of English.
Mixing anecdotes, sample student writing, and specific teaching and learning strategies, Pearse offers a detailed description of a writing-to-learn approach for the high school literature class.

662. Peterson, D. (1985). Writing to learn German. In A. R. Gere (Ed.), *Roots in the sawdust: Writing to learn across the disciplines* (pp. 46–59). Urbana, IL: National Council of Teachers of English.
Discusses uses of writing-to-learn strategies in a foreign language class.

663. Pletcher, G. K. (1983). Literacy and the study of philosophy. *Teaching Philosophy, 6,* 109–115.
Contends that philosophers must oppose the "increasing illiteracy" of today's students. While class discussion may help in this endeavor, writing is crucial.

664. Popoff, L. A. (1986). In-class writing to faciliate learning in music theory courses. In K. O'Dowd & E. Nolan (Eds.), *Learning to write, writing to learn* (pp. 27–31). Livonia, MI: Madonna College Humanities Writing Program.
Describes the content, successes, and limitations of writing activities the author has used in classes at Madonna College in Michigan.

665. Rebhorn, M. (1985). What does "writing across the disciplines" mean to historians? *Teaching English in the Two-Year College, 12,* 265–268.
It means, argues Rebhorn, that students must learn "to write like historians." They must learn to identify, assess, and replicate the structure of historical arguments, which consist of hypothesis and proof.

666. Redmon, J. (1986). If music be the food of thought, write on: Writing in the general music class. In K. O'Dowd & E. Nolan (Eds.), *Learning to write, writing to learn* (pp. 72–74). Livonia, MI: Madonna College Humanities Writing Program.
Explains how vocabulary exercises, freewriting, and journal writing can improve learning by music students.

667. Reif, B., & Davis, J. S. (1987). Choice produces results. In T. Fulwiler (Ed.), *The journal book* (pp. 210–216). Portsmouth, NH: Heinemann.
Describes an elementary-level writing and research project that allows students maximum autonomy in the selection and development of topics.

668. Reilly, J. (1986). Goodbye Mr. Chips: An informal evaluation of the group inquiry method. In K. O'Dowd and E. Nolan (Eds.), *Learning to write, writing to learn* (pp. 32–38). Livonia, MI: Madonna College Humanities Writing Program.
An English professor uses personal experience and student evaluations to conclude that the group inquiry method is an effective strategem for learning and teaching literature.

669. Ricci, M. N. (1985, March). *Writing across the curriculum: Strategies for social studies.* Paper presented at the annual meeting of the National Council of Teachers of English, Houston, TX. (ERIC Document Reproduction Service No. ED 264 558)
Describes how journal writing can improve learning in eighth grade social studies. Gives detailed descriptions of journaling activities and of two collaborative projects attempted at the author's school (between social studies and English) to promote learning through writing.

670. **Richmond, S. (1979). When to begin writing.** *Teaching Philosophy, 3,* **181–183.**
Typically, students feel they must gather all their information before they begin writing, and this overwhelms them and prevents them from writing successfully. Richmond suggests that students write constantly, and that their formal papers undergo multiple drafts and successive refinements over time.

671. **Rico, G. L. (1989). Daedalus and Icarus within: The literature/ art/art/writing connection.** *English Journal, 78,* **14–23.**
Argues that learning is enhanced when students are asked to explore the connection between art and literature.

672. **Rouse, J. (1983). On children writing poetry.** *Language Arts, 60,* **711–716.**
Describes two approaches to the writing of poetry in the elementary classroom: the "methodological," which is narrow and restrictive; and the "experimental," which works against institutional mechanism in favor of freedom.

673. **Rubano, G. (1987). Using writing to teach political decision making.** *Social Education, 51,* **278–279.**
Presents a creative, sequenced writing assignment for the high school history class. Students write using role-play, collaboration, and readings as means of understanding the contexts in which historic political decisions are made.

674. **Russell, K., & Robertson, L. (1986). Teaching analytic reading and writing: A feminist approach.** *Teaching Philosophy, 9,* **207–217.**
Argues that students can only learn to think analytically by reading and writing regularly in a student-centered classroom. The authors show how they utilized a feminist pedagogy in a team-taught philosophy course at Denison University in Ohio.

675. **Saidel, J. R., Thorstensen, M., & O'Connell, P. S. (1980). Historical perspective, imagination, and writing: A museum-high school collaboration.** *History Teacher, 13,* **327–340.**
Describes a project to involve high school students actively in the study of history and English. Students used Old Sturbridge Village in Massachusetts as a "laboratory" for historical investigation. The project included many writing activities, some of which are described in the article.

676. **Sandler, K. (1987). Letting them write when they can't even talk? Writing as discovery in the foreign language classroom. In T. Fulwiler (Ed.),** *The journal book* **(pp. 312–320). Portsmouth, NH: Heinemann.**
Shows how she uses journals and expressive writing in the foreign language class.

677. **Sautter, R. C. (1992). Student-written philosophical journals.** *Teaching Philosophy, 15,* **239–250.**
Describes a method of assigning philosophical journals as a tool for students to explore and define their individual beliefs and values. Diverse in scope, the journal comprises all of the writing students do in Sautter's course; there are no exams or final papers.

678. Scali, N. (1991). Writing and art: Tools for self-expression and understanding (a literature, writing, and art activity). *Writing Notebook: Creative Word Processing in the Classroom, 9*(2), 19–20.

679. Simon, L. (1991). De-coding writing assignments. *The History Teacher, 24,* 149–155.
Traces much of students' difficulty with writing to an inability to de-code assignments. Simon suggests how instructors can clarify such common writing instructions as "discuss," "compare," "argue," and "summarize" for their students.

680. Spader, P. H. (1979). Writing a philosophy paper. *Teaching Philosophy, 3,* 177–179.
Offers a handout for making philosophy papers a less "traumatic experience" for many young college students.

681. Sparling, R. (1976). Interdisciplinary pursuit of the American dream. *Journal of English Teaching Techniques, 9,* 18–25.
Describes a two-semester course that combines history and literature of the United States.

682. Steffens, H. (1987). Journals in the teaching of history. In T. Fulwiler (Ed.), *The journal book* **(pp. 219–226). Portsmouth, NH: Heinemann.**
Argues for more informal and expressive forms of writing in the teaching and learning of history. Discusses different types of entries in journals in history classes and how the instructor should evaluate these journals.

683. Steffens, H. (1989). Designing writing assignments for student success. *The Social Studies, 80,* 59–63.
Shares how he incorporates WAC strategies of process writing and peer review into university-level history classes. Steffens illustrates his method with a sample writing assignment on Martin Luther.

684. Steffens, H. (1991). Helping students improve their own writing: The self-conference sheet. *The History Teacher, 24,* 239–241.
Provides a sample self-evaluation sheet he requires students to submit with their final drafts of papers and suggests ways of adapting the sheet to different writing tasks.

685. Stotsky, S. (1987). *Civic writing in the classroom.* **Bloomington, IN: Social Studies Development Center and ERIC Clearinghouse for Social Studies/Social Science Education. (ERIC Document Reproduction Service No. ED 285 800)**
Describes several school programs around the United States that integrate writing with student participation in civic affairs. Also provides samples of civic writing by students and suggests kinds of civic writing that teachers can assign in classrooms.

686. Strenski, E. (1982). Lightening the burden of assigned writing: Editing guides for self and peer evaluation. *History Teacher, 16*(1), 9–17.

Describes a peer-evaluation method that takes responsibility for critiquing students' papers off of the teacher and places it on students.

687. Summerfield, J. F. (1987). Golden notebooks, blue notebooks: Re-readings. In T. Fulwiler (Ed.), *The journal book* (pp. 137–147). Portsmouth, NH: Heinemann.
Uses the journal format to reflect on journal writing and its fundamentally exploratory, open-ended, and recursive character.

688. Sweterlitsch, R. C. (1987). The honest voice of inquiry: Teaching folklore through writing. In T. Fulwiler (Ed.), *The journal book* (pp. 239–245). Portsmouth, NH: Heinemann.
Journals enabled students in the author's college folklore class to write without the formal constraints imposed by grading. Sweterlitsch describes four journal assignments and quotes and analyzes several sample student entries.

689. Swope, J. W. (1985). Journals: Capturing students' individual responses to literature. *Virginia English Bulletin, 35*, 35–41.
Describes how he has students respond to a text in three ways: by giving their emotional response; by making free associations to connect what they have read with their personal experience; and by examining the text for features that attract them. Also explains how he reads and evaluates the journals.

690. Tashlik, P. (1987). I hear voices: The text, the journal, and me. In T. Fulwiler (Ed.), *The journal book* (pp. 171–178). Portsmouth, NH: Heinemann.
Describes how students in her junior high English class kept two types of journals: fictional, in which they used texts to generate creative writing; and reader-response, in which they recorded their affective reactions to texts.

691. Thaiss, C. (1987). A journal in the arts. In T. Fulwiler (Ed.), *The journal book* (pp. 246–253). Portsmouth, NH: Heinemann.
Focusing on the experiences of one student, Thaiss discusses the purposes and applications of journal writing in an interdisciplinary undergraduate arts course, "Reading the Arts."

692. Thaler, R. (1980). Art and the written word. *Journal of Basic Writing, 2* (4), 72–81.
Shares five exercises designed to help students in an art history course to understand the relationship between art and the written word.

693. Thieman, G. Y. (1992). Using fictional journals to study underrepresented groups in history. *Social Education, 56*, 185–186.
Describes an assignment in which middle and high school students write journals from the perspective of fictional historical figures who are women and/or people of color. The assignment incorporates writing, group collaboration, oral presentations, and research.

694. Ventre, R. (1979). Developmental writing: Social studies assignments. *Social Education, 43*, 181–183.
Outlines a writing assignment (for an American history class) which requires

students to move from simpler to increasingly complex cognitive tasks. Explores ways in which developmentally-based writing assignments can aid learning.

695. Verriour, P. (1983). Toward a conscious awareness of language through written drama. *Language Arts, 60,* 731–736.
Argues for the incorporation of written drama into elementary and secondary language classes. Verriour discusses drama as a vehicle for understanding, for teaching and increasing language awareness, and for reflection.

696. Vitiello, J. (1983). The development of poetic intuition in children: A study in the practice of nonviolence. *Language Arts, 60,* 740–748.
A poet describes his experience teaching poetry to children at the Germantown Friends School in inner-city Philadelphia.

697. Watson, T. (1985). Writing to learn history. In A. R. Gere (Ed.), *Roots in the sawdust: Writing to learn across the disciplines* **(pp. 137–147). Urbana, IL: National Council of Teachers of English.**
A high school teacher shares writing activities to help students learn about history as well as geology, geography, and other subjects.

698. Yosida, J. (1985). Writing to learn philosophy. In A. R. Gere (Ed.), *Roots in the sawdust: Writing to learn across the disciplines* **(pp. 117–136). Urbana, IL: National Council of Teachers of English.**
Describes a range of writing-to-learn activities—such as dialectics, dialogues, metaphorical questions, biopoems, and role-playing—to help students examine their lives, know themselves (i.e., in the Socratic sense), confront the problems of existence, and clarify beliefs.

699. Zimmerman, P. (1985). Writing for art appreciation. In A. R. Gere (Ed.), *Roots in the sawdust: Writing to learn across the disciplines* **(pp. 47–59). Urbana, IL: National Council of Teachers of English.**
Explains how to use writing-to-learn strategies (listing, clustering, freewriting, and others) in an art appreciation class.

Math, Science, and Engineering

700. Abel, J. P., & Abel, F. J. (1988). Writing in the mathematics classroom. *Clearing House, 62*(4), 155–158.
Suggests a variety of writing activities—journals, story problems, written algorithms, microthemes, letters, interviews, etc.—and shares ideas for designing and evaluating writing assignments.

701. Ambron, J. (1987). Writing to improve learning in biology. *Journal of College Science Teaching, 16,* 263–266.
Explains how freewriting, journal writing, and microthemes can help students understand course material better and think critically.

702. Andrews, D. C. (1975). Teaching writing in the engineering classroom. *Engineering Education, 66,* 169–174.
Describes a pilot program at Ohio State University in which students earn English composition credit and engineering credit in courses collaboratively taught by English and engineering faculty.

703. Armes, R. A., & Sullenger, K. (1986). Learning science through writing. *Science and Children, 23,* 15–19.
A second grade teacher and a middle school teacher describe several innovative writing activities that involve children in science and the outside community.

704. Bagley, T., & Gallenberger, C. (1992). Assessing students' dispositions: Using journals to improve students' performance. *The Mathematics Teacher, 85,* 660–663.
Discusses how journal writing benefits students and suggests creative ways of incorporating journals into the math class.

705. Bahns, M. (1989). Writing in science education classes for elementary school teachers. In P. Connolly & T. Vilardi (Eds.), *Writing to learn mathematics and science* (pp. 178–189). New York: Teachers College Press.
Describes her experience teaching elementary school science to pre- and in-service teachers. Bahns' courses stimulate reflective and critical thinking

through writing-to-learn activities, which the teachers can, in turn, pass on to their students.

706. Bailey, R. A., & Geisler, C. (1991). An approach to improving communication skills in a laboratory setting. *Journal of Chemical Education,* **68, 150–152.**
Describes a writing-intensive chemistry program at Rensselaer Polytechnic Institute (NY). The program utilizes graduate students from the Department of Language, Literature, and Communication as "writing consultants."

707. Bakos, J. D., Jr. (1986). A departmental policy for developing communication skills of undergraduate engineers. *Engineering Education,* **77, 101–104.**
Describes a successful effort by a civil engineering department to incorporate writing and speaking into the department curriculum.

708. Beall, H. (1991). In-class writing in general chemistry. *Journal of Chemical Education,* **68, 148–149.**
Contends that writing in a large lecture course can improve student learning and writing ability.

709. Bell, E. S., & Bell, R. N. (1985). Writing and mathematical problem solving: Arguments in favor of synthesis. *School Science and Mathematics,* **85, 210–221.**
Bell and Bell argue that expository writing is an effective and practical means of teaching mathematics.

710. BeMiller, S. (1987). The mathematics workbook. In T. Fulwiler (Ed.), *The journal book* (pp. 359–366). Portsmouth, NH: Heinemann.
Describes how he incorporates writing-to-learn workbooks into math courses. Two-thirds of writing in the workbooks is "transactional" (e.g., directed writings during class, mini-reports on designated problems) and one-third is "expressive" (i.e., informal writing for oneself as a means of thinking).

711. Berlinghoff, W. P. (1989). Locally original mathematics through writing. In P. Connolly & T. Vilardi (Eds.), *Writing to learn mathematics and science* (pp. 88–94). New York: Teachers College Press.
Describes how to use writing "to get non-science majors to do 'locally original' mathematics, that is, to engage in independent exploration of mathematical ideas that are new to them."

712. Beurk, D. (1986). *Carolyn Werbel's journal: Voicing the struggle to make meaning of mathematics.* **Working paper No. 160. Wellesley, MA: Wellesley College Center for Research on Women. (ERIC Document Reproduction Service No. ED 297 977)**
Considers the role and impact of journals in the math class by examining extended quotations from the journal of one math-avoidant student.

713. Birken, M. (1989). Using writing to assist learning in college mathematics classes. In P. Connolly & T. Vilardi (Eds.), *Writing to learn mathematics and*

science (pp. 33–47). New York: Teachers College Press.
Describes four formal and informal writing activities that have improved learning in her own math classes.

714.   **Borasi, R., & Rose, B. J. (1989). Journal writing and mathematics instruction.** *Educational Studies in Mathematics, 20,* 347–365.
Identifies ways that journal writing can help students learn math and encourage a supportive classroom environment.

715. **Botstein, L. (1989). Foreword: The ordinary experience of writing. In P. Connolly & T. Vilardi (Eds.),** *Writing to learn mathematics and science* **(pp. xi–xviii). New York: Teachers College Press.**
Reviews trends in American education since the 1938 publication of John Dewey's *Education and Experience,* which called for education based on the "intelligently directed development of the possibilities inherent in ordinary experience." Botstein then links the essays in the Connolly and Vilardi volume to Dewey's philosophy. The essays "take language and writing…as elements of 'ordinary experience' that can be used to enhance the teaching of science and mathematics."

716.   **Briand, P. L., Jr. (1967).   The nonsense about technical writing.** *Engineering Education, 57,* 507–508.
Urges English and engineering departments to collaborate in the teaching of technical writing.

717.   **Brillhart, L. V., & Debs, M. B. (1979).   Team-teaching and faculty development: A simultaneous process.** *Educational Research and Methods, 12* **(1), 18–20.**
Describes ways in which English and engineering faculty can collaborate to team-teach English courses.

718.   **Brillhart, L. V., & Debs, M. B. (1981).   Teaching writing—A scientist's responsibility.** *Journal of College Science Teaching, 10(5),* 303–304.
Contends that communication instruction should be emphasized in science courses and that lab reports are an important part of this instruction.   The authors then outline a structured method for teaching lab report writing.

719.   **Brillhart, L. V., & Debs, M. B. (1983).   A survey of writing and technical writing courses in engineering colleges.** *Engineering Education, 74,* 110–113.
Based on a survey of 108 American undergraduate engineering programs, the authors conclude that a) most curricula value writing, but do so "minimally"; and b) most program administrators express "a personal commitment to the value of writing."

720.   **Bump, J. (1985).   Metaphor, creativity, and technical writing.** *College Composition and Communication, 36,* 444–453.
Challenging notions that effective writing must be "objective" and impersonal, Bump argues that writing textbooks and assignments should encourage student engineers and scientists to think in bold, metaphorical terms.   Bump quotes writings by scientists and engineers to show how metaphor has

facilitated breakthrough problem-solving discoveries and suggests several classroom activities using metaphor.

721. Burns, M. (1988). Beyond "the right answer"...helping your students make sense out of math. *Learning, 16*(5), 30–32, 36.
Describes four strategies for using writing to promote learning in math.

722. Burton, G. M. (1985). Writing as a way of knowing in a mathematics education class. *Arithmetic Teacher, 33*(4), 40–45.
Shares techniques for teaching undergraduate and graduate mathematics methods courses.

723. Carre, C. (1981). *Science: Book four of the language teaching and learning series.* **London: Ward Lock Educational.**
Advocates writing, along with talking and reading, as a crucial means of active learning in science.

724. Cherkas, B. M. (1992). A personal essay in math? Getting to know your students. *College Teaching, 40*, 83–86.
Describes a personal essay assignment that promotes "student-teacher bonding" and familiarizes teachers with the subject-related needs of students.

725. Comprone, J. J. (1989). Narrative topic and the contemporary science essay: A lesson from Loren Eiseley's notebooks. *Journal of Advanced Composition, 9*, 112–123.
Criticizes WAC textbook/readers and teachers for favoring a mode-centered approach to science writing. Eiseley's use of narrative shows how contemporary science essayists (such as Oliver Sacks, Stephen Jay Gould, and Lewis Thomas) create forms to satisfy contextual aims rather than simply writing to fit prescribed formal patterns.

726. Connolly, P. (1989). Writing and the ecology of learning. In P. Connolly & T. Vilardi (Eds.), *Writing to learn mathematics and science* **(pp. 1–14). New York: Teachers College Press.**
Articulates the relevance of writing-to-learn to science and math. Writing-to-learn helps students to see mathematical/scientific knowledge not as something that is found "raw in nature" but as socially constructed and negotiated. Thus, while helping students to problem-solve, writing-to-learn also broadens students' view of themselves and of their teachers as members of mathematical/ scientific communities.

727. Connolly, P., & Vilardi, T. (Eds.). (1989). *Writing to learn mathematics and science.* **New York: Teachers College Press.**
A collection of articles on the integration of writing into math and science teaching. Articles are individually annotated in this section. See 1989 entries for: Botstein; Connolly; Rose; Birken; Tobias; Marwine; Kenyon; Berlinghoff; White & Dunn; Martin; Layzer; Keith; Lesnak; Powell & Lopez; Bahns; Snow; Mullin; Gopen & Smith; Duncan; Lax; Whitney; Worsley; John-Steiner; and Hersh.

728. Cooley, A. P. (1980). Writing in science—An innovation. *The American Biology Teacher, 42,* **534–536.**
A high school biology teacher criticizes emphasis on multiple choice testing in science classes and describes an extended writing assignment he gave to his class.

729. Cory, W. (1982). A comprehensive bibliography on scientific and technical writing. *Journal of College Science Teaching, 11,* **351–355.**
Lists over 200 books and articles.

730. Countryman, J. (1992). *Writing to learn mathematics: Strategies that work, K–12.* **Portsmouth, NH: Heinemann.**
Shows how journals, learning logs, letters, autobiographies, formal papers, and other writing activities can improve student learning of math at all grade levels.

731. Covington, D. H., Brown, A. E., & Blank, G. B. (1984). A writing assistance program for engineering students. *Engineering Education, 75,* **91–93.**
Describes how a program at North Carolina State University's School of Engineering addresses the technical writing problems of students through teaching, tutorials, workshops, and advisory services.

732. Covington, D. H., & Keedy, H. F. (1979). A technical communication course using peer evaluation reports. *Engineering Education, 69,* **417–419.**
Shows how to simulate, in class, the kinds of contexts that surround actual written and oral technical reports.

733. Creager, J. G. (1980). Teaching writing is every teacher's job. *The American Biology Teacher, 42,* **273.**
Argues that teachers in all discplines should require writing, and offers five suggestions for overcoming the particular problems students face when writing about science.

734. Davison, D. M., & Pearce, D. L. (1988a). Using writing activities to reinforce mathematics instruction. *Arithmetic Teacher, 35*(8), **42–45.**
Davison and Pearce classify writing activities in mathematics into five categories: direct use of language (copying and recording information); linguistic translation (translation of mathematical symbols into written language); summarizing; applied use of language (application of a mathematical idea to a problem context); and creative use of language. They then present some writing exercises in each category.

735. Davison, D. M., & Pearce, D. L. (1988b). Writing activities in junior high mathematics texts. *School Science and Mathematics, 88,* **493–499.**
Reports their study of the quality and quantity of writing activities suggested in junior high math textbooks. The authors conclude that "the five series examined…contained few writing activities, very few longer writing tasks, little or no instructional support, and no assistance for teachers on how to use writing in their mathematics classrooms in either the form of explanation or additional references."

736. **DeBruin, J. E., & Gibney, T. C. (1984). If you teach science and mathematics, then write!** *School Science and Mathematics, 84,* 33–42.
Advises science and math teachers who aspire to write and publish.

737. **Denten, L. W. (1978). Continuing engineering education in technical writing.** *Engineering Education, 66,* 760–762.
A nationwide survey of American colleges and universities shows that 25% offer technical writing through continuing education programs.

738. **Donavan, T. R. (1977).** *Math and English as integrated discourse.* **Unpublished manuscript, Northeastern University.   (ERIC Document Reproduction Service No. ED 146 598)**
Proposes a composition course that integrates the traditionally separated discourses of mathematics and English.

739. **Dorman, W. W., & Pruett, J. M. (1985). Engineering better writers: Why and how engineers can teach writing.** *Engineering Education, 75,* 656–658.
In addition to suggesting methods for teaching writing, the authors stress that engineering teachers can motivate better student writing by stressing the importance of writing on the job. Includes an annotated bibliography of books, essays and articles on the teaching of writing.

740. **Duncan, E. (1989). On preserving the union of numbers and words: The story of an experiment. In P. Connolly & T. Vilardi (Eds.),** *Writing to learn mathematics and science* **(pp. 231–248). New York: Teachers College Press.**
Describes an experiment to bring a language-linked approach to mathematics into several Brooklyn schools. The experiment, conducted collaboratively by a math teacher and a writer, emphasizes the role of imagination in mathematics as well as in writing.

741. **Fagan, E. R. (1987). Interdisciplinary English: Science, technology, and society.** *English Journal, 76*(5), 81–83.
Calls for syllabi and curricula that broaden student awareness of the interconnectedness of English with science, technology, and other disciplines.

742. **Feinberg, S. (1979). Feedback on format improves technical writing.** *Engineering Education, 69,* 339–342.
Argues that students' writing improves when they receive "immediate and constructive feedback and…information on formats and criteria."

743. **Feirn, M. (1989). Writing in the health sciences: A short course for graduate nursing students.** *Writing Lab Newsletter, 13*(5), 5–8.
Describes a short course in writing for nursing students offered through the University of Wisconsin-Madison writing lab.

744. **Fennell, F., & Ammon, R. (1985). Writing techniques for problem solvers.** *Arithmetic Teacher, 33*(1), 24–25.
Outlines a four-stage process to have elementary students write their own word problems. The authors provide specific ideas for each stage—prewriting, writing, revising, and publication/sharing.

745. **Fisher, R. J., & Fisher, R. L. (1985). Reading, writing, and science.** *Science and Children*, **[Sept.], 23–24.**
Advocating a "hands on" emphasis in science instruction, the authors contend that "doing science" can make children better readers and writers and that reading and writing can (in turn) make them better "doers" of science.

746. **Flynn, E. A., McCulley, G. A., & Gratz, R. K. (1986). Writing in biology: Effects of peer critiquing and analysis of models on the quality of biology laboratory reports. In A. Young & T. Fulwiler (Eds.),** *Writing across the disciplines: Research into practice* **(pp. 160–175). Upper Montclair, NJ: Boynton/Cook.**
A comparative analysis of 140 lab reports from four college biology classes leads the authors to conclude that "techniques such as peer critiquing and analysis of models may be helpful in the preparation of lab reports and that further investigation of these approaches in courses other than composition would be worthwhile."

747. **Foos, K. M. (1987). Abstracts can enhance writing skills.** *Journal of College Science Teaching, 16,* **254–255.**
Argues that writing scientific abstracts helps students to develop as writers and thinkers.

748. **Friday, C. (1986). An evaluation of graduating engineers' writing proficiency.** *Engineering Education, 77,* **114–116.**
Based on a comparative study of writing performance by engineering and non-engineering undergraduates at California State University, Sacramento, Friday suggests that "the poor writing performance" of engineering students may be related to the engineering curriculum. Urges a greater integration of writing into engineering curricula.

749. **Fulwiler, T., & Jones, R. (1979). Writing in biology.** *College Composition and Communication, 30,* **308–310.**
In a seminar with 14 biology teachers, the authors discovered that these teachers identify writing problems and offer solutions consistent with current writing pedagogy, dispelling the myth that teachers in content areas are concerned only with mechanics and usage problems.

750. **Ganguli, A. B. (1989). Integrating writing in developmental mathematics.** *College Teaching, 37(4),* **140–142.**
Describes a study to examine the effects of integrating writing into an algebra class. Results indicated that writing did not detract from coverage of course material and improved performance on tests.

751. **Gopen, G. D., & Smith, D. A. (1989). What's an assignment like you doing in a course like this? Writing to learn mathematics. In P. Connolly & T. Vilardi (Eds.),** *Writing to learn mathematics and science* **(pp. 209–228). New York: Teachers College Press.**
Describes an experimental calculus course that is part of Duke University's WAC program. The course uses writing to emphasize conceptualization of mathematical problems rather than rote learning and calculational skill.

752. **Gordon, C. J., & MacInnis, D. (1993). Using journals as a window on students' thinking in mathematics.** *Language Arts, 70,* 37–43.
Describes how dialogue journals help student learning and enhance student-teacher communication in an intermediate grade math class.

753. **Gordon, J. T. (1988). Writing: A teaching strategy for elementary algebraic fractions.** *Focus on Learning Problems in Mathematics, 10*(1), 29–36.
Describes a study of six developmental studies elementary algebra classes at Georgia State University. While the results of the study were inconclusive, writing seemed to make students more motivated and excited to do math.

754. **Graves, D. H. (1989). Research currents: When children respond to fiction.** *Language Arts, 66,* 776–783.
Describes a research project in which students and teachers write letters to each other about the books they read. The letters improve learning, foster community and understanding among students and teachers, and provide an important means of evaluating children's growth as readers of fiction.

755. **Greenes, C., Schulman, L., & Spungin, R. (1992). Stimulating communication in mathematics.** *Arithmetic Teacher, 40,* 78–82.
Illustrates a method of using writing and other types of communication to enhance students' powers of observation, analysis, and creativity in math.

756. **Greenleaf, C. (1990). Taking charge of curriculum.** In N. Atwell (Ed.), *Coming to know: Writing to learn in the intermediate grades* (pp. 149–159). Portsmouth, NH: Heinemann.
Describes an effort to develop a third-grade curriculum "that integrates writing and literature with content-area studies and the fine arts."

757. **Grumbacher, J. (1987a). How writing helps physics students become better problem solvers.** In T. Fulwiler (Ed.), *The journal book* (pp. 323–329). Portsmouth, NH: Heinemann.
Describes his use of learning logs in physics classes. Sample passages from the logs suggest that writing enhances learning and also illustrate the resistance of some students to logs.

758. **Grumbacher, J. (1987b). Writing to understand science: Theory and practice.** In J. Self (Ed.), *Plain talk: About learning and writing across the curriculum* (pp. 27–35). Commonwealth of Virginia: Virginia Department of Education.
Shares strategies for integrating writing into science courses. Discusses journal writing, freewriting, reader response to texts, writing to discover prior knowledge, writing to solve problems, lab reports, research papers, publishing students' writing, and evaluating science writing.

759. **Haggerty, D. J., & Wolf, S. E. (1991). Writing in the middle school mathematics classroom.** *School Science and Mathematics, 91,* 245–246.
Acknowledging that students should write more in mathematics classes, the authors suggest numerous math-related writing exercises under the headings of "narrative writing," "descriptive writing," and "expository writing."

760. Hamilton, D. (1978). Writing science. *College English, 40,* 32–40.
Argues that the greatest benefit of science writing is shaping scientific knowledge more thoroughly and coherently.

761. Hamilton, D. (1980). Interdisciplinary writing. *College English, 41,* 780–796.
Reiterates key ideas of Hamilton (1978).

762. Haney, J. (1990). A puffin is a bird, I think. In N. Atwell (Ed.), *Coming to know: Writing to learn in the intermediate grades* (pp. 139–148). Portsmouth, NH: Heinemann.
Describes a "hands-on" learning project for elementary students involving writing and other activities.

763. Havens, L. (1989). Writing to enhance learning in general mathematics. *The Mathematics Teacher,* [Oct.], 551–554.
Math-resistant high school students do a variety of writing assignments—such as letter-writing, diary entries, and word problems—to explore mathematics.

764. Hersh, R. (1989). A mathematician's perspective. In P. Connolly & T. Vilardi (Eds.), *Writing to learn mathematics and science* (pp. 290–292). New York: Teachers College Press.
A math professor, newly exposed to WAC, ruminates on the resistance of some math instructors to writing, the role of writing in the math class, and the potential impact of WAC on his discipline.

765. Hoffman, M., & Powell, A. (1989). Mathematical and commentary writing: Vehicles for student reflection and empowerment. *Mathematics Teaching,* [March], 55–57.
Illustrates how writing can build confidence among underprepared math students in a university setting.

766. Hotchkiss, S. K., & Nellis, M. K. (1988). Writing across the curriculum: Team-teaching the review article in biology. *Journal of College Science Teaching, 18*(1), 45–47.
A biology professor and an English professor explain how they collaborate to teach students to write review articles in an introductory science course.

767. Irons, C., & Irons, R. (1991). Ideas. *Arithmetic Teacher, 39*(4), 18–25.
Shares exercises that allow students to discuss, describe, read, and write about numbers they find in familiar real-world situations.

768. Jensen, V. (1987). Writing in college physics. In T. Fulwiler (Ed.), *The journal book* (pp. 330–336). Portsmouth, NH: Heinemann.
Contends that journal writing, freewriting, and other write-to-learn activities can be incorporated into a physics course without significantly altering the traditional approach to teaching physics. Jensen lists numerous topics for journal writing about physics, quotes sample student journal entries, and describes the results of an experiment to assess the impact of freewriting on learning in his classes.

769. Jewett, J. W., Jr. (1991). Learning introductory physics through required writing assignments. *Journal of College Science Teaching, 21*(1), 20–25.
Argues that writing skills in the basic physics class "can be improved without loss of physics content learning."

770. Johnson, M. L. (1983). Writing in mathematics classes: A valuable tool for learning. *Mathematics Teacher, 76*(2), 117–119.
Suggests ways to incorporate writing into algebra, computer-mathematics, calculus, and other math-related classes. Includes a bibliography of books and articles suitable for student-written books reports.

771. John-Steiner, V. (1989). Is mathematics a language? In P. Connolly & T. Vilardi (Eds.), *Writing to learn mathematics and science* **(pp. 285–289). New York: Teachers College Press.**
Relates the movement for writing-to-learn in math and science to the work of Jerome Bruner, L. S. Vygotsky, and other innovative psychologists, educators, and social theorists of thought. John-Steiner also describes ordinary language and the language of mathematics as mutually reinforcing symbol systems: "The drive to achieve precision in words or symbols can be empowered by using these two symbol systems in interaction with each other."

772. Johnston, P. (1985). Writing to learn science. In A. R. Gere (Ed.), *Roots in the sawdust: Writing to learn across the disciplines* **(pp. 92–103). Urbana, IL: National Council of Teachers of English.**
Explains how she uses writing to help students explore concepts in natural and physical sciences. Exercises used include role-playing, in which biology students must write about daily existence from an animal's point of view by imagining they are that animal.

773. Keith, S. Z. (1988). Explorative writing and learning mathematics. *Mathematics Teacher,* **[Dec.], 714–719.**
Shows how writing assignments can help teachers expose and address learning problems at all levels of mathematics instruction. Describes a variety of writing activities (e.g., summaries, synopses, definitions and proofs, group projects) and gives examples of each.

774. Keith, S. Z. (1989). Exploring mathematics in writing. In P. Connolly & T. Vilardi (Eds.), *Writing to learn mathematics and science* **(pp. 134–146). New York: Teachers College Press.**
Describes several short, in-class "exploratory" writing exercises for university math classes. The assignments invite risk-taking, stimulate discussion, and improve collaboration and communication between teacher and students.

775. Keith, S. Z., & Keith, P. (1985, June). *Writing and learning college mathematics.* **Paper presented at the annual meeting of the Conference on English Education, Cedar Rapids, IA. (ERIC Document Reproduction Service No. ED 264 570)**
The authors (teachers of mathematics and English, respectively) present a progress report after one year of using write-to-learn activities in freshman pre-calculus classes at St. Cloud State University in Minnesota.

776. **Kennedy, B. (1985). Writing letters to learn math.** *Learning, 13*(6), 58–59, 61.
Has students write letters to the instructor, keep learning logs, and devise and solve math problems in writing to learn more about math and develop better teacher-student communication.

777. **Kennedy, J. (1980). Mathematics and the art of writing. In J. Z. Flinn (Ed.),** *Reflections on writing: Programs and strategies for classrooms K–12* (pp. 71–74). St. Louis: Gateway Writing Project.
Describes a variety of ways to incorporate writing into the arithmetic class. Activities include story problems, graph stories, secret codes, math crosswords, weather charts, "at home" work, roll keeping, and class books of records.

778. **Kenyon, R. W. (1987).** *Writing IS problem solving.* Amherst, MA: University of Massachusetts, Scientific Reasoning Research Institute. (ERIC Document Reproduction Service No. ED 300 427). Reprinted in P. Connolly & T. Vilardi (Eds.), 1989, *Writing to learn mathematics and science* (pp.73–87). New York: Teachers College Press.
Sumarizes a variety of long- and short-term writing activities for advancing cognitive growth in math.

779. **King, B. (1982). Using writing in the mathematics class: Theory and practice. In C. W. Griffin (Ed.),** *Teaching writing in all disciplines* (pp. 39–44). San Francisco: Jossey-Bass.
Discusses ten kinds of "transactional" and "expressive" writing assignments to use in a mathematics class.

780. **Kirkpatrick, L. D., & Pittendrigh, A. S. (1984). A writing teacher in the physics classroom.** *Physics Teacher, 22*(3), 159–164.
The authors (a physics teacher and a writing teacher, respectively) outline exercises they developed to promote writing-to-learn and better finished writing in an undergraduate physics class at Montana State University. The exercises encourage students to explore the functions of role, audience, format, and task in physics writing.

781. **Kiyama, K., & Nold, E. (1979). Engineering students teach each other to write.** *Engineering Education, 69*, 334–337.
Describes the Stanford School of Engineering's Communication Project, a tutoring program in which a composition expert trains engineering students with strong writing abilities to instruct other students in writing.

782. **Kliman, M., & Richards, J. (1992). Writing, sharing, and discussing mathematics stories.** *Arithmetic Teacher, 40*, 138–141.
Offers an alternative to traditional story-problem instruction in which students use writing and talk to compose and share their own story problems.

783. **Kumar, L., Burke, D. D., & O'Connor, C. (1989). An innovative biology lab for underprepared biology majors.** *American Biology Teacher, 51*(3), 155–158.
Describes a year-long sequence of biology labs that uses writing and other skills to foster learning.

784. Labianca, D. A., & Reeves, W. J. (1985). Writing across the curriculum: The science segment. *Journal of Chemical Education, 62,* 400–402.
Argues against WAC, contending that writing in science classes "can interfere with the main business of teaching science."

785. *Language everywhere—Math.* **(1985). Urbana, IL: National Council of Teachers of English. (ERIC Document Reproduction Service No. ED 262 427)**
A compilation of columns from NCTE's publication *Live Wire* (October and December, 1984, and February and April, 1985) which focus on the integration of writing into mathematics instruction, particularly in elementary and secondary education.

786. Lavoie, D., & Backus, A. (1990). Students write to overcome learning blocks. *Journal of College Science Teaching, 19,* 353–358.
The authors argue that writing helps students break through "impedances" to learning—i.e., "any hindrance, resistance, or barrier that interferes with the transfer of knowledge between the knower and the learner." They then map out several writing strategies to reduce impedances.

787. Lax, A. (1989). They think, therefore we are. In P. Connolly & T. Vilardi (Eds.), *Writing to learn mathematics and science* **(pp. 249–265). New York: Teachers College Press.**
Describes an empowering and "leisurely" approach to learning math, in which students talk and write their way through problems rather than learning by rote memorization and drill. The approach allays math anxiety and encourages students to take responsibility for their own learning.

788. Layzer, D. (1989). The synergy between writing and mathematics. In P. Connolly & T. Vilardi (Eds.), *Writing to learn mathematics and science* **(pp. 122–133). New York: Teachers College Press.**
Argues that "There is a peculiar synergy between mathematics and ordinary language. Writing and talking about mathematical subject matter stimulates the efforts needed to master abstract mathematical ideas. Conversely, mastery of these ideas enables students to write and speak more articulately about the contexts in which these ideas figure."

789. Leesley, M. E., & Williams, M. L., Jr. (1978). All a chemical engineer does is write. *Chemical Engineering Education, 12* (4), 188–192.
Outlines the writing component of an introductory engineering course.

790. Leesley, M. E., & Williams, M. L., Jr. (1979). Improving the writing of freshman chemical engineers. *Engineering Education, 69,* 337–339.
Discusses the structure and merits of a freshman-level writing course offered to undergraduate chemical engineering students.

791. LeGere, A. (1991). Collaboration and writing in the mathematics classroom. *The Mathematics Teacher, 84,* 166–171.
Describes techniques she has used to integrate collaboration and writing into math classes at the community college level.

792. Lesnak, R. J. (1989). Writing to learn: An experiment in remedial algebra. In P. Connolly & T. Vilardi (Eds.), *Writing to learn mathematics and science* (pp. 147–156). New York: Teachers College Press.
Summarizes an experiment measuring the benefits of writing-to-learn in the teaching of basic algebra. Lesnak concludes that writing-to-learn helped reduce students' "math block" and math anxiety.

793. Levine, D. S. (1985). The biggest thing I learned but it really doesn't have to do with science.... *Language Arts, 62,* 43–47.
Summarizes some successful writing assignments in junior high science classes.

794. Licata, K. (1980). Writing is part of literacy, too! *The Science Teacher, 47,* 24–26.
Discusses the use of fantasy/narrative and factual modes of writing in science, and offers over a dozen assignments in these two genres for teachers to use or adapt.

795. Linn, M. M. (1987). *Effects of journal writing on thinking skills of high school geometry students.* Unpublished master's thesis, University of North Florida, Jacksonville. (ERIC Document Reproduction Service No. ED 289 692)
Concludes that writing in journals can enhance students' "metacognitive ability" and learning, improve communication between teacher and student, and provide instructors with a valuable tool for assessing student needs.

796. Love, E., & Tahta, D. (1977). Language across the curriculum: Mathematics. *Mathematics Teacher, 79,* 48–49.
Members of the Association of Teachers of Mathematics (Great Britain) speculate on the pedagogical relevance to mathematics of class discussion, writing, and recent linguistic theories.

797. Madigan, C. (1987a). Writing across the curriculum resources in science and mathematics. *Journal of College Science Teaching, 16,* 250–253.
Annotates over 30 resources under the headings "General," "Biology," "Chemistry," "Physics," and "Mathematics."

798. Madigan, C. (1987b). Writing as a means, not an end. *Journal of College Science Teaching, 16,* 245–249.
States the case for including writing-to-learn activities in math and science classes. Madigan explains WAC and its theoretical background, gives examples of types of informal classroom writing, and surveys successes of specific WAC programs around the United States.

799. Martin, K., & Miller, E. (1988). Storytelling and science. *Language Arts, 65,* 255–259.
Argues that "science is a story" and that "narrative is the most appropriate mode for exposing children to science." Most science books used in schools "offer children no stories, no connections between forms and forces, between observers and observed....Through a storytelling mode, scientific knowledge can be kept alive for children."

800. Martin, K. H. (1989). Writing "microthemes" to learn human biology. In P. Connolly & T. Vilardi (Eds.), *Writing to learn mathematics and science* (pp. 113–121). New York: Teachers College Press.
Describes how microthemes (short optional writings inviting individual and creative responses to lectures and readings) help marginal students in a general education biology course to gain ownership of course content. Includes a course syllabus and 36 microtheme assignments.

801. Marwine, A. (1989). Reflections on the uses of informal writing. In P. Connolly & T. Vilardi (Eds.), *Writing to learn mathematics and science* (pp. 56–69). New York: Teachers College Press.
Shows how informal writing helps students to learn concepts they don't yet know by drawing, individually and collaboratively, on what they do know (i,.e., their tacit knowledge). Marwine offers suggestions for writing topics and guidelines and describes the evolution of his own thinking about informal writing.

802. Mathes, J. C., & Stevenson, D. W. (1976). Completing the bridge: Report writing in "real life" engineering courses. *Engineering Education, 67*, 154–158.
Contrasts engineering communication in the classroom to that in industry, indentifying purpose and audience as significantly different in each setting.

803. Mathes, J. C., Stevenson, D. W., & Klaver, P. (1979). Technical writing: The engineering educator's responsibility. *Engineering Education, 69*, 331–334.
Argues that engineering colleges and departments, rather than English departments or Composition programs, should teach writing to engineering students.

804. Matz, K. A., & Leier, C. (1992). Word problems and the language connection. *Arithmetic Teacher, 39*(8), 14–17.
Shows how students can use writing and other devices to become better solvers of word problems.

805. McIntosh, M. E. (1991). No time for writing in your class? *The Mathematics Teacher, 84*, 423–433.
Addressing teachers skeptical about WAC, McIntosh shows how math instructors can incorporate writing activities into their classes without substantially changing course content. Activities described are classified into four categories: logs, journals, expository writing, and creative writing.

806. Meese, G. (1987). Focused learning in chemistry research: Suzanne's journal. In T. Fulwiler (Ed.), *The journal book* (pp. 337–347). Portsmouth, NH: Heinemann.
Under faculty directorship, a senior undergraduate in chemistry kept a journal of her work as a lab assistant. Meese concludes that the journal helped Suzanne to learn the technical practices and social implications of her discipline.

807. Mett, C. L. (1989). Writing in mathematics: Evidence of learning through writing. *Clearing House, 62*, 293–296.

Contending that journal writing helps to personalize students' knowledge of math, Mett shares several out-of-class and in-class writing activities.

808. Miller, L. D. (1991). Writing to learn mathematics. *The Mathematics Teacher, 84,* **516–521.**
Answers questions commonly asked by math teachers skeptical about WAC.

809. Miller, L. D., & England, D. A. (1989). Writing to learn algebra. *School Science and Mathematics, 89,* **299–312.**
Suggests how various affective and/or subject-oriented writing prompts can help "teachers to teach and...students to learn algebra."

810. Moger, S., & Wlezien, R. G. (1983). Using current technological issues in a writing course for engineers. *Engineering Education, 73,* **316–318.**
Describes a class that increases student interest in technical writing by using current technological issues (e.g., product liability, government regulation, technology assessment) as topics for writing assignments.

811. Moore, R. (1991). How we write about biology. *The American Biology Teacher, 53,* **388–389.**
Deplores the excessive use of passive voice in writings about biology and proposes remedies.

812. Mullin, W. J. (1989a). Qualitative thinking and writing in the hard sciences. In P. Connolly & T. Vilardi (Eds.), *Writing to learn mathematics and science* **(pp. 198–208). New York: Teachers College Press.**
While many regard physics as an exclusively quantitative and formal discipline, Mullin asserts that intuitions, feelings, and qualitative concerns are also important—to professional physicists and students alike—and suggests ways of using writing to stimulate such qualitative thinking in the classroom.

813. Nahrgang, C. L., & Petersen, B. T. (1986). Using writing to learn mathematics. *The Mathematics Teacher, 79,* **461–465.**
Discusses the value of writing-to-learn activities (specifically journal writing) in the mathematics classroom.

814. Nevin, M. L. (1992). A language arts approach to mathematics. *Arithmetic Teacher, 40,* **142–146.**
Describes a program of mathematics instruction for pre-school children that incorporates writing, talk, dramatization, and other "hands-on" and whole language activities.

815. Owen, D. (1987). Math discovery. In J. Self (Ed.), *Plain talk: About learning and writing across the curriculum* **(pp. 21–26). Commonwealth of Virginia: Virginia Department of Education.**
Tells how writing-to-learn changed the author's approach to high-school math instruction.

816. Paik, M. K., & Norris, E. M. (1983). Writing to learn in statistics, mathematics, and computer science: Two views. In C. Thaiss (Ed.), *Writing to*

learn: Essays and reflections on writing across the curriculum (pp. 107–115). Dubuque, IA: Kendall Hunt.
Shares techniques to incorporate writing into statistics, mathematics, and computer science courses.

817. Powell, A. (1985). A chemist's view of writing, reading, and thinking across the curriculum. *College Composition and Communication, 36,* 414–418.
Invites colleagues in the hard sciences to use discipline-based writing and reading assignments in their courses. Powell extends the writing activities in his chemistry classes to include abstracts based on outside readings; project papers; concept papers exploring abstract ideas in the field of chemistry; and lecture or laboratory journals.

818. Powell, A. B., & Lopez, J. A. (1989). Writing as a vehicle to learn mathematics: A case study. In P. Connolly & T. Vilardi (Eds.), *Writing to learn mathematics and science* (pp. 157–177). New York: Teachers College Press.
Describes a case study to assess the impact of writing on student learning in a developmental math course.   Concludes that writing-to-learn improved student-instructor communication, student feelings about math, and learning.

819. Richards, L. (1990). "Measuring things in words": Language for learning mathematics. *Language Arts, 67,* 14–25.
Describes numerous strategies to integrate language into middle school math classes.

820. Rideout, C. (1983). Applying the writing across the curriculum model to professional writing. In B. L. Smith (Ed.), *Writing across the curriculum* (pp. 27–32). Washington: American Association for Higher Education.   (ERIC Document Reproduction Service No. ED 243 391)
Synthesizes information on the use of writing in professional or "utilitarian" programs (engineering, law, math, etc.) at U.S. colleges.

821. Risk, T. A. (1988). Understanding math through language. *Exercise Exchange, 34*(1), 34–36.
Shows how journal writing can help elementary students learn math.

822. Rose, B. (1989a). Using expressive writing to support the learning of mathematics (Doctoral dissertation, The University of Rochester, 1989). *Dissertation Abstracts International, 50,* 04A.

823. Rose, B. (1989b). Writing and mathematics: Theory and practice. In P. Connolly & T. Vilardi (Eds.), *Writing to learn mathematics and science* (pp. 15–30). New York: Teachers College Press.
In a review essay, Rose presents a rationale for incorporating writing into the math class. Borrowing the taxonomy of Britton et al. (1975), she also reviews the literature on various kinds of "transactional" writing in math (e.g., summaries, definitions, word problems, term papers, essays, books, notetaking, projects) and "expressive" writing (e.g., freewriting, letters, autobiographical writing, and journals).

824. Rosenthal, L. C. (1987). Writing across the curriculum: Chemistry lab reports. *Journal of Chemical Education, 64,* 996–998.
Suggests ways of grounding lab reports in the tenets of WAC as articulated by Britton et al. (1975) and other WAC researchers and theorists.

825. Rueter, G., & Dunn, T. M. (1983). Science writing and literacy. In P. L. Stock (Ed.), *Fforum: Essays on theory and practice in the teaching of writing* (pp. 32–38). Upper Montclair, NJ: Boynton/Cook.
Arguing that literacy today requires interdisciplinary knowledge, Rueter and Dunn contend that "English teachers who want to help their students become literate…can and should introduce them to the literature of science."

826. Salem, J. (1982). Using writing in teaching mathematics. In M. Barr, P. D'Arcy, & M. K. Healy (Eds.), *What's going on? Language/learning episodes in British and American classrooms, grades 4–13* (pp. 123–134). Upper Montclair, NJ: Boynton/Cook.
Describes her use of learning logs in first-year algebra classes.

827. Scarnati, J. T., & Weller, C. J. (1992). The write stuff. *Science and Children, 29*(4), 28–29.
Argues that writing in science classes can help students improve their overall composing skills.

828. Schaible, R., & Rhodes, G. (1992). Metaphor in science and literature: Creating an environment for active interdisciplinary learning. *Journal of College Science Teaching, 22*(2), 100–105.
Describes an interdisciplinary course that uses writing and other assignments to explore the power of metaphoric thinking in science and literature.

829. Schmidt, D. (1985). Writing in math class. In A. R. Gere (Ed.), *Roots in the sawdust: Writing to learn across the disciplines* (pp. 104–116). Urbana, IL: National Council of Teachers of English.
Shares writing exercises to improve communication between teachers and students. Exercises include admit slips (i.e., brief written responses collected as tickets of "admission" to class), unsent letters, dialectics (i.e., students write numbers or calculations on the left side of a page and their explanations on the right), and book reports.

830. Schubert, B. (1987). Mathematics journals: Fourth grade. In T. Fulwiler (Ed.), *The journal book* (pp. 348–358). Portsmouth, NH: Heinemann.
Shares methods of assigning, reading, and responding to journals.

831. Selfe, C. L. (1983). Decoding and encoding: A balanced approach to communication skills. *Engineering Education, 74,* 163–164.
Arguing that many engineering educators have stressed students' "encoding" abilities of speaking and writing while slighting complementary "decoding" abilities of listening and reading, Selfe reports the results of a survey in which representatives from 100 companies stated that decoding skills are as vital to success on the job as encoding skills. She concludes that courses in engineering communication should pay increased attention to listening and reading.

832. Shapland, J. (1984). Worksheets—my changing attitudes toward them. In N. Martin (Ed.), *Writing Across the Curriculum Pamphlets* (pp. 120–124). Upper Montclair, NJ: Boynton/Cook.
Discusses the limitations of science worksheets and proposes alternatives that encourage students to learn through writing.

833. Shaw, J. G. (1983). Mathematics students have a right to write. *Arithmetic Teacher, 30*(9), 16–18.
Shows how writing can help students with common mathematical problems, such as long division, percentage problems, and story problems. Shaw suggests a range of exercises that incorporate writing, including games, definitions, peer editing, daily logs, reports, interviews, and the writing of computer programs.

834. Shires, N. P. (1991). Teaching writing in college chemistry: A practical bibliography 1980–1990. *Journal of Chemical Education, 68*, 494–495.
An annotated bibliography of 48 sources emphasizing "practical ideas" for classroom teaching.

835. Sides, C. H. (1980). What should we do with technical writing? *Engineering Education, 70*, 743–744.
Challenging the conclusions of Mathes, Stevenson & Claver (1979, this section), Sides argues that the teaching of technical writing should remain the responsibility of English departments.

836. Snow, J. E. (1989). The advanced writing requirement at Saint Mary's College. In P. Connolly & T. Vilardi (Eds.), *Writing to learn mathematics and science* (pp. 193–197). New York: Teachers College Press.
Describes Saint Mary's advanced writing program in math. The program emphasizes production of formal papers (e.g., technical or analytical papers, a senior project) rather than informal writings.

837. Sommers, J. (1992). Statistics in the classroom: Written projects portraying real-world situations. *The Mathematics Teacher, 85*, 310–313.
Shows how she involves eighth-grade math students in "real-world" situations that require the use of statistics and writing.

838. Soriano, J. R. (1989). Thinking through writing. *Science Teacher*, [March], 70–73.
Presents a variety of assignments to help high school science students respond creatively to textbook readings.

839. Squitieri, L. (1988). Cue: How to get started writing in anatomy and physiology. *Journal of College Science Teaching, 17*(4), 279–280.
Shows how she helps students write by teaching them how to interpret the "cue" words in essay or exam questions—i.e., the words that indicate the type or form of writing requested in the question.

840. Srulowitz, F. (1992). Diary of a tree. *Science and Children, 29*(5), 19–21.
Shows how students can use a combination of writing, talk, and drawing to complete an intensive study of trees.

841. St. Germain, A. (1983). A survey of ET writing programs. *Engineering Education, 73, 782–783.*
Based on a survey of engineering technology programs, St. Germain concludes that most schools surveyed share a belief in the importance of writing in engineering curricula.

842. Stempien, M., & Borasi, R. (1985). Students' writing in mathematics: Some ideas and experiences. *For the Learning of Mathematics 5(3), 14–17.*
Describes exercises and formats for writing-to-learn in math, including story-writing, writing mathematical essays, expressing feelings and beliefs about mathematics through diaries and anecdotes, and dialogues.

843. Strauss, M. J., & Fulwiler, T. (1987). Interactive writing and learning chemistry. *Journal of College Science Teaching, 16, 256–262.*
In a large course in introductory chemistry, students are invited to drop written queries, comments, reactions, etc., in exit boxes near the lecture hall doors. By sharing these with the class, and responding to them, the faculty develop an interactive relationship with students that facilitates learning and enhances teacher-student understanding.

844. Strauss, M. J., & Fulwiler, T. (1990). Writing to learn in large lecture classes. *Journal of College Science Teaching, 19, 158–163.*
Offers a rationale and methods for incorporating learning logs, question-writing, and other "creative language" activities into science lecture courses.

845. Sullivan, P. A. (1980). Teaching the writing process in scientific and technical writing classes. *Technical Writing Teacher, 9(1), 10–16.*
Arguing that scientific and technical writing textbooks emphasize formal and stylistic considerations to the relative neglect of the writing process, Sullivan suggests ways for instructors to teach the writing process (e.g., prewriting) in their classes. Offers examples of exercises that emphasize process in the writing of titles, introductory sections of reports, resumes, and instructions.

846. Tebeaux, E. (1980). Technical writing is *not* enough. *Engineering Education, 70, 741–743.*
Rejects the view that writing instruction for engineers can or should be limited to one upper-division technical writing course.

847. TePaske, E. R. (1982). Writing in biology: One way to improve analytical thinking. *The American Biology Teacher, 44(2), 98–99.*
Shares exercises to improve student skill in biology and in writing.

848. Thall, E., & Bays, G. (1989). Utilizing ungraded writing in the chemistry classroom. *Journal of Chemical Education, 66, 662–663.*
The authors have students in an introductory chemistry class write for 10 to 15 minutes, once a week, in response to questions derived from demonstrations, labs, discussions, lectures, and readings.

849. Thompson, A. (1990). Letters to a math teacher. In N. Atwell (Ed.), *Coming to know: Writing to learn in the intermediate grades* (pp. 87–93).

Portsmouth, NH: Heinemann.
How elementary students learn more about math by writing letters about math to their teacher.

850. Thompson, P. (1970). Why lab reports? *Physics Teacher, 8,* **204.**
Stresses the importance of communication to the natural sciences, and sketches a method for assigning and evaluating high school lab reports.

851. Tobias, S. (1989). Writing to learn science and mathematics. In P. Connolly & T. Vilardi (Eds.), *Writing to learn mathematics and science* **(pp. 48–55). New York: Teachers College Press.**
Describes ways of using writing to reduce math anxiety and math avoidance. The techniques include journal writing; "divided-page" exercises, in which students do calcuations on one side of a page and express their feelings and thoughts about the process on the other; peer perspectives; and "minute papers about muddiest points," in which students communicate with their instructors by taking a minute at the end of a class period to record what confuses them in the day's lesson.

852. VanOrden, N. (1987). Critical-thinking writing assignments in general chemistry. *Journal of Chemical Education, 64,* **506–507.**
Shares three writing assignments designed to promote critical thinking and improve student writing in chemistry.

853. VanOrden, N. (1988). Write an autobiography of an element. *Journal of Chemical Education, 65,* **995.**
Describes a creative and "fun" assignment to give on the first day of a general chemistry class.

854. Venne, G. (1989). High-school students write about math. *English Journal, 78*(1), **64–66.**
An English teacher describes how he collaborated with a math teacher to integrate writing into an algebra class.

855. Vukovich, D. (1985). Ideas in practice: Integrating math and writing through the math journal. *Journal of Developmental Education, 9*(1), **19–20.**
Shows how journal writing helps basic math students at the post-secondary level. Students share their journals with their instructors and with each other to promote learning and encourage teacher-student understanding.

856. Wadlington, E., Bitner, J., Partridge, E., & Austin, S. (1992). Have a problem? Make the writing-mathematics connection! *Arithmetic Teacher, 40,* **207–209.**
Explains a three-step process for connecting writing and cooperative problem-solving to each other and to various mathematical skills and concepts.

857. Walpole, P. (1987). Yes, writing in math. In J. Self (Ed.), *Plain talk: About learning and writing across the curriculum* **(pp. 51–59). Commonwealth of Virginia: Virginia Department of Education.**
Shares six strategies for using writing as a tool for learning mathematics:

"rulesheets" (students use their own words to explain methods or solve problems); "card files" (in which students write down formulas and theorems in a cumulative personal index file); "flowcharts" (step-by-step directions showing how to perform certain computational skills); "homework questions"; "class logs" (a notebook in which a different student enters the notes from the class each day); and "exam review booklets" (each student writes a one-page summary of an assigned topic and they are published together as a collaborative review for a final exam).

858. Watson, M. (1980). Writing has a place in a mathematics class. *Mathematics Teacher, 73,* 518–519.
Suggests ways of using journals to encourage learning and exploration in math.

859. Watts, S. (1984). Science: Writing and understanding—writing and learning. In N. Martin (Ed.), *Writing across the curriculum pamphlets* **(pp. 114–119). Upper Montclair, NJ: Boynton/Cook.**
A science teacher calls for more talk and writing in science classes. Quotes samples of expressive writing by first-form students.

860. Weaver, L. H. (1985, March). *Writing for mathematics discovery-learning: A model for composition courses.* **Paper presented at the annual meeting of the Conference on College Composition and Communication, Minneapolis, MN. (ERIC Document Reproduction Service No. ED 266 449)**
Presents the techniques of mathematician Clark Kimberling as a model "for students to re-enact learning in all subject areas."

861. White, D. L., & Dunn, K. (1989). Writing and the teacher of mathematics. In P. Connolly & T. Vilardi (Eds.), *Writing to learn mathematics and science* **(pp. 95–109). New York: Teachers College Press.**
Describes a National Science Foundation project to use writing as a means of changing teachers' beliefs about mathematics instruction.

862. Whitney, H. (1989). Writing and reading for growth in mathematical reasoning. In P. Connolly & T. Vilardi (Eds.), *Writing to learn mathematics and science* **(pp. 266–275). New York: Teachers College Press.**
Argues for an approach to math instruction that encourages students to take risks and assume responsibility for their own learning. Whitney illustrates how students of all ages can use writing, collaboration, and creative thinking to solve problems—and have fun doing it.

863. Wilde, S. (1991). Learning to write about mathematics. *Arithmetic Teacher, 38*(6), 38–43.
Describes a variety of writing activities to promote learning in the elementary-level math class. Activities discussed include composing word and process problems, writing to "reframe knowledge," and writing in course journals.

864. Wilkinson, A. M. (1985). A freshman writing course in parallel with a science course. *College Composition and Communication, 36,* 160–165.
Reports on an experimental freshman writing course taught in collaboration

with a biology course, with students enrolled concurrently. Wilkinson concedes several disadvantages of the experiment; he also notes advantages, including giving students access to the rhetorical forms most likely to produce the precise writing demanded of scientists, and providing motivation to study both writing and biology.

865. Willson, K. J. (1991). Calculators and word problems in the primary grades. *Arithmetic Teacher, 38*(9), 12–14.
How a first-grade class created and worked through their own book of story problems, using calculators for problems involving large numbers.

866. Winsor, D. (1990). Engineering writing/writing engineering. *College Composition and Communication, 41,* 58–70.
Contends that writing is an indispensable means of creating and preserving knowledge and of helping an engineer to articulate ideas.

867. Wood, K. D. (1992). Fostering collaborative reading and writing experiences in mathematics. *Journal of Reading, 36,* 96–103.
Outlines several collaborative strategies that integrate reading and writing with mathematics instruction. Wood also provides sample lessons to show how the strategies can be applied "across grade levels and across topics in mathematics."

868. Worsley, D. (1989). The dignity quotient. In P. Connolly & T. Vilardi (Eds.), *Writing to learn mathematics and science* **(pp. 276–282). New York: Teachers College Press.**
Perceives a correlation between students' success at writing and their sense of dignity.

The Social and Behavioral Sciences

869. **Allen, H., & Fauth, L. (1987). Academic journals and the sociological imagination. In T. Fulwiler (Ed.), *The journal book* (pp. 367–374). Portsmouth, NH: Heinemann.**
The authors describe their use of journal-writing in undergraduate sociology classes. Journal entries range from reactive responses to texts and lectures to elementary sociological analyses, and thus initiate students to be "entry-level" members of the sociological discipline.

870. **Anderson, L., & Holt, M. (1990). Teaching writing in sociology: A social constructionist approach. *Teaching Sociology, 18,* 179–184.**
The authors, a sociologist and an English professor, outline a social constructionist approach to teaching writing and describe a course which they team-taught using the social constructionist paradigm. Anderson and Holt argue that sociological writing at the post-secondary level is best taught by sociologists who are familiar with composition pedagogy.

871. **Anderson, T. (1990). A psychodynamic approach to the teaching of writing: A hermeneutic dialogue. *Teaching of Psychology, 17,* 18–22.**
Proposes the "hermeneutic dialogue" as a method of teaching writing. Anderson sees the hermeneutic dialogue as superior to traditional cognitive and behavioral approaches to writing instruction because it is "dialogue centered" and because it rejects positivism in favor of a social constructionist view of knowledge. Includes two classroom examples of the hermeneutic dialogue.

872. **Anderson, W. P. (1982). The use of journals in a human sexuality course. *Teaching of Psychology, 9,* 105–107.**
Offers his guidelines for assigning journals in a graduate course on "Human Sexuality for Psychotherapists." Class reactions suggest that the journals improve students' understanding of sexuality issues and increase their comfort with addressing those issues.

873. **Beaman, B. (1985). Writing to learn social studies. In A. R. Gere (Ed.), *Roots in the sawdust: Writing to learn across the disciplines* (pp. 60–71). Urbana, IL: National Council of Teachers of English.**

Describes journal-writing exercises he uses in his psychology, sociology, and contemporary problems courses to help students develop self-esteem, broaden their concept of peer pressure, and gain insight into the complexities of world problems. These journal strategies involve peer dialogue, focused writing, unsent letters, and dramatic scenarios.

874. Becker, H. S. (1986). *Writing for social scientists: How to start and finish your thesis, book, or article.* Chicago: University of Chicago Press.

875. Beers, S. E. (1985). Use of a portfolio writing assignment in a course on developmental psychology. *Teaching of Psychology, 12,* 94–96.
Describes a portfolio assignment used in the author's course in life span developmental psychology. Portfolios included autobiographical essays, observations, exercises, interviews, and summaries of outside reading. Of the 26 students involved, 93% found the portfolio to be helpful.

876. Beers, S. E. (1986). Questioning and peer collaboration as techniques for thinking and writing about personality. *Teaching of Psychology, 13,* 75–77.
Describes the author's attempt to support the link between thinking and writing by making question-asking and peer collaboration in writing the central activities in her course in personality.

877. Bennett, S. M. (1985). Coordinated teaching of psychology and composition: A valuable strategy for students and instructors. *Teaching of Psychology, 12,* 26–27.
Report and performance evaluation of a coordinated experiment in which introductory composition and psychology classes were taught back-to-back in the same classrooms. Teachers coordinated readings and activities to complement the partner course.

878. Bennett, S. M., & Strauss-Noll, M. (1981). A rewarding approach: coordinated composition and psychology. *Peabody Journal of Education, 58,* 168–172.
Reports the outcomes of the authors' first coordinated courses in composition and psychology. [Also see Bennett (1985) this section]

879. Berg, E. Z. (1992). An introduction to sociology using short stories and films: Reshaping the cookie cutter and redecorating the cookie. *Teaching Sociology, 20,* 265–269.
Describes how she uses short stories and films as examples to help students analyze sociological processes and patterns. Students produce their analyses, which link sociology with "everyday life," in the form of "prep papers."

880. Blevin-Knabe, B. (1987). Writing to learn while learning to write. *Teaching of Psychology, 14,* 239–241.
Explains how she uses writing to improve learning in a developmental psychology course.

881. Boice, R. (1982). Teaching of writing in psychology: A review of sources. *Teaching of Psychology, 9,* 143–147.

Reviews recent literature in the field of writing theory and pedagogy, as well as that which has come from the field of psychology about writing and its processes. Boice concludes that there is much "information available about writing that lends itself nicely to teaching writing in psychology."

882. Boice, R. (1990). Faculty resistance to writing-intensive courses. *Teaching of Psychology, 17,* 13–17.
Examines the causes of faculty resistance to WAC and suggests a sequence of steps for overcoming it.

883. Brodsky, D., & Meagher, E. (1987). Journals and political science. In T. Fulwiler (Ed.), *The journal book* (pp. 375–386). Portsmouth, NH: Heinemann.
The authors describe their experience integrating journals into the political science class.

884. Cadwallader, M. L., & Scarboro, C. A. (1982). Teaching writing within a sociology course: A case study in writing across the curriculum. *Teaching Sociology, 9,* 359–382.
An exploration of the role that teachers of sociology and other social sciences can and should take in helping students to be better writers.

885. Calhoun, L. G., & Selby, J. W. (1979). Writing in psychology: A separate course? *Teaching of Psychology, 6,* 232.
Concerned that a blanket requirement for writing in all courses threatens academic freedom, Calhoun and Selby recommend that psychology departments offer "Writing in the Behavioral Sciences" as a distinct and separate course.

886. Camplese, D. A., & Mayo, J. A. (1982). How to improve the quality of student writing: The colleague swap. *Teaching Sociology, 9,* 122–123.
Shares a system in which students swap papers in draft form to proofread and critique each other's drafts before revising and turning them in. The authors provide a list of questions for students and an evaluation form to help them organize evaluative information.

887. Carlson, J. F. (1992). From metropolis to never-neverland: Analyzing fictional characters in a personality theory course. *Teaching of Psychology, 19,* 153–155.
Has students write analyses of characters from children's stories and comic strips using different theoretical orientations (e.g., psychoanalytic, phenomenological, behavioral).

888. Charbonneau, G. (1986). Writing in the social sciences: Fostering critical thinking and values formation through micro-themes. In K. O'Dowd & E. Nolan (Eds.), *Learning to write, writing to learn* (pp. 57–63). Livonia, MI: Madonna College Humanities Writing Program.
A social work professor assigns microthemes (very short essays) as a means of promoting students' cognitive growth. Charbonneau's assignments utilize principles of Rogerian rhetoric and measure success in terms of William Perry, Jr.'s model of cognitive development.

889. **Chrisler, J. C. (1990). Novels as case-study materials for psychology students.** *Teaching of Psychology, 17,* 55–57.
Has students use fictional or nonfictional characters from books (on mental illness) as case-studies for writing about psychology.

890. **Coker, F. H., & Scarboro, A. (1990). Writing to learn in upper-division sociology courses: Two case studies.** *Teaching Sociology, 18,* 218–222.
The authors describe two upper-division writing-intensive courses at Millsaps College in Jackson, Mississippi. The courses utilize freewriting, journals, collaboration, peer review, and other write-to-learn techniques.

891. **Crew, K. (1989, fall). Writing processes and the sociological imagination.** *Cross-over: A WAC Newsletter,* 3–6.

892. **Denscombe, M., & Robins, L. (1980). Self-assessment and essay writing.** *Teaching Sociology, 8,* 63–77.
Reports a study of the effects of self-assessment on essay-writing in sociology. Although no statistical data are reported, the authors saw "observable improvements" in the quality of essay work and some "moderate benefits" for communication between staff and students about their writing.

893. **Dynia, P. (1981, October).** *A case for course journals.* **Paper presented at the meeting of the Wisconsin Sociological Association, Beloit, WI.**
Discusses how journal-writing can help students become more actively engaged with the subject matter of sociology and other courses.

894. **Fauth, G., Gilstrap, R., & Isenberg, J. (1983). Teaching teachers to teach writing: A modeling approach.** In C. Thaiss (Ed.), *Writing to learn: Essays and reflections on writing across the curriculum* (pp. 72–89). Dubuque, IA: Kendall Hunt.
Discusses the use of writing in education classes.

895. **Freeman, D. E., & Freeman, Y. S. (1991). "Doing" social studies: Whole language lessons to promote social action.** *Social Education, 55,* 29–32, 66.
Outlines a program for involving students as critical readers and transformers of their communities. The program includes writing.

896. **Friedrich, J. (1990). Learning to view psychology as a science: Self-persuasion through writing.** *Teaching of Psychology, 17,* 23–27.
Reports an experiment which suggests that writing in the psychology class encourages students to view psychology as a science.

897. **Glaze, B. (1987). When writing to learn didn't work in social studies.** In J. Self (Ed.), *Plain talk: About learning and writing across the curriculum* (pp. 69–76). Commonwealth of Virginia: Virginia Department of Education.
Describes a third-grade social studies class that tested the author's beliefs in writing-to-learn and small group discussion.

898. **Green, C. S., III, & Klug, H. G. (1990). Teaching critical thinking and writing through debates: An experimental evaluation.** *Teaching Sociology, 18,*

462–471.
The authors tentatively argue "that the debate format in the context of large classes is an effective way to modify students' opinions on social issues and to teach critical thinking and writing skills."

899. Hegtvedt, K. A. (1991). Teaching sociology *of* literature *through* literature. *Teaching Sociology*, 19, 1–12.
Describes an advanced undergraduate sociology seminar that uses writing activities to help students explore relationships between literature and society.

900. Hettich, P. (1976). The journal: An autobiographical approach to learning. *Teaching of Psychology*, 3, 60–63.
Students in a psychology class keep autobiographical journals in which they relate course material to their thoughts and experiences. The journals stimulate student involvement with course content and help teachers understand the needs of each student.

901. Hettich, P. (1980). The journal revisited. *Teaching of Psychology*, 7, 105–106.
A brief follow-up to Hettich (1976). The author reports additional student data and teachers' experiences to support the use of journals as a teaching technique in various psychology courses. Teacher surveys showed that journals were most highly favored as a supplement to, rather than as a substitute for, exams and formal papers.

902. Hettich, P. (1988). Journal writing: An autobiographical approach to learning. *High School Psychology Teacher*, 19(3), 4, 6–7.

903. Hettich, P. (1990). Journal writing: Old fare or nouvelle cuisine? *Teaching of Psychology*, 17, 36–39.
Offers a rationale and guidelines for journal writing in psychology classes. Hettich also reviews the adaptability of journals to diverse classes and assesses the effectiveness of journals as a device for teaching and learning.

904. Hinkle, S., & Hinkle, A. (1990). An experimental comparison of the effects of focused freewriting and other study strategies on lecture comprehension. *Teaching of Psychology*, 17, 31–35.
The Hinkles' experiment suggests that, in some circumstances, focused freewriting can improve students' writing skills and comprehension of course content.

905. Hinrichs, D. W. (1990). Teaching communication skills in the context of introductory sociology. *Teaching Sociology*, 18, 32–38.
Describes an introductory sociology course that integrates writing, speaking, and listening with the learning of course content. Hinrichs also reports the results of a research experiment which shows that the course described improves students' communication skills more than do conventional courses.

906. Jensen, E. L. (1979). *Student journals in the social problems course: Applying sociological concepts.* Paper presented at the annual meeting of the

Pacific Sociological Association.
Describes the author's use of student journals in a social problems course. Students are required to select one social problem each term for extended analysis, including journal writing. Students are encouraged to apply concepts (e.g., from journal and magazine articles) to their own lives.

907. Jolley, J. M., & Mitchell, M. L. (1990). Two psychologists' experiences with journals. *Teaching of Psychology, 17,* 40–41.
Contending that journals should be used to explore "other people's ideas" rather than simply to reinforce students' "dogmatic beliefs," the authors propose two adaptations of journal writing that encourage dialectical reasoning and thereby promote critical reading and writing.

908. Junn, E. N. (1989). "Dear Mom and Dad": Using personal letters to enhance students' understanding of developmental issues. *Teaching of Psychology, 16,* 135–139.
To enhance learning, Junn has students in human development classes write semi-autobiographical letters a) to a future or actual child on the occasion of the child's 18th birthday; and b) to one or both of the student's parents.

909. Kalia, N. N. (1984). The sociological book review: A substitute for the standard term paper. *Teaching Sociology, 11,* 213–217.
Shows how to teach a sociological book review using literacy materials. The review teaches students "the art and craft of hypothesizing, testing, and explicating the sociologically significant in everyday situations, without time-consuming field work or statistical concatenation."

910. Karcher, B. C. (1988). Sociology and writing across the curriculum: An adaptation of the sociological journal. *Teaching Sociology, 16,* 168–172.
Advocates journal writing to enhance learning in sociology courses.

911. Keller, R. A. (1982). Teaching from the journals. *Teaching Sociology, 9,* 407–409.
Shows how to use professional journals in sociology as a way of helping students learn research skills. Students were asked to locate 6 readings from 12 journals in sociology, write critiques of these readings in the form of letters to their parents, and actually send these home. The exercise resulted in improved class discussions, better research skills among students, and gratitude and attention from parents.

912. Kiernan, H. (1992). Teaching civic identity and civic writing. *Social Education, 56,* 9–12.
Describes an interdisciplinary program, undertaken at the Southern Regional HIgh School District in Manahawkin, New Jersey, to involve students in innovative research and writing about their own communities.

913. King, K. M. (1987). Using retrospective autobiographies as a teaching tool. *Teaching Sociology, 15,* 410–413.
Discusses an exercise in which students imagine themselves to be 72 years old and write retrospective autobiographies. Such autobiographies can help

instructors learn about their students and also provide a basis for class lectures and discussions.

914. Klugh, H. E. (1983). Writing and speaking skills can be taught in psychology classes. *Teaching of Psychology, 10,* 170–171.
Describes how to integrate writing and speaking in an Industrial Psychology course. The course requires frequent abstracts of readings from journals, and the students must make oral presentations of their articles to a small group.

915. Lehmann, T. S. (1990). Academic research guides: Aids to the dissertation writer. *Teaching of Psychology, 17,* 59–61.
Reviews and evaluates a variety of academic research guides and how they can help the dissertation writer.

916. Levine, J. R. (1990). Using a peer tutor to improve writing in a psychology class: One instructor's experience. *Teaching of Psychology, 17,* 57–58.
Describes a pilot program, at SUNY College of Technology at Farmingdale, to enhance student writing through peer tutoring.

917. Madigan, R., & Brosamer, J. (1990). Improving the writing skills of students in introductory psychology. *Teaching of Psychology, 17,* 27–30.
Describes an experiment using writing assignments (i.e., weekly essay exams) in a first-year psychology class.

918. McGovern, T. V., & Hogshead, D. L. (1990). Learning about writing, thinking about teaching. *Teaching of Psychology, 17,* 5–10.
The authors discuss how learning about writing led them "to think more about our teaching and about how our students learn."

919. Miller, R., & Miller, R. S. (1976). The student's sociological diary. *Teaching Sociology, 4,* 67–82.
Describes a "diary technique" which required students to write several times a week about events in their everyday lives that were connected to course topics and concepts. The diaries provided interesting reading, led to new teaching material, provided personal contact, warned of students who were having difficulty, and demonstrated patterns of growth in writing.

920. Miller, S. U. (1979). Keeping a psychological journal. *Gifted Child Quarterly, 23,* 168–175.
Tells how to initiate and maintain a psychological journal, which is a resource for addressing the "internal themes" of one's life. Miller also suggests numerous themes and topics for such a journal, such as "peak experiences," "subpersonalities," dreams, meditations, "bright ideas," questions, "the inner dialogue," "dialogue with ideas," "dialogue with and about persons," etc. Finally, she notes various classroom applications of the journal.

921. Moynihan, M. M. (1989). Writing in sociology classes: Informal assignments. *Teaching Sociology, 17,* 346–350.
Describes three informal writing activities which stimulate learning without adding to the instructor's workload. The activities are: "Diary Entry of a 75-

Year-Old," in which students role-play the part of a 75-year-old diarist; "Marriage Contract," in which they play the part of a prospective bride or groom drafting a wedding contract; and "The Work-Alienation Letter," in which they describe their "worst work experience" in a letter to a friend.

922. Nadelman, L. (1990). Learning to think and write as an empirical psychologist: The laboratory course in developmental psychology. *Teaching of Psychology, 17,* 45–48.
Argues that students must write and converse within a discipline in order to understand it. By doing a variety of writing assignments and oral presentations, students in a laboratory course begin developing the writing skills and audience awareness of empirical psychologists.

923. O'Flaherty, K. M. (1992). Introducing students to the concept of the sociological imagination: A written assignment. *Teaching Sociology, 20,* 326–328.
Defines "the sociological imagination" as the "patterns of questioning and understanding" that are habitual to sociologists. O'Flaherty then describes a writing assignment that helps inculcate this habit of thinking in students, enabling them to appreciate "the intersection between personal biography and social history."

924. Pittendrigh, A. S., & Jobes, P. C. (1984). Teaching across the curriculum: Critical communication in the sociology classroom. *Teaching Sociology, 11,* 281–296.
Argues that through the process of planning, writing, and revising a paper, "students practice fundamental intellectual skills needed for professional life— the abilities to identify issues, ask meaningful questions, and evaluate and defend answers before a rational, critical audience." The authors describe a new sociology course that adapts instructional techniques used in composition courses to help students through the thinking and writing process.

925. Poe, R. E. (1990). A strategy for improving literature reviews in psychology courses. *Teaching of Psychology, 17,* 54–55.
Outlines a sequence of writing exercises designed to help students prepare literature reviews.

926. Polyson, J. (1985). Students' peak experiences: A written exercise. *Teaching of Psychology, 12,* 211–212.
Undergraduates in three of the author's introductory psychology classes were asked to write a two-page descriptive essay on a "peak experience," as described in the work of Abraham Maslow. These essays then served as a way for the students to interpret the theoretical construct by relating it to events in their own lives.

927. Price, D. W. W. (1990). A model for reading and writing about primary sources: The case of introductory psychology. *Teaching of Psychology, 17,* 48–53.
Explains how he integrates writing and reading from primary sources into an introductory psychology course.

928. Riedmann, A. (1991). We wrote our own book: Teaching introductory sociology by helping students to tell their own stories with sociological insight. *Teaching Sociology, 19,* 477–482.
Describes a classroom strategy in which students learn sociology by writing sociologically about themselves. Students write their individual stories and collect them, as a class, in a self-published book.

929. Roth, R. L. (1985). Learning about gender through writing: Student journals in the undergraduate classroom. *Teaching Sociology, 12,* 325–338.
Shares experiences using journals to enhance learning in sex/gender courses. Roth explains her methods, shares excerpts from students' journals, and discusses the advantages and disadvantages of journals.

930. Sanford, J. F. (1983). Multiple drafts of experimental laboratory reports. In C. Thaiss (Ed.), *Writing to learn: Essays and reflections on writing across the curriculum* (pp. 119–126). Dubuque, IA: Kendall Hunt.
A psychology professor requires multiple drafts of lab reports so that students become familiar with writing as a process. The processes of redrafting and receiving feedback improve the quality of reports and make students more conscious of how they write.

931. Selcher, W. A., & McClellan, E. F. (1990). Sequential writing assignments in international relations and American government survey courses. *Political Science Teacher, 3*(3), 14–16.

932. Seligman, L. (1983). Writing in counseling and clinical psychology. In C. Thaiss (Ed.), *Writing to learn: Essays and reflections on writing across the curriculum* (pp. 90–97). Dubuque, IA: Kendall Hunt.
Defines four broad categories of writing in psychology: research papers and articles; case studies, intake reports, and progress reports; test and referral reports; and proposals. Seligman then describes several techniques to help students with writing and learning. These include the use of models, freewriting, simulated counseling sessions, revision groups, and creative organization and mapping.

933. Sills, C. K. (1991). Paired composition courses: "Everything relates." *College Teaching, 39,* 61–64.
Argues in favor of "paired" courses (i.e., courses taught by two-person teams which involve pairing composition courses with courses in other disciplines, such as sociology). Sills contends that such pairings provide a sense of interdisciplinarity and also bolster writing across the curriculum.

934. Simon, B. L., & Soven, M. (1989). The teaching of writing in social work education: A pressing priority for the 1990s. *Journal of Teaching in Social Work, 3*(2), 47–63.
Argues that "students can and should begin receiving preparation to write professionally from the time that they are introduced to the social work curriculum, and this initiation should be followed by continuous integration of specially designed writing assignments in intermediate and advanced courses." The authors show how they have integrated such writing

assignments as personal and double-entry journals, annotated bibliographies, and analyses of historical sources into social work programs at both the graduate and undergraduate levels.

935. Singh, R. N., & Unnithan, N. P. (1989). Free to write: On the use of speculative writing in sociology courses. *Teaching Sociology, 17,* 465–470.
Compares speculative writing (or freewriting) in a sociology class with traditional writing assignments. The authors conclude that speculative writing has a unique value in sociology instruction and suggest guidelines for incorporating it into lecture-discussion classes.

936. Snodgrass, S. E. (1985). Writing as a tool for teaching social psychology. *Teaching of Psychology, 12,* 91–94.
Shows how writing can be a teaching tool (rather than an evaluative tool) in a social psychology class. Exercises include a course log to stimulate thinking and discussion; analyses and syntheses of journal articles; and a course project in which students design an unobtrusive observational study to examine a social psychological phenomenon.

937. Spiegel, T. A., Cameron, S. M., Evans, R., & Nodine, B. F. (1980). Integrating writing into the teaching of psychology: An alternative to Calhoun and Selby. *Teaching of Psychology, 7,* 242–243.
Disagrees with Calhoun and Selby's (1979) solution to the problem of students' deficient writing abilities, in which they advocate instituting a separate course on writing within the department of psychology.

938. Stoddart, K. (1991). Writing sociologically: A note on teaching the construction of a qualitative report. *Teaching Sociology, 19,* 243–248.
Contending that "sociology is as much a representational style as it is anything else," Stoddart describes a class handout that helps students learn the formal conventions involved in writing an ethnographic essay.

939. Stoddart, R. M., & Loux, A. K. (1992). And, not but: Moving from monologue to dialogue in introductory psychology/English writing courses. *Teaching of Psychology, 19,* 145–149.
The authors, a psychology and English professor, respectively, describe their linked psychology and English courses. Students read classic psychology texts alongside literary works and write papers on topics that reflect increasingly complex intellectual tasks.

940. Tamura, E. H., & Harstad, J. R. (1987). Freewriting in the social studies classroom. *Social Education, 51,* 256–259.
Advises teachers of social studies to assign freewriting journals. The authors illustrate brief and practical steps for two kinds of freewriting, "unedited" and "edited."

941. Ventis, D. G. (1990). Writing to discuss: Use of a clustering technique. *Teaching of Psychology, 17,* 42–44.
Has students in an introductory psychology course "cluster" to promote class discussion. Students write down and free associate from a key word, share, and

do follow-up writing at the end of discussion to summarize points and issues raised.

942. Wagenaar, T. C. (1984). Using student journals in sociology courses. *Teaching Sociology, 11,* **419–437.**
Provides a pedagogical and sociological rationale for integrating journal writing into sociology courses. Wagenaar offers practical advice for using and evaluating journals and shares journal excerpts from an introductory sociology course and a course in human sexuality.

943. Weintraub, S., & Stark, M. (1982). "I wish the punk had written back." In M. Barr, P. D'Arcy, & M. K. Healy (Eds.), *What's going on? Language/learning episodes in British and American classrooms, grades 4–13* **(pp. 175–195). Upper Montclair, NJ: Boynton/Cook.**
The authors, teachers at culturally dissimilar high schools (one inner-city and the other suburban) had students in their American government classes exchange letters as a means of clarifying "their own values and opinions about various social, political, and economic problems by explaining them in letters to someone else in a very different area." Students sustained the correspondence throughout the school term. Writing and sharing enabled students to recognize and address prejudice and other issues on a personal level, while also "incorporating the class curriculum into their letters."

944. Weitz, R. (1991). Teaching writing for publication. *Teaching Sociology, 19,* **414–417.**
Describes a graduate-level course on writing for scholarly publication.

945. Willingham, D. B. (1990). Effective feedback on written assignments. *Teaching of Psychology, 17,* **10–13.**
Offers advice for responding effectively to student writing. Willingham suggests that comments be specific without being simply prescriptive, that minimal attention be paid to mechanical errors, and that comments "form a hierarchy of importance that students can easily discern."

Business, Law, Finance, and Economics

946. **Addams, H. L. (1981). Should the big 8 teach communication skills?** *Management Accounting, 62*(11), 37–40.
Results of a survey suggest that the big 8 CPA firms should provide junior members with more training in writing and other communication skills. Addams briefly suggests implications for communication and accounting instructors at the post-secondary level.

947. **Andrews, J. D., & Pytlik, B. P. (1983). Revision techniques for accountants: Means for more efficient written communication.** *Issues in Accounting Education 1983,* 152–163.

948. **Atkinson, T. (1982). Politics and the business writing student: An approach to finding real writing projects.** *ABCA Bulletin, 45*(4), 11–12.
Describes a collaboration between business writing students and a local state senator's office. Students performed nonpartisan writing tasks for the senator as a means of gaining "real" world experience with writing.

949. **Baltensperger, B. H. (1987). Journals in economic geography. In T. Fulwiler (Ed.),** *The journal book* **(pp. 387–390). Portsmouth, NH: Heinemann.**
Explains how he uses journals in a sophomore-level economic geography course to promote active learning as opposed to passive memorization of facts and information. Baltensperger describes several kinds of journal assignments and assesses their effects on students.

950. **Coffinberger, R. L. (1983). Evaluating the classroom journal as a supplemental teaching strategy in business law. In C. Thaiss (Ed.),** *Writing to learn: Essays and reflections on writing across the curriculum* **(pp. 101–106). Dubuque, IA: Kendall Hunt.**
Describes how he has used journals in a business law course for undergraduates. In their journals students prepare narrative versions of class lectures and "identify and analyze the reasons for and alternatives to the rules of law presented in those lectures."

951. **Coleman, E. B. (1992). Writing to learn, writing to think in a computer course for preservice teachers.** *Journal of Computing in Teacher Education, 8*(3), 4–9.

952. Collins, T. (1981). What's new in freshman comp? Some gleanings for the business writing teacher. *ABCA Bulletin,* **44(1), 10–12.**
Observes that much of the literature in composition studies is relevant to teachers of business writing. Collins then reviews recent work, by composition theorists, in three areas: the composing process, rhetorical modes, and classroom peer groups.

953. Coppage, R. E. (1991). Student motivation from beyond the classroom. *Management Accounting,* **72(11), 65.**
Explains how he motivates accounting students to write by requiring them to compose either for publication or for entry in a contest.

954. Corman, E. J. (1986). A writing program for accounting courses. *Journal of Accounting Education,* **4(2), 85–95.**
Outlines a program of writing to help students learn course content while also improving as writers.   Corman advises instructors to balance short writing assignments with long, to encourage projects involving research, and to exploit such modern technologies as computer aided instruction.

955. Crosser, R., & Laufer, D. (1990, November). An empirical analysis of student attitudes towards the value of written communication skills. *DSI (Decision Science Institute) National Conference Proceedings.*
Reports a study evaluating the effects of a writing-intensive accounting course on students' motivation and attitudes towards writing.

956. Crosser, R., & Laufer, D. (1991, March). Journal writing in tax courses: A preliminary evaluation of a writing-to-learn endeavor. *DSI (Decision Science Institute) Western Regional Conference Proceedings.*
Presents a preliminary empirical assessment of the effects of informal writing assignments (i.e., journals) on student learning in an undergraduate tax course.

957. Crosser, R., & Laufer, D. (1992, March). A survey of faculty attitudes about writing-across-the-curriculum workshops. *DSI (Decision Science Institute) Western Regional Conference Proceedings.*
In two separate surveys at Weber State University in Ogden, Utah, the authors measured the effects of WAC workshops on WAC faculty and the use of writing in business courses.

958. Crowe, D., & Youga, J. (1986).   Using writing as a tool for learning economics. *Journal of Economic Education,* **17, 218–222.**
Crowe and Youga begin by describing writing, generally, as a mode of learning, as "a record of thought," and as a means of monitoring "students' progress toward understanding." They then list eight kinds of writing activities for the economics class along with suggested techniques for responding to writing.

959. David, C. (1980). Explaining business communication to English departments. *ABCA Bulletin,* **43(3), 16–18.**
Suggests ways of fostering better "PR" between teachers of business communication and English departments.

960. Deitrick, J. W., & Tabor, R. (1987). Improving the writing skills of accounting majors: One school's approach. *Advances in Accounting, 4,* 97–110.

961. DeLespinasse, D. (1985). Writing letters to clients: Connecting textbook problems and the real world. *Journal of Accounting Education, 3*(1), 197–200.
To simulate the difficulty of "real world" writing tasks, students in accounting classes at Adrian College (MI) write letters to explain complex accounting problems to imaginary clients. The problems are drawn from textbook readings.

962. Dickerson, R. (1978). Legal drafting: Writing as thinking, or talk-back from your draft and how to exploit it. *Journal of Legal Education, 29,* 373–379.
Viewing drafting as an ongoing "conversation" between the writer and her material, Dickerson discusses ways of balancing the demands of drafting with those of research. Rather than postponing writing till after the research is done, he advocates writing early in the research process to test out ideas, organize thoughts, and recognize gaps in information. The resultant "talk-back" from drafts can help the writer to organize and complete her research efficiently.

963. Drenk, D. (1982). Teaching finance through writing. In C. W. Griffin (Ed.), *Teaching writing in all disciplines* (pp. 53–58). San Francisco: Jossey-Bass.
Shares his rationale and objectives for incorporating writing into finance classes and discusses the hardships and rewards that have resulted.

964. Evans, O. H. (1981). Using transmittal correspondence as a teaching tool. *ABCA Bulletin, 44*(3), 18–19.
A writer uses a transmittal memo to clarify the rhetorical context (audience, purpose, etc.) of the particular report or document she is submitting. Evans has students attach such a memo to each written class assignment in order to strengthen their sensitivity to the contextual issues involved in every piece of writing.

965. Farkas, D. K. (1981). An invention heuristic for business and technical communication. *ABCA Bulletin, 44*(4), 16–19.
Analyzes how his "Heuristic of Professional Communication Goals" enables a communicator to identify all the pertinent goals of a particular communicative situation and to generate subject matter that will achieve those goals.

966. Field, W. J., Wachter, D. R., & Catanese, A. V. (1985). Alternative ways to teach and learn economics: Writing, quantitative reasoning, and oral communication. *Journal of Economic Education, 16,* 213–217.
Three members of the economics department at DePauw University describe how writing and other communication/critical thinking skills are integrated into their economics curriculum.

967. Flatley, M. (1984). Improving business writing skills with reactive writing. *ABCA Bulletin, 47*(1), 25–26.
Has students in her business classes keep a journal in which they write one

paragraph reactions to articles they read. Such "reactive" composing helps students to write better and can be adapted to provide practice in documentation and organization as well.

968. France, A. W. (1990). Teaching the dialectics of "objective" discourse: A progressive approach to business and professional writing. *Writing Instructor,* **9(3–4), 79–86.**

969. Gabriel, S. L., & Hirsch, M. L., Jr. (1992). Critical thinking and communication skills: Integration and implementation issues. *Journal of Accounting Education, 10,* **243–270.**
Discusses assignment design, response, revision, and other issues confronting accounting faculty interested in establishing "an integrated approach to critical thinking and communication skills."

970. Gingras, R. T. (1987). Writing and the certified public accountant. *Journal of Accounting Education, 5,* **127–137.**
Surveyed over 650 practicing accountants about the role of writing in their professional lives. Results showed that the CPAs do a significant amount of technical and non-technical writing. Gingras urges a stronger integration of writing into classroom accounting curricula.

971. Gollen, S. (1981). Communications: Its role in accounting education. *ABCA Bulletin, 44(4),* **37–40.**
Studies the importance of communication in accounting education, noting universal requirements for comprehensible writing in any type of accounting communication and the need to develop strong interpersonal communication skills.

972. Hagge, J. (1989). Ties that bind: Ancient epistolography and modern business communication. *Journal of Advanced Composition, 9,* **26–44.**
Finds parallels between the structure and principles of contemporary business writing textbooks and those of the ancient Greek and Roman letter-writing tradition.

973. Halpern, J. W. (1981a). How to start a business lab. *ABCA Bulletin, 44(4),* **9–14.**
Explains how to create a business writing laboratory. Halpern discusses how to select and train good tutors, which types of materials and services to offer in order to meet student need, and how to develop public relations to "sell" the benefits of the lab.

974. Halpern, J. W. (1981b). What should we be teaching students in business writing? *The Journal of Business Communication, 18(3),*   **39–53.**
Based on an informal survey of 125 writers in business, government, and industry, the author identifies six composing processes as crucial preparation for on-the-job writing: invention, adaptation for audience, clarification of purpose, organization, control of voice or persona, and polishing. Halpern illustrates the process with respect to one assignment (a memo) while stressing its adaptability to all other business writing tasks.

975. Hemmeter, T., & Conners, D. (1987). Research papers in economics: A collaborative approach. *Journal of Advanced Composition, 7*, 81–91.
Describes a model for teaching the process of research in a writing course taught parallel to a college economics course. The parallel course uses all the phases of the economics research project to guide its writing assignments.

976. Henry, L. H. (1986). Clustering: Writing (and learning) about economics. *College Teaching, 34*, 89–93.
Argues that techniques of expressive writing (e.g., clustering) can be used to enhance learning in a basic economics course. Includes two sample clusters.

977. Hilton, C. B. (1989). Reading journals in the business communication classroom. *Journal of Education for Business, 65*, 34–36.
Contending that a curriculum for critical thinking in business should balance attention to writing with attention to reading, Hilton has students keep a reading journal in which they summarize and respond to articles in two kinds of journals—general and field-specific. Students write in the reading journal throughout the semester.

978. Hirsch, M. L., Jr., & Collins, J. D. (1988). An integrated approach to communication skills in an accounting curriculum. *Journal of Accounting Education, 6*, 15–31.
Describes a program for integrating writing and other communication skills into the accounting curriculum. Hirsch and Collins argue that such skills are best taught in core courses within professional accounting programs rather than as part of general education or in a special business communication class.

979. Hirsh, K. F. (1980). Writing about the law: A composition course for pre-law students. *Journal of Basic Writing, 2*(4), 82–94.
Describes an undergraduate English course in Writing About the Law.

980. Hoff, K. T., & Stout, D. E. (1990). Practical accounting/English collaboration to improve student writing skills: The use of informal journals and the diagnostic reading technique. *The Accounting Educators' Journal, 2*(2), 83–96.
Describes a collaboration in which an English instructor used diagnostic readings of student texts and other techniques to acquaint an accounting instructor with English composition skills and methods of response. The aim was to develop "an autonomous accounting-writing instructor" and thus undercut the assumption that accounting and communication are two separate disciplines.

981. Horning, A. S. (1980). The business of business is English! *English Quarterly, 13*(2), 23–28.
Argues that English departments and colleges of business administration should offer a double major in business and English. Provides a detailed outline of a curriculum for such a double major.

982. Jacobi, M. J. (1987). Using the enthymeme as a heuristic in professional writing courses. *Journal of Advanced Composition, 7*, 41–51.

Describes ways in which the Aristotelian "enthymeme" can be used to enhance the writing processes of students in professional writing courses. Offers a sample assignment—a cover letter to accompany a questionnaire—as a model of how the enthymeme can be used.

983. Kelly, K. (1985). Professional writing in the humanities course. *College Composition and Communication, 36,* 234–237.
Asks if business and technical writing courses should be offered by English or professional departments. Argues that advanced expository writing courses may blend humanities subjects with professional forms through assignments for informing and recommending.

984. Kettering, R. C. (1989). Meeting the needs of the accounting profession: Requiring more student writing. *Journal of Education for Business, 65,* 64–66.
Describes a program to promote writing in business courses.

985. Kogen, M. (1983). The role of audience in business and technical writing. *ABCA Bulletin, 46*(4), 2–4.
Reviews recent literature on audience and writing and discusses its relevance to teachers of business and technical communication. Also suggests classroom exercises for stimulating audience awareness.

986. Kogen, M., Book, V. A., Cunningham, D. H., Gieselman, R. D., & Pickett, N. A. (Eds.). (1989). *Writing in the business professions.* Urbana: National Council of Teachers of English and the Association for Business Communication.

987. Laufer, D., & Crosser, R. (1989, March). Integration of the "writing-across-the-curriculum" concept into upper division accounting and tax courses. *Southwest AAA Conference Proceedings.*
See Laufer & Crosser (1990).

988. Laufer, D., & Crosser, R. (1990). The "writing-across-the-curriculum" concept in accounting and tax courses. *Journal of Education for Business, 66,* 83–87.
Citing "an educational gap" between writing in the workplace and the amount of writing generally done in school, the authors describe their program to integrate writing into accounting and tax courses. The courses utilize a variety of WAC strategies, including: treatment of writing as a multi-step process; creation of authentic contexts for writing, in which students compose for diverse audiences besides the instructor; and peer review.

989. Lynch, D. H. (1985). For teachers of business communication: A review of research on peer evaluation of writing. *NABTE Review, 12,* 42–46.
Reviews a variety of studies which compare the effects of instructor- and student-evaluated assessment of students' writing skills. The studies reviewed suggest that the two approaches are generally comparable in effectiveness.

990. Lynch, D. H., & Golen, S. (1992). Peer evaluation of writing in business communication classes. *Journal of Education for Business, 68,* 44–48.

Results of a questionnaire show how selected members of the Association for Business Communication employ peer evaluation of writing in their business communication classes.

991. Marcoulides, G. A., & Simkin, M. G. (1991). Evaluating student papers: The case for peer review. *Journal of Education for Business, 67,* 80–83.
Based on an experiment to test the reliability of peer review, the authors conclude that "students can be both consistent and fair in their assessments" of each other's writing.

992. May, G. S., & Arevalo, C. (1983). Integrating effective writing skills in the accounting curriculum. *Journal of Accounting Education, 1*(1), 119–126.
The authors describe their school's program to integrate writing into the accounting curriculum. Students take a three quarter sequence of writing-intensive accounting courses. Instruction is supported by an outside consultant who has graduate training in English.

993. May, G. S., & May, C. B. (1989). Communication instruction: What is being done to develop the communication skills of accounting students? *Journal of Accounting Education, 7,* 233–244.
Reports the results of a survey "to determine what colleges and universities are doing to improve accounting students' communication skills and how they are doing it."

994. Mohrweis, L. C. (1991). The impact of writing assignments on accounting students' writing skills. *Journal of Accounting Education, 9,* 309–325.
Describes a year-long study to determine the impact of writing assignments on the composing skills of undergraduate accounting students. The results provide empirical evidence that writing assignments enhanced the students' writing skills.

995. Orem, E. E., & Burns, J. O. (1988, spring). The problems and challenges of teaching accounting students to communicate. *Georgia Journal of Accounting,* 9–24.
Provides an overview of the roles of writing and other communication skills in accounting education and suggests more effective methods for incorporating writing into accounting classes.

996. Phillips, M. J., & Davis, C. H. (1991). Writing requirements in financial accounting courses. *Journal of Education for Business, 66,* 144–146.
Summarizes the results of a nationwide questionnaire devised to obtain descriptive information on the writing requirements of undergraduate financial accounting programs. Despite hopeful signs of a growing attention to writing, "the results suggest that educators are just beginning to respond to the AICPA's [American Institute of Certified Public Accountants'] call to improve the written communication skills of accounting graduates."

997. Phillips, M. J., & Jackson, F. R. (1989). Mapping: An aid to studying and teaching accounting. *Journal of Education for Business, 64,* 210–214.
Explains how to incorporate mapping, a well-known invention technique, into

a lower division accounting class. Mapping can help students understand accounting concepts and methods while also providing instructors with an instrument for assessing student learning. Includes four sample maps.

998. Pierce, E. M. (1983). Reinforced learning through written case studies. In C. Thaiss (Ed.), *Writing to learn: Essays and reflections on writing across the curriculum* **(pp. 64–71). Dubuque, IA: Kendall Hunt.**
Argues that written case studies provide "a unique and powerful" vehicle for learning. Pierce first describes how he has assigned and used case studies in his finance course for MBA students. He then relates the process of writing case studies in finance to the theoretical literature on writing-to-learn.

999. Polanski, V. G. (1987). Integrating the real world into the writing class. *Journal of Education for Business, 62,* **327–329.**
Discusses ways of enlisting the collaboration of business professionals to promote learning in the business class.

1000. Pomerenke, P. J. (1984). Rewriting and peer evaluation: A positive approach for business writing classes. *ABCA Bulletin, 47*(3), 33–36.
Emphasizes a need to make revision a more integral part of writing in business classes. Pomerenke also contends that peer review can make the revision process more "positive" by providing students with early feedback and by creating an authentic context and audience for writing.

1001. Redish, J. C. (1981). The document design course. In A. Humes (Ed.), *Moving between theory and practice: Proceedings of the NIE-FIPSE grantee workshop* **(pp. 153–158). Los Alamitos: SWRL Educational Research and Development.**

1002. Roundy, N. (1982). A process approach to teaching the abstract. *ABCA Bulletin, 45*(3), 34–38.
To help business students through one of their most difficult writing tasks, Roundy breaks the process of composing an abstract into multiple steps.

1003. Roundy, N. (1983). A program for revision in business and technical writing. *The Journal of Business Communication, 20*(1), 55–66.
Suggests a program of revision based on five criteria: amount/kind of detail, appropriate emphasis of content, logical progression, stylistic appropriateness, and mechanical accuracy.

1004. Shibli, A. (1992). Increasing learning with writing in quantitative and computer courses. *College Teaching, 40,* **123–127.**
A business professor, Shibli suggests writing assignments to use in statistics and computer classes and discusses "hurdles" he has faced in incorporating writing into courses on quantitative subjects.

1005. Sides, C. H. (Ed.). (1989). *Technical and business communication: Bibliographic essays for teachers and corporate trainers.* **Urbana and Washington, D. C.: National Council of Teachers of English and the Society for Technical Communications.**

A collection of 17 essays on diverse aspects of business and technical communications, ranging from ethics and reading theory to graphics, software documentation, and advertising and sales literature. The first part of the book, "Issues and Abilities in Technical Communication," contains pieces on a range of technical documents; the second part, "Genres in Technical Communication," includes essays on diverse business and technical forms, such as proposals, annual reports, instructions, software documentation, newsletters, and press releases.

1006. Smeltzer, L. (1981). An integrated approach for a graduate course in business communication. *ABCA Bulletin*, 44(3), 27–29.
Describes a graduate seminar designed to (1) integrate written, oral, and organizational communication into one course; (2) meet the needs of both masters and doctoral students; and (3) integrate the disciplines of management and communication.

1007. Stine, D., & Skarzenski, D. (1979). Priorities for the business communication classroom: A survey of business and academe. *The Journal of Business Communication*, 16(3), 15–30.
A survey of 120 businesses and 70 people in academe suggests priorities for writing instruction in the business communication classroom.

1008. Stine, L. (1990). Computing across the curriculum: New friends for WAC. *Writing Notebook: Creative Word Processing in the Classroom*, 7(4), 37–38.

1009. Stocks, K. D., Stoddard, T. D., & Waters, M. L. (1992). Writing in the accounting curriculum: Guidelines for professors. *Issues in Accounting Education*, 7, 193–204.
Addresses specific problems (e.g., assignment design, distinguishing learning-to-write from writing-to-learn, evaluation) faced by accounting faculty desiring to integrate writing into their classes.

1010. Summers, M. K. (1990). Writing across the curriculum techniques in computer information systems. *The Journal of Computer Information Systems*, 30(4), 43–46.
Outlines several writing assignments that can be incorporated into Computer Information Systems courses, including journals, short communications, reviews, documentation, and formal research papers. Summers also offers advice on time management, responding to student writing, and using writing centers and other support services.

1011. Swindle, R. E. (1982). Making certain that graduates can write. *ABCA Bulletin*, 45(1), 7–10.
Addressing complaints about the poor writing of college graduates entering business, Swindle sketches his own strategy for improving writing abilities among students in business classes.

1012. Tebeaux, E. (1985). Redesigning professional writing courses to meet the communication needs of writers in business and industry. *College*

Composition and Communication, 36, 419–428.
Surveys traditional methods and textbooks in the teaching of writing to students in business, science, and engineering courses. Tebeaux recommends several changes in the writing curriculum for business and science students: (1) heterogeneous grouping of students in basic writing courses; (2) emphasis on common rhetorical principles that underlie design and development of all writing; (3) emphasis on adapting communication to varying audiences; and (4) emphasis on an integrated model of communication including writing, oral presentation, group conferences, and word processing.

1013. Tobey, D. M. (1979). Writing instruction in economics courses: Experimentation across disciplines. *Journal of the Northeastern Agricultural Economics Council, 8*(2), 159–164.
Argues that writing, as a process of critical thinking, has close affinities to the analytical emphases of economics.

1014. Varner, I. I. (1988). Writing in groups. *Journal of Education for Business, 64,* 274–276.
Offers guidelines for assigning group writing tasks in business courses.

1015. West, L. J. (1992). How to write a research report for journal publication. *Journal of Education for Business, 67,* 132–136.
Discusses differences between writing for an academic degree and writing for publication, and suggests strategies for getting successfully published.

1016. White, J. B. (1983). The invisible discourse of law: Reflections on legal literacy and general education. In P. L. Stock (Ed.), *Fforum: Essays on theory and practice in the teaching of writing* (pp. 46–59). **Upper Montclair, NJ: Boynton/Cook.**
Begins by exploring the "invisible discourse of law"; that is, "the unstated conventions by which the [legal] language operates." White then suggests ways of teaching this discourse in advanced high school or college writing courses as a means of reducing "the gap between the specialized language of the law and the ordinarily literate person." In particular, he proposes exercises in "law-like writing," in which students write, in their own language, about analogues to the law in their own lives.

1017. Wintz, K. A. (1981, October). *The use of the WATC [writing across the curriculum] model in teaching law to undergraduates.* **Paper presented at the meeting of the Wisconsin Sociological Association, Beloit, WI.**
An adaptation of WAC to courses in law, the program described involves students in a variety of writing activities, including freewriting, journaling, peer-conference groups, and revision sessions.

1018. Woolever, K. R. (1986). Untangling the law: Verbal design in legal argument. *Journal of Advanced Composition, 6,* 151–165.
The "seamless web" of the law, Woolever argues, often ensnares law students in tangles of discourse from which they can't seem to escape to clarity of expression. Woolever offers strategies for teaching five of the most common problems with students' legal writing: addiction to the passive voice, overuse

of the verb "to be," nominalization, overly embedded sentences, and repetitive sentence structure.

1019. Wygal, D. E., & Stout, D. E. (1989). Incorporating writing techniques in the accounting classroom: Experience in financial, managerial, and cost courses. *Journal of Accounting Education, 7,* **245–252.**
Describes ways of using various informal writing techniques (i.e., freewriting, course logs, letters, and peer review) to foster learning in financial, managerial, and cost accounting courses.

Textbooks

1020. Barnet, S. (1992). *A short guide to writing about literature* **(6th ed.). New York: HarperCollins.**
Part One provides overviews on the reading and writing processes and on writing about literature. Part Two includes chapters on writing about essays, fiction, drama, poetry, and film. Part Three addresses issues of style, format, the research process, and essay examinations.

1021. Barnet, S. (1993). *A short guide to writing about art* **(4th ed.). New York: HarperCollins.**
A text for teachers who "lack the time—and perhaps the skill—to teach writing in addition to...art." Barnet illustrates various principles of writing about art with model compositions by students, professors, and scholars. Chapters include: (1) "Writing about Art"; (2) "Analysis" (heuristics for discovering and developing ideas for writing); (3) "Writing a Comparison"; (4) "In Brief: How to Write an Effective Essay"; (5) "Style in Writing"; (6) "Manuscript Form" (issues of manuscript preparation and documentation, conventions of usage); (7) "The Research Paper" (defining a topic, finding and using outside sources, writing the paper); and (8) "Essay Examinations."

1022. Bazerman, C. (1985). *The informed writer: Using sources in the disciplines* **(2nd ed.). Boston: Houghton Mifflin.**
Introduces students to the forms and procedures of writing in the disciplines while encouraging originality and creativity in writing. The text consists of four parts, each of which contains between two and seven chapters. They are: "Writing About Reading," "Writing Using Reading," "Writing in Disciplines," and "The Craft of Writing." Each chapter includes writing assignments.

1023. Behrens, L., and Rosen, L. J. (1991). *Writing and reading across the curriculum* **(4th ed.). New York: HarperCollins.**
A text-reader aimed at helping freshmen develop college-level thinking and writing skills. Part One introduces the skills of summary, synthesis, and critique. Each chapter in Part Two consists of related readings on a particular topic. Readings for each topic represent a variety of perspectives drawn from the different disciplines.

1024. Biddle, A. W., & Bean, D. J. (with T. Fulwiler). (1987). *Writer's guide: Life sciences.* **Lexington, MA: D. C. Heath.**
Based on the premise that "the best way to learn biology is by writing about it," this text offers a process-based writing guide to biology students at all levels and is "adaptable to virtually any course." Topics and writing assignments are sequenced from the less to the more sophisticated, with chapters on "Writing in the Life Sciences," "Keeping a Journal," "Learning Biology through Writing," research methods and "Basic Bibliography," "Documentation of Sources," and other subjects. Includes sample student writings for a variety of assignments and from all stages of the writing process.

1025. Biddle, A. W., & Holland, K. M. (with T. Fulwiler). (1987). *Writer's guide: Political science.* **Lexington, MA: D. C. Heath.**
A process-centered writing guide for majors and non-majors in political science. Includes chapters on "Writing in Political Science," "Keeping a Journal," "Learning Political Science Through Writing," "Issues and Arguments," and "Principles of Research and Basic Bibliographies."

1026. Bond, L. A., & Magistrale, A. S. (with T. Fulwiler) (1987). *Writer's guide: Psychology.* **Lexington, MA: D. C. Heath.**
A process-centered writing guide for majors and non-majors in psychology. Includes chapters on "Writing in Psychology," "Using a Journal," "Writing Exams and Short Essay Assignments," "Writing to Summarize," and "Principles of Library Research and Basic Bibliographies."

1027. Bowen, M. E., & Mazzeo, J. A. (Eds.). (1979). *Writing about science.* **New York: Oxford University Press.**
An anthology intended to show that scientific writing "can be as rewarding to the reader, and as demanding of the writer, as the greatest belles lettres, essay, or story." Contains "models of good scientific writing," popular and professional, by physical and biological scientists of the past and present. Readings are categorized by rhetorical mode and by source and method of exposition. Questions for discussion and writing follow each essay.

1028. Brundage, A. (1989). *Going to the sources: A guide to historical research and writing.* **Arlington Heights, IL: Harlan Davidson.**
A text based on the author's "History Methods" course for history majors. Chapter One addresses historiography; Chapter Two discusses the nature of primary and secondary historical sources; Chapter Three explains how to locate sources; Chapters Four and Five deal with preparing historiographic essays and research papers.

1029. Charrow, V. R., & Erhardt, M. K. (1986). *Clear and effective legal writing.* **Boston: Little, Brown.**
A guide to writing for law students and lawyers. Chapter One defines the nature of legal writing. Chapter Two explores the history, methods, and purposes of legal writing. Chapters Three through Eight consider the process of writing, including prewriting, writing, and post-writing (practice exercises are included with each step of the process). Chapters Nine and Ten guide readers through the process of composing a legal memorandum and an appellate brief.

1030. Chittenden, P., & Kiniry, M. (Eds.). (1986). *Making connections across the curriculum: Readings for analysis.* **New York: St. Martin's.**
A cross-disciplinary reader aimed at improving analytical thinking. Consists of ten chapters, each organized around a theme (e.g., "The Origins of the Nuclear Arms Race," "The Urban Experience," etc.) and comprised of several readings drawn from the works of scholars, thinkers, and writers across the disciplines. The readings provide different, interdisciplinary perspectives on the common theme. Each selection is followed by "Considerations," which raise questions about the individual reading; and "Connections," which require the student to compare the selection with others in the same chapter. Chapters conclude with "Further Connections" and "Extensions," which invite the student to take a comparative outlook on the contents of the chapter.

1031. Clegg, C. S. (1988). *Critical reading and writing across the disciplines.* **New York: Holt.**
A two-part text/anthology. Part One "presents chapters on process-centered writing and critical reading and a chapter on drawing upon reading for writing." Part Two "contains essays by recognized authorities in a format encouraging students' critical responses." Readings are drawn from the natural and social sciences, history, art and literature, and are followed by questions for discussion and writing.

1032. Comley, N. R., Hamilton, D., Klaus, C., Scholes, R., & Sommers, N. (Eds.). (1984). *Fields of writing: Readings across the disciplines.* **New York: St. Martin's.**
A textbook anthology of model writings by major scholars and thinkers across the disciplines. Readings are arranged by rhetorical category ("Reporting," "Explaining," "Arguing," "Reflecting") and discipline, and are followed by questions and suggestions for study and writing. Later chapters discuss reading-writing relationships and trace E. B. White's composing process—from first notes to final draft—for a *New York Times* feature article. The concluding chapter contains broader suggestions for writing across the disciplines.

1033. Corrigan, T. (1988). *A short guide to writing about film.* **New York: HarperCollins.**

1034. Cuba, L. (1993). *A short guide to writing about social science* **(2nd ed.). New York: HarperCollins.**
Cuba describes his book as a supplementary text for any social science course. Chapters One and Eight present the writing process from drafting to revising. Chapters Two through Five discuss specific kinds of writing "that are often a part of both undergraduate and graduate curriculums," including "Summaries and Reviews of Literature," "Papers Based on Original Research," "Library Research Papers," and "Oral and Written Presentations." Chapters Six and Seven provide a general guide to "Using the Library" and "Form."

1035. Day, R. A. (1983). *How to write and publish a scientific paper* **(2nd ed.). Philadelphia: ISI.**
Addressing professional scientists as well as students, Day describes his text as a "cookbook" for writing and publishing scientific papers. Concise chapters

explain the ingredients of a scientific paper—from title (Chapter 2) to results (Chapter 8) to illustrations (Chapter 13)—and survey the how-to's of submitting and publishing a manuscript. Later chapters discuss usage, jargon, and such common types of scientific writing as review papers, conference reports, and oral presentations.

1036. Dougherty, B. N. (1985). *Composing choices for writers: A cross-disciplinary rhetoric.* **New York: McGraw-Hill.**
Dougherty builds her text on several premises: that composing is the making of meaning; that every writing task involves a "series of choices" concerning topic, audience, purpose, and other contextual features; and that writing is a recursive process of planning, drafting, and revising. The text emphasizes the writing process and examines a range of topics (audience, narration, argument, reader-response, etc.) from the standpoint of how they stimulate specific rhetorical choices. Chapters include exercises and assignments and are illustrated with numerous cross-disciplinary writing examples—student and professional, academic and nonacademic—for discussion and analysis.

1037. Field, J., & Weiss, R. H. (1979). *Cases for composition.* **Boston: Little, Brown.**
Fifty cases involving different problems in campus life. Students must place themselves in realistic contexts for writing, and these are interdisciplinary in nature.

1038. Friedman, S., & Steinberg, S. (1989). *Writing and thinking in the social sciences.* **Englewood Cliffs, NJ: Prentice Hall.**
Written by a writing specialist and a social scientist, this text addresses the entire domain of the social sciences. Discusses the common research tools and methodologies (observation, interview, experiment) and provides information on the various types of social science writing with special focus on academic forms such as the book review, critical essay, essay exam, and research paper. Includes an appendix of reference works in the social sciences; manuscript form, footnotes and bibliography; and a student research paper.

1039. Gordon, W. I., & Nevins, R. J. (1993). *We mean business: Building communication competence in business and professions.* **New York: HarperCollins.**

1040. Gregg, J. Y., & Russell, J. (1985). *Science and society: A reading-writing text.* **Belmont, CA: Wadsworth.**

1041. Grinols, A. B. (Ed.). (1984). *Critical thinking: Reading across the curriculum.* **Ithaca, NY: Cornell University Press.**

1042. Hirschberg, S. (Ed.). (1988). *Patterns across the disciplines.* **New York: Macmillan.**
A reader containing "classic, modern, and contemporary readings by major writers, scholars, and scientists in the liberal arts, political and social sciences, and sciences." Readings are grouped traditionally by discipline and rhetorical mode.

1043. Hubbuch, S. M. (1985). *Writing research papers across the curriculum.* **New York: Holt.**
A step-by-step guide to the research process for students in any discipline. Characterizing research as "detective work," Hubbuch emphasizes that the student's ideas form "the central element in the research process, from its inception to the final paper that evolves." Basic to this process is the "researcher's notebook," in which students keep an ongoing record of their thinking and research on their topics. The book's seven chapters take the reader step by step through the researching/writing process by focusing on two kinds of papers—the secondary research paper and the primary research report. Appendices describe bibliographic and documentation formats for papers in the humanities and sciences (natural, social, and applied), and offer suggestions for copyediting and proofreading.

1044. Hult, C. A. (1990). *Researching and writing across the curriculum* **(2nd ed.). Belmont, CA: Wadsworth.**
An introduction to research in science and technology, social sciences, humanities, and business. The text is intended as a guide to research methodologies and as a reference tool for students and professionals. Part One, "Research Methods and Resources," begins with a general introduction to college research and continues with chapters on primary research, library resources, and other research, and the steps involved in planning, writing, and presenting a research paper. Part Two, "Model Research Projects," describes the research processes and documentation formats peculiar to each of the four disciplinary areas and includes exercises and a sample research paper for each.

1045. Johnson, J. (1987). *The Bedford guide to the research process.* **New York: St. Martin's.**
A cross-disciplinary, step-by-step guide to research. Part One, "Searching," provides an overview of the research process and explains the fundamentals of choosing a topic, compiling a working bibliography, and finding, evaluating, and recording information. Part Two, "Researching and Writing," discusses outlining, drafting, revising, and editing and includes full-length samples of research papers in the humanities, the social sciences, and science and technology. Brief exercises follow each chapter. Appendices contain annotated bibliographies of general and reference works and reference materials and professional journals in 25 individual disciplines.

1046. Kiniry, M., & Rose, M. (1993). *Critical strategies for academic thinking and writing* **(2nd ed.). Boston: Bedford Books of St. Martin's Press.**
Aims "to provide a miniature course in university inquiry—one that ranges across the disciplines and raises a number of the fundamental questions that students will find in courses ranging from biology to women's studies." This text-reader includes 150 readings from 20 different content areas and is divided into two parts. Part One introduces students to methods of defining, summarizing, serializing, classifying, comparing, and analyzing. Part Two consists of writing exercises based on readings across the disciplines.

1047. Kinneavy, J. L., McCleary, W., & Nakadate, N. (1985). *Writing in the liberal arts tradition: A rhetoric with readings.* **New York: Harper & Row.**

A volume of readings for freshman students stressing the aims and modes of discourse. Includes topics for writing across the curriculum.

1048. Lynch, R. E., & Swanzey, T. B. (Eds.). (1981). *The example of science: An anthology for college composition.* **Englewood Cliffs, NJ: Prentice-Hall.**
Addressing a college audience, the editors stress the value of good writing in science, technology, and engineering. Part One, "Writing and the Scientific Method," is divided into five chapters ("Defining the Problem," "Observing the Evidence," "Forming the Hypothesis," "Experimenting," "Presenting the Theory"), each of which illustrates a different step in the scientific method. Part Two, "Fiction, Science, and Science Fiction," provides additional prose models and illustrates the changing roles of science and scientists in culture. Reading selections are followed by questions about "language and structure" and "content and ideas," and each chapter ends with suggestions for writing.

1049. Maimon, E. P., Belcher, G. L., Hearn, G. W., Nodine, B. F., & O'Connor, F. W. (1981). *Writing in the arts and sciences.* **Cambridge, MA: Winthrop.**
Provides "an introduction to academic writing, reading, and studying." The text is organized into two parts with important sections on "Writing in the Humanities," "Writing in the Social Sciences," and "Writing in the Natural Sciences." All 14 chapters are followed by various questions and exercises that help students of different disciplines become better writers and learners. The authors teach in different departments at Beaver College in Pennsylvania.

1050. Maimon, E. P., Belcher, G. L., Hearn, G. W., Nodine, B. F., & O'Connor, F. W. (Eds.) (1984). *Readings in the Arts and Sciences.* **Boston: Little, Brown.**
A companion guide to *Writing in the Arts and Sciences.* Reading is seen as access to membership in the academic community and its ongoing "conversations." Reading in the content areas is supplemented by suggestions for journal writing.

1051. Marius, R. (1989). *A short guide to writing about history.* **New York: HarperCollins.**

1052. Martinish, A. P. (1989). *Philosophical writing: An introduction.* **Englewood Cliffs, NJ: Prentice Hall.**
An ancillary text for philosophy courses. Discusses the process of writing the philosophical essay and contains tips on argumentative strategies and basic philosophical terms. Includes discussions of audience, author, drafting, outlining, note-taking, revising, and conducting research. Also includes an overview of basic concepts in logic and various types of arguments used in philosophical reasoning.

1053. Miles, T. H. (1990). *Critical thinking and writing for science and technology.* **San Diego: Harcourt.**
A guide to academic and professional writing in engineering and the sciences. Part One focuses on writing in the professional career in science and technology and includes chapters on the writing process and the audiences for technical writing. Part Two shows how thinking and writing are connected in science and technology, and includes models of descriptive, explanatory,

analytical, and persuasive writing; innovative or "revolutionary" writing; exploratory writing; and speculative or reflective writing. Part Three shows how technical reports and scientific papers are put together, and includes sections on library research, documentation, revision and style, computers, and graphics. Appendices contain recent literature on science and technology, "other forms of communication" (letters, memos, oral presentations), and a guide to the conventions of correct grammar and punctuation.

1054. Miller, R. K. (1986). *The informed argument: A multidisciplinary reader and guide.* **San Diego, CA: Harcourt.**
Combines 74 multidisciplinary readings with an introduction to argument and a guide to research and documentation.

1055. Neman, B. S., & Smythe, S. H. (1992). *Writing effectively in business.* **New York: HarperCollins.**

1056. Pechenik, J. A. (1993). *A short guide to writing about biology* **(2nd ed.). New York: HarperCollins.**
Intended as a supplementary textbook for lecture courses or seminars at the undergraduate or graduate level. Chapter One provides an overview of writing in biology and describes the "key principles that characterize all sound scientific writing." Subsequent chapters focus on laboratory reports, essays and term papers, research proposals, summaries and critiques, oral presentations, letters of application, sentence-level revision, and answering essay questions.

1057. Rosnow, R. L., & Rosnow, M. (1986). *Writing papers in psychology: A student guide.* **Belmont, CA: Wadsworth.**
A short guide to preparing term papers or reports in psychology. Chapters include: "Getting Started," "Using the Library," "Outlining the Term Paper," "Planning the Research Report," "Writing and Revising," and "Layout and Typing." Appendices provide a sample term paper and research report.

1058. Sayre, H. M. (1989). *Writing about art.* **Englewood Cliffs, NJ: Prentice Hall.**
Designed to complement art history or art appreciation courses, this text addresses the processes of "seeing and writing," selecting a work of art to write about, using visual information, and working with words and images. Includes one finished model essay and four others in various draft stages.

1059. Sociology Writing Group. (1986). *A guide to writing sociology papers.* **New York: St. Martin's.**
Group-authored by sociology and English faculty at UCLA, this text is intended for college sociology courses at all levels and for advanced writing courses emphasizing the social sciences. The authors take a process approach to social science writing that is adaptable to courses other than sociology. Contains three parts: 1) "Essentials" defines sociology as a discipline and discusses the general processes of writing research in sociology; 2) "Writing from Various Data Sources" addresses writing problems relevant to particular types of sociological research, such as literature reviews, ethnographies, and quantitative research papers; and 3) "Finishing Up" discusses editing and submitting a final paper.

1060. Steffens, H. J., & Dickerson, M. J. (with T. Fulwiler). (1987). *Writer's Guide: History.* **Lexington, MA: D.C. Heath.**
A process-centered writing guide for majors and non-majors in history. Parallels the philosophy, structure and purpose of other volumes in Heath's "Writer's Guide" series (see entries for Biddle & Bean, Biddle & Holland, Bond & Magistrale, this section). Includes chapters on "Writing to Learn History," "Journal Writing in History," "Approaches to Writing and Learning History," "Writing Short Essays," "The Research Paper," "Principles of Library Research and Basic Bibliographies," and "Documentation Techniques."

1061. Steward, J. S., & Smelstor, M. (1984). *Writing in the social sciences.* **Glenview, IL: Scott, Foresman & Co.**
A textbook-reader intended both for classroom use and for use by individual students and professionals. Readings (all by prominent authors in the social sciences) are followed by discussion questions and writing activities. Selections in Part One, "About Writing," introduce students to the writing process. Readings in Part Two, "Writing for Many Purposes," illustrate papers that "investigate and report," "clarify and discuss abstractions," "analyze events and their causes," and "argue and persuade." Readings in Part Three, "Longer Projects," indicate how audience, purpose, and other contextual factors influence a writer's rhetorical choices. Two full-length student research papers are also included in this section. Part Four, "Tools for the Social Science Writer," lists reference materials and other resources for social science students and professionals.

1062. Sunderman, P. (1985). *Connections: Writing across disciplines.* **New York: Holt.**
A cross-curricular textbook for ESL students, particularly those enrolled in scientific, business, or technical disciplines. Part One concentrates on the writing process, effective paragraphing, organization, and writing the essay. Part Two discusses rhetorical patterns of exposition (comparision/contrast, cause/effect, etc.) and common technical writing tasks such as process descriptions and instruction manuals.

1063. Vesper, J., & Ruggiero, V. R. (1993). *Contemporary business communication: From thought to expression.* **New York: HarperCollins.**

1064. Walvoord, B. F. (1985). *Writing: Strategies for all disciplines.* **Englewood Cliffs, NJ: Prentice-Hall.**
Addressing students of freshman composition and of writing in any discipline, Walvoord characterizes her book as "an overview of the creative process we call writing and a specific guide to using writing to think, to learn, and to transmit ideas in every discipline." Section One, "Strategies for the Writing Process," discusses planning, organization, researching, drafting, revising, and editing. Section Two, "Modes for Thinking and Writing," considers "ways of discovering ideas, ways of organizing data, and ways of thinking about a topic" through explorations of narration, summary, comparison, analysis, logical argument, and other modes. Section Three, "Reference," describes strategies for library research, documentation styles, and methods for designing and using visual aids. Writing exercises follow each chapter.

1065. Williams, J. D., Huntley, D., & Hanks, C. (Eds.). (1992). *The interdisciplinary reader: A collection of student writing.* **New York: HarperCollins.**
A text "designed for writing-across-the-curriculum courses that introduce nonmajors to composing in a range of subject areas." Sample student papers in life and applied sciences, social sciences, humanities, and business are interspersed with commentary and suggestions regarding the specific demands of writing within the particular subject area.

1066. Wingell, R. J. (1990). *Writing about music: An introductory guide.* **Englewood Cliffs, NJ: Prentice Hall.**
A short, practical textbook which addresses both general writing issues as well as the special features and challenges of writing about music. Includes chapters on "Words and Music"; writing a research paper on a musical topic; other kinds of writing about music (i.e., concert reports and program notes); and writing effective prose. Includes an appendix with a sample paper.

1067. Zimbardo, R., & Stevens, M. (1985). *Across the curriculum: Thinking, reading, writing.* **New York: Longman.**
A textbook offering an interdisciplinary approach to reading, writing, and thinking. The book consists of four sections, each organized around a theme ("Love and Sexuality," "Work," "Death," and "The Future") and comprised of several readings by scholars, thinkers, and writers across the disciplines. The readings provide different interdisciplinary perspectives on the common theme. Each selection is preceded by a brief introduction and followed by questions and exercises.

Author Index

The numbers refer to entries, and not to pages, with the exception of the roman numerals, which relate to pages in the front matter.

Subject Index

The numbers refer to entries, and not to pages, with the exception of the roman numerals, which relate to pages in the front matter.

About the Compilers

CHRIS M. ANSON is Associate Professor of English and Director of the Program in Composition and Communication at the University of Minnesota, where he teaches courses in writing theory and research. He is co-author of *Writing in Context* (1988) and *A Field Guide to Writing* (1992), and is editor of *Responding to Writing: Theory, Practice and Research* (1989). He has published articles on composition in several edited collections and scholarly journals. His research interests include writing across the curriculum, the language of self-assessment, and response to writing.

JOHN E. SCHWIEBERT is Associate Professor of English and Director of the Writing Center at Weber State University in Ogden, Utah. He is author of *The Frailest Leaves: Whitman's Poetic Technique and Style in the Short Poem* (1992) and has published articles on Whitman, nineteenth-century British poetry, and creativity. He is currently completing a book which explores relationships between intertextuality and creativity across the disciplines. His research interests include writing across the curriculum, reader-oriented theory and criticism, and reading/writing relationships.

MICHAEL M. WILLIAMSON is Professor of English and Director of Graduate Studies at Indiana University of Pennsylvania, where he teaches courses in English education, psycholinguistics, linguistics for the teaching of English, research methodology, and composition research and theory. He has published articles on composition in several edited collections and scholarly journals. His research interests include writing across the curriculum, linguistic approaches to writing research, and computers in writing.